Voice of Georgia

Senator Richard B. Russell Jr.

Voice of Georgia

Speeches of
Richard B. Russell,
1928-1969

Edited by

Calvin McLeod Logue
&
Dwight L. Freshley

Mercer University Press
Macon, Georgia

ISBN 0-86554-586-3   MUP/H438

Copyright ©1997
Mercer University Press, Macon, Georgia 31210-3960 USA
All rights reserved
Printed in the United States of America

The paper used in this publication meets the minimum requirements
of American National Standard for Information Sciences—
Permanence of Paper for Printed Library Materials, ANSI Z39.48-1984.

Library of Congress Cataloging-in-Publication Data

Russell, Richard B. (Richard Brevard), 1897-1971.
   Voice of Georgia: Speeches of Richard B. Russell, 1928-1969 /
edited by Calvin McLeod Logue & Dwight L. Freshley
     x + 379 pp.   6" x 9" (15 x 22 cm.)
   Includes index.
   ISBN 0-86554-586-3 (alk. paper)
   1. United States—Politics and government—20th century.
2. Constitutional history—United States. 3. Agriculture—Economic aspects—United States—History—20th century. 4. United States—Defenses—History —20th century. 5. Civil rights—United States—History—20th century. I. Logue, Calvin M. (Calvin McLeod), 1935-II. Freshley, Dwight L., 1924- . III. Title.
E742.5.R875   1997
328.73'092—dc21   97-37100
                                                                                         CIP

CONTENTS

Introduction: "Not Afraid to Stand, and to Stand Alone"   1

I. Speeches on Constitutional Principles   39

United Daughters of the Confederacy, October 1930   41
Campaign for Senate Re-election, 4 July 1936   47
Freedom Train, 29 December 1947   57
Association of Attorneys General, 9 December 1952   64
University of Georgia Law Day, 1 May 1954   71
George Washington Award, 30 April 1958   79
On the United Nations, 4 April 1962   85
Georgia Jaycees Breakfast, 6 February 1966   102

II. Speeches on Agriculture and Industry   109

Jute, The Arch Competitor of Cotton, 5 June 1936   111
Hart County Crimson Clover Festival, 28 April 1939   119
4-H Clubs, ca. 1941   129
National Rural Electric Cooperative Association,
    19 January 1943   135
American Farm Bureau, 10 December 1946   142
Tufted Textile Manufacturing Convention, 30 May 1947   153
Presidential Campaign, 19 June 1952   158
Turner County Chamber of Commerce, 15 October 1959   167
Georgia Crop Improvement Association,
    18 February 1963   175
Carters Dam, 14 November 1964   185
Georgia Press Association, 9 July 1965   194

III. Speeches on Military Preparedness   201

Armistice Day, 11 November 1928   203
Defense Savings Program, 10 November 1941   212

The Navy's Challenge for Service, August 1942	217
Report on Visit to War Theaters, 28 October 1943	223
University of Georgia Alumni, 13 June 1946	244
American Legion Convention, 15 October 1951	256
Douglas Chamber of Commerce, 8 December 1959	264
Dalton High School, 13 December 1962	270
Gordon Military School, 26 May 1963	277
Georgia Association of Broadcasters, 13 June 1965	287
Veterans of Foreign Wars Congressional Dinner, 12 March 1968	294
Admiral James Forrestal Memorial Award, 20 March 1969	298
IV. Speeches on Civil Rights	305
The Poll Tax, 17 November 1942	307
President Harry S. Truman's Civil Rights Commission, 23 March 1948	322
Message to Constituents, 24 January 1950	329
Civil Rights Referendum, 2 July 1957	333
Georgia General Assembly, 8 February 1960	348
Coosa Valley Area Planning and Development Commission, 15 July 1964	354
Index	359

DEDICATED
to
VETERANS
of
UNITED STATES MILITARY SERVICE
FOR WHOM SENATOR RICHARD B. RUSSELL
SPOKE SO UNTIRINGLY

List of Photographs

1. Frontispiece: Senator Richard B. Russell Jr.
2. Handwritten notes, speech at the Georgia State College for Women graduation, Milledgeville, Georgia, September 24, 1945
3. Handwritten notes, speech at a Rural Ministers meeting, Emory University, Atlanta, Georgia, ca. 1942.
4. Handwritten notes, speech at a meeting of the Turner County Chamber of Commerce, 15 October 1959
5. Handwritten notes, speech on Armistice Day, Atlanta, Georgia, 11 November 1953
6. Handwritten notes, speecha meeting of the Rural Electric Association, Cairo, Georgia, 29 October 1953

All photographs courtesy of the Richard B. Russell Library, University of Georgia. Frontispiece photograph also courtesy of the *Atlanta Journal-Constitution*.

To girls →

United States Senate
WASHINGTON, D. C.

Young ladies of student body fortunate — Are coming into the Kingdom in most exciting period of our civilization — We are just emerging from a great & costly war. Many hearts have been saddened — Many homes lost loved ones — Lives of 15 million interrupted by being called to service — Great cost in money and natural resources —

But with all its horrors it has brought us to the threshold of a new era — an era which presents the greatest challenge the human race has ever known — Technological inventions and improvements have shrunken the world — It is smaller than the continents 25 years ago. Americans have served in every part of world, however remote — Have come to know how other peoples live — More than that — other peoples all of them from heart of Africa — Asia — Middle East — have become acquainted with sons & daughters of a democracy —

Handwritten notes, speech at the Georgia State College for Women graduation, Milledgeville, Georgia, September 24, 1945

Introduction:
"Not Afraid to Stand, and to Stand Alone"

In 1957 Richard Brevard Russell, Jr. told an Atlanta audience that he had "tried to speak the voice of Georgia."[1] Russell represented the views of Georgians well enough that they elected him to the Georgia House in 1920, to the Governor's Mansion in 1931, and to the United States Senate in 1933. Just out of college, he was elected to the Georgia House of Representatives from Barrow County at the age of twenty-three, and held that office until 1931. Colleagues thought enough of his leadership abilities to make him Speaker of the Georgia General Assembly in 1929. In the Georgia House he made lasting political ties that enabled him as governor to restructure state government. Russell was elected governor of Georgia at the age of thirty-three.

As governor from 1931 to 1933, Russell was confronted with making a state government devastated by the Great Depression more efficient and affordable. He sponsored legislation consolidating more than 100 state agencies into eighteen. For example, he improved the administration of the colleges and universities in Georgia. Before his Reorganization Act of 1931, each of twenty-three institutions of higher education operated under the control of its own Board of Trustees with only four colleges sponsoring accredited programs. Russell had the General Assembly create a Board of Regents with authority to administer a central University System. Under this plan, educational programs were abolished or consolidated, and by 1941 all

---

[1] States Rights Council Speech, October 8, 1957, Congressional Appreciation Dinner, Atlanta, Georgia, 1, Speech File, Speech/Media Series, Richard B. Russell Collection, Richard B. Russell Library for Political Research and Studies [hereinafter, RRLPRS], University of Georgia, Athens, GA.

institutions of higher education were accredited. In 1940 the senate of Phi Beta Kappa, composed of educators from throughout the United States, judged that New York and Georgia had made the most progress in developing their systems of higher education.[2]

There were severe limits on what a state government in debt could do to relieve the economic hardships of Georgians. Under Russell's leadership, selection of textbooks for public schools was made uniform so that persons moving to another county did not have to buy new ones, the salaries of highest paid officials, including his own, were cut, and taxes on farm property were reduced. When funds were unavailable for teachers, they were paid in script. By economizing, Russell and supporters were able to balance the state budget.[3]

In 1932, the year Franklin D. Roosevelt won the presidency, Russell was elected to the United States Senate. He served there until his death on January 21, 1971. During that period the Senator addressed topics such as the economy, industry, agriculture, education, immigration, space, military preparedness, natural resources, Communism, civil rights, and nature of government.

Russell held significant Senate appointments during the administrations of Franklin D. Roosevelt, Harry S. Truman, Dwight D. Eisenhower, John F. Kennedy, Lyndon B. Johnson, and Richard M. Nixon. During his first term in the Senate, Russell was appointed to standing committees on Appropriations, Immigration, Manufactures, and Naval Affairs. He chaired the Appropriations Subcommittee on Agriculture. Later he chaired the Subcommittee on Defense. In 1945 Russell was appointed to the Special Senate Committee on Atomic

---

[2] Speech by Marion Smith to Atlanta Rotary Club, *Atlanta Constitution*, July 22, 1941.

[3] Marion Smith's speech to Atlanta Rotary Club, *Atlanta Constitution*, July 22, 1941; Karen Kalmar Kelly, "Richard B. Russell: Democrat From Georgia," (Ph.D. diss., University of North Carolina at Chapel Hill, 1979), 123-125, 130-131, 147-150; Gilbert C. Fite, *Richard B. Russell, Jr., Senator from Georgia* (Chapel Hill: University of North Carolina Press, 1991), 82, 89.

Introduction 3

Energy, and in 1959 to the Senate Standing Committee on Aeronautical and Space Sciences. He was a member of the Armed Services Committee from 1947 to 1971, and chaired it from 1951 to 1953 and 1955 to 1969.

Colleagues highly valued his judgment because of his authority on committees, the personal respect he commanded, and his diligence in studying the issues. Senator Winston L. Prouty, Republican of Vermont, told how, when Russell was scheduled to speak in the Senate, "most of us . . . made it a point to be there." He enjoyed the same respect back home. When he returned to Georgia to speak to civic clubs, students, farmers, political organizations, and business people, many listened in awe of his political authority. They appreciated what he had achieved for the economy of Georgia and, in 1954, 1960, and 1966, returned him to the Senate with little or no opposition.[4]

The Senator appreciated the support of rural Georgians, whose votes were crucial for being elected to public office in 1920. In that year, only 25.1 percent of Georgians lived in urban areas, and the county unit system of determining elections favored rural voters. The candidate receiving a plurality of county unit votes won an election. Each county had twice as many county unit votes as it had representatives in the Georgia House of Representatives. Eight counties with the largest population had only six unit votes each, thirty counties had four unit votes each, while 121 rural counties had two unit votes each. To win a state-wide election, one had to satisfy voters outside the cities who lived on farms, in the mountains, the piney woods, and on the coastal plain.[5] By 1962, when the county

---

[4]Hugh Cates's interview with Winston L. Prouty, April 21, 1971, RRLPRS, OH 04, 4; Numan V. Bartley and Hugh D. Graham, *Southern Elections County and Precinct Data, 1950-1972* (Baton Rouge: Louisiana State University Press, 1978), 94.

[5]Dewey W. Grantham, *Southern Progressivism: The Reconciliation of Progress and Tradition* (Knoxville: University of Tennessee Press, 1983), 6; Barton C.

unit system was ruled unconstitutional and when the General Assembly of Georgia was required to reapportion on the basis of population, Russell had become so popular and influential that no change in election procedure could deny him office.

"A People Expert"

Russell was called the "spiritual leader" of the Senate and the "actual leader" of southerners in that body. A number of qualities and practices enabled Russell to become "one of the few Senate giants in the twentieth century." Russell's public personality and professional deportment won wide respect. Senator Henry M. Jackson of Washington emphasized Russell's deep sense of "honor," observing how his "word was it. . . . He was intellectually honest." Colleagues "liked" and "trusted" him. He was hailed as a "gentleman lawyer in politics." The Senator was considered by many to be "courteous," "modest," and "diplomatic" in manner to the point of being "gravely courteous." Observers found Russell to be "courtly," "rigid," and "serious" but not "stuffy," more "Olympian" than "chummy." He was a "private" person who was reluctant to share the "depth of" his "feelings." Certainly Russell was an imposing figure. Clothed in a blue serge suit, his dignity and unobtrusiveness created an "innocent rectitude" that caused persons to be reluctant to offend him.[6]

Shaw, *Wool-Hat Boys Georgia's Populist Party* (Baton Rouge: Louisiana State University Press, 1984), 1.
  [6]Harold Davis, "Dick Russell Blasts a Rights Myth," *Atlanta Journal*, July 28, 1957, Section C, 1; Fite, 502, 77, 199, 125, 208, 199; ; Cates's interview with Henry M. Jackson, April 29, 1971, RRLPRS (hereinafter *RRLPRS*), OH 103, 2-7; Cates's interview with William H. Darden, March 5, 1971, OH 71, 1 (*RRLPRS*); *Evening Star*, Washington, D. C., February 29, 1960, A-4; Frederic W. Collins, "Senator Russell `in the Last Ditch'," *New York Times Magazine*, October 20, 1936, 16; *Evening Star*, Washington, D. C., February 29, 1960, A-4; Meg Greenfield, "The Man Who Leads the Southern Senators," *Reporter*, 30 (May 21, 1964), 18.

Introduction 5

Russell often personified the civility expected of persons debating in the Senate. In 1942, for example, when Senators Harry Flood Byrd of Virginia and Alben W. Barkley of Kentucky asked that a vote concerning the school lunch plan be reconsidered, Russell responded:

> I should be very glad to agree to the request; but I have just objected to a similar request by the Senator from Oklahoma (Mr. Josh Lee) with regard to another amendment. . . . I cannot make fish of one Senator and foul of another.[7]

The school lunch legislation led to one of the programs that Russell sponsored and of which he was justifiably proud.

Russell studied and addressed issues judiciously. Observers praised the Senator's ability to concentrate upon a problem and his "poise under pressure." Senator Jackson concluded that Russell "was a genius for zeroing in on the central issue." Jackson indicated that Russell had a "judicial temperament" that made him a good judge of character and a reliable assessor of problems and their causes. Russell "could restrain himself" and not allow any "evidence of a temper ever to appear in connection with anything he was saying or doing." When questioning witnesses who appeared before Senate committees, Russell treated them with "dignity," but he was also "skeptical and probing." Driven by an "inner passion" for conscientious and effective public service, before reaching a decision, Russell asked "penetrating questions." Margaret Appleby McCormick, secretary in Russell's Washington office from 1935 to 1948, recalled the Senator's "quick mind." William H. Darden, Press Secretary to Russell from 1948 to 1951, noted the Georgian's "uncanny insight into human nature. He was a

---

[7]United States Senate Speech, *Congressional Record: Proceedings and Debates of the 77th Congress*, Second Session, Vol. 88, Part 3, May 15, 1942, 4251.

people expert I had the feeling that he could talk to a person for a few minutes and really size him up and know what made him tick."⁸

After studying a problem and deciding upon what he considered the best solution, Russell comfortably assumed responsibility for having it implemented. Although often a "tolerant man," stated William M. Bates, Russell's press secretary from 1958 to 1961, and 1964 to 1966, the Senator was also "a commanding person." Earl T. Leonard, the Senator's Press Secretary from 1961 to 1964, explained that Russell tried "very hard . . . to exert his own control over the situation." Another perceived that Russell was confident enough to take "for granted" that he was "the authoritative voice on how the Senate should conduct its affairs."⁹

While generally realistic politically and, on occasions, willing to compromise, on issues vital to him and his constituents, he refused to budge. One colleague suggested that, among Senators, Russell was "most respected" but not necessarily the "most loved." When defending a position, Russell could "express cold, outraged indignation." Suspicious of the press, he became "mad as fire" when misquoted. He could be a "ferocious antagonist" when challenged personally and when defending the South. Whether pressured by Commissioner of Agriculture Eugene Talmadge to call a special session of the Georgia General Assembly to curtail the planting of cotton for a year, or President Franklin D. Roosevelt to oppose Georgia's Walter F. George's reelection to the Senate, he held his ground. Senator Jackson explained that Russell "hated phoniness.

---

⁸Letter, June 23, 1927, in Correspondence/Speech File, (RRLPRS); Cates's interview with Jackson, 2-7 (RRLPRS); Cates's interview with Earl T. Leonard, Jr., February 15, 1971, OH 73, 22 (RRLPRS); Collins, "Senator Russell 'in the Last Ditch'" 16; Cates's interview with Darden, 27-28 (RRLPRS); letter to Calvin M. Logue, September 23, 1981; Cates's interview with Darden, 36-37 (RRLPRS), emphasis added.

⁹Cates's interview with William M. Bates, February 25, 1971, OH 72, 14 (RRLPRS); Cates's interview with Leonard, 42 (RRLPRS); Collins, "Senator Russell `in the Last Ditch'," 16.

Introduction

He'd just say what he thought, whether it was favorable or unfavorable."[10] In Senate debate in 1933, while speaking on a New Deal program, Russell challenged the conclusion of Kentucky's Alben W. Barkley:

> *Mr. Russell.* The Senator from Kentucky has said . . . that the Reconstruction Finance Corporation is now limiting the amount each county may expend for administrative expenses. I should like to know what that amount is.
> *Mr. Barkley.* It is not a uniform amount. . . .
> *Mr. Russell.* I think the Senator must be in error about that.[11]

Russell's political toughness found expression in his 1936 campaign against Eugene Talmadge. As governor, Talmadge used soldiers and persuasive coercion to enforce his will upon opponents. Turning the tables, during a number of rallies in 1936, Russell ridiculed "Gene's soldiers" by contrasting them with his own "body guard," consisting of the "Winder Girls' Drum and Trumpet Corps." During a speech in Swainesboro, Russell had a "group of men" walk to the speaker's stand, "strip off their red suspenders" (worn by Talmadge and his followers) and announce that they had been "converted" to his campaign. Russell informed the radio audience gleefully that "it's raining red suspenders."[12]

Even in the heat of the 1936 campaign, however, Russell relied more upon good reasoning than extravagant promises. "All legislation

---

[10]Fite, *Richard B. Russell, Jr.,* 65, 81, 92-93, 200, 208-209, 211, 225, 299, 348, 365, 402; Collins, "Senator Russell `in the Last Ditch'," 16; *Evening Star,* Washington, D. C., February 29, 1960, A-4; Calvin McLeod Logue, *Eugene Talmadge: Rhetoric and Response* (New York: Greenwood Press, 1989), 86-97; Cates' interview with Jackson, April 29, 1971, 2-7 (RRLPRS).

[11]United States Senate Speech, *Congressional Record: Proceedings and Debates of the 77th Congress,* Second Session, Vol. 76, Part 4, February 17, 1933, 4338.

[12]Ralph McGill, *Atlanta Constitution,* August 15, 1936; Swainesboro, Georgia speech, *Atlanta Constitution,* August 19, 1936.

passed" in the New Deal "was not perfect," he told an Eatonton audience, but "the house was on fire when President Roosevelt was elected" and the administration could not "take time to look in every cupboard." In his successful bid for re-election to the Senate, Russell told Georgia voters he was proud to have helped farmers by voting for an increase in funding for programs from $58,000,000 to $107,000,000.[13]

Russell was also a formidable opponent in Senate hearings and debates. Quite simply, he left nothing to chance. Russell often outprepared the opposition. A tireless worker, he arrived at the office early and worked late. When she worked in his office from 1935 to 1948, McCormick found him to be "wedded to his job." Russell "went about everything with a vigor that inspired all of us." During the "early, middle, and late years," Leonard said, Russell "worked himself to death."[14]

He diligently and systematically mastered the science and the art of politics. Russell followed a "highly developed sense of strategy," working at "politics all the time." He explained to Leonard that he "never had time to get married" because his "ambitions were all" in the "way." "When I got to be Speaker" of the House of Representatives in Georgia, "I tasted power. . . . I wanted to be Governor." To "do well" in Washington, he recalled studying the rules of the Senate "very, very vigorously."[15]

Russell carefully examined issues to be debated. Erle Cocke, Jr., who worked in Russell's 1936 Senate reelection campaign and his 1952 presidential primary campaign, recalled that the Senator's

---

[13] Eatonton, Georgia speech, *Atlanta Constitution*, August 22, 1936.

[14] McCormick letter to Logue, September 23, 1981; Cates interview with Leonard, 33 (RRLPRS).

[15] Greenfield, "The Man Who Leads the Southern Senators," 18; Collins, "Senator Russell 'in the Last Ditch'," 16; Cates's interview with Leonard, 31 (RRLPRS); see Dwight Freshley's interview with Erle Cocke, Jr., OH 165, 17-18 (RRLPRS); Fite, *Richard B. Russell, Jr.*, 170-173.

Introduction 9

"memory was extremely good. He had photostatic ability to quote figures." McCormick observed him to be an "inveterate reader" of history and current events. "His mind worked all the time, applying the lessons of history to his job, and storing away nuggets to pull out when presenting his views in a speech." Correspondence among secretaries, press secretaries, and others working in Russell's Senate office indicates the Senator gave careful attention to researching specific issues with which he dealt. For example, during World War II, Russell asked the Library of Congress for "the most authentic information" available on "Japan and Germany proper before their period of expansion." In 1946, while on a speaking tour in Georgia, Russell wired his press secretary Leeman Anderson to find out "how low wheat" had fallen in 1932.[16]

Russell perfected the parliamentary rules by which government functioned. Senator Fulbright maintained that democracy is largely a matter of parliamentary procedure, and that Russell was one of the Senate's most knowledgeable strategists and skilled practitioners. Senator Alan Cranston, Democrat from California, described how Russell worked "magic" in the Senate. News correspondent Roger Mudd quoted Russell saying that "this government works" by "pressure blocks."[17]

Senators cooperated to appropriate funds for projects of special interest to their home states. Barboura G. Raesly, Russell's personal secretary from 1956 until his death, explained how Russell obtained results by helping colleagues. He "was willing to do a favor for another

---

[16]Freshley interview with Cocke, 12 (RRLPRS); McCormick letter to Logue, September 23, 1981; Speech File/Correspondence (RRLPRS); telegram to Leeman Anderson, November 7, 1946, Farm Continued folder, #1, 1941-1947 (RRLPRS).

[17]Cates's interview with William Fulbright, April 19., 1971, OH 50, 2-3; Cates's interview with Alan Cranston, April 23, 1971, OH 62, 2-3; Cates's interview with Roger H. Mudd, March 4, 1971, OH 117, 4, 6. All interviews in RRLPRS.

Senator. But he rarely asked another Senator to do a favor for him." Russell, however, did keep a list of favors owed to him by Lyndon B. Johnson.[18] Raesly indicated that reciprocal bartering was one of the "sources of his tremendous power in his later years." She explained how Russell would "tell" Clinton Anderson, chair of the Public Works Committee:

> "I sure would appreciate your putting in an authorization for a dam at Clarke Hill," and it was put in. . . . Once you get it in the authorization bill, Russell was on the public works subcommittee of Appropriations and he'd get the money for it.[19]

Senator Jackson indicated how Russell practiced the art of personalized politics: "I chaired the Military Construction Subcommittee for him. There are a lot of projects in Georgia that I was able to be of some help to him. . . . I didn't need to talk to him about it and he didn't talk to me about it. I just understood what his interest was and concern." Through this potent combination of collegiality and committee structure, Russell obtained funds for dams, military bases, military equipment, and research centers in Georgia. Senator William Fulbright concluded that Russell had "more influence among other Senators on a personal basis" than any individual he had ever known.[20]

With the groundwork for decisions laid interpersonally, Russell often managed their defense in formal committee hearings. Russell had great faith in the legislative process. He insisted that all proposals go to an appropriate committee before being debated on the Senate

---

[18] Fite, 475.

[19] Angus Hepburn's interview with Barboura G. Raesly, June 16, 1975, RRLPRS, OH 157, 40.

[20] Cates's interview with Jackson, 40; Cates's interview with Fulbright, 2. Both interviews in RRLPRS.

Introduction   11

floor. For example, in 1954, while speaking on a proposition to lower the national voting age to eighteen, Russell argued that such a vital issue must undergo a "thorough hearing" prior to consideration by the Senate as a whole.[21]

Preferring to "give common sense and reason time to work its will," Russell believed in "taking the heat out of an issue" before acting upon it.[22] Russell could frustrate a colleague by his insistence upon following legislative procedure. During Senate debate in 1961, Senator Frank M. Clark of Pennsylvania expressed "deep disappointment" to Russell for the "striking of the authorization of $4 million for maintenance facilities at the naval shipyard" in Philadelphia. Russell defended the decision:

> I can understand the deep concern. . . . However . . . there is no Bureau of the Budget clearance for this item. In the second place, representatives of the Department of the Navy, when they appeared before the Committee, stated . . . that they were not requesting . . . additional authorization.[23]

Russell effectively addressed issues on the floor of the Senate. The *Evening Star* reported how, when Russell spoke, "the Senate listens."[24] The Senator was adept at marshaling support for his causes. In 1941, for example, to bolster Georgia agriculture, Russell argued for a food stamp plan in the form of a veiled threat. He warned colleagues that they would be courting criticism by constituents if they reduced "surplus commodities." He further demonstrated how the project would be as advantageous to the city dweller in the North as the

---

[21] United States Senate Speech, *Congressional Record: Proceedings and Debates of the 87th Congress*, Second Session, Vol. 100, Part 5, May 21, 1954, 6975.

[22] Cates's interview with Leonard, 22.

[23] United States Senate Speech, *Congressional Record: Proceedings and Debates of the 87th Congress*, First Session, Vol. 107, Part 6, May 8, 1961, 7515.

[24] [Washington, D. C.] *Evening Star*, February 29, 1960, A-4.

farmer in Georgia: "It has . . . been as much of a relief program for the benefit of those who are on the direct relief rolls as it has been an agricultural program."[25]

In Senate debates, Russell seized the levity of a situation for advantage. In 1933, when the Senate seriously assessed the "untapped market for shoes in the South," Russell wryly introduced the principle of states' rights: "In the event an effort is made to force the people of the South to wear shoes by legislative fiat," he demanded an "exemption permitting those under 14 to go barefooted in the summertime." The Senator enjoyed teasing people, often pestering colleagues with whom he felt familiar. In 1960, during a civil rights debate, Russell had the floor, but yielded periodically to other Senators. When Senator Spessard L. Holland caught Illinois Senator Everett Dirksen in a mistake, Dirksen responded: "I will confess my sins in public any old time." Russell rebutted: "Mr. President, I refuse to yield for that long a time, at any time (Laughter)."[26]

By nature, Russell was not a teller of jokes in public. He usually spoke with a "deadly purpose." The Senator was more concerned with the "realities of the Senate" than "its imagery."[27] He was more interested in informing and influencing colleagues than merely entertaining them. Newsman Mudd observed that the Georgian "never showboated. He could get very dramatic and had a lot of oratorical stops and half stops that he could use, but he was never comical." Atlanta reporter Celestine Sibley recalled that Russell, in his campaigning for governor, could be "pretty eloquent," but that he

---

[25] United States Senate Speech, *Congressional Record: Proceedings and Debates of the 77th Congress*, First Session, Vol. 87, Part 5, June 30, 1941, 5746.

[26] Darden letter to Logue, June 30, 1980; United States Senate Speech, *Congressional Record: Proceedings and Debates of the 73rd Congress*, First Session, Vol. 77, Part 4, May 25, 1933, 4156; Cates's interview with Leonard, 29; United States Senate Speech, *Congressional Record: Proceedings and Debates of the 85th Congress*, Vol. 106, Part 2, February 15, 1960, 2470.

[27] Davis, "Dick Russell Blasts A Rights Myth," 1; Greenfield, "The Man Who Leads the Southern Senators," 17.

Introduction   13

"grew less colorful as he grew older and more burdened by affairs of the country." Senator Prouty concluded that Russell was not a "dramatic speaker," but was "logical and convincing." Senator Jackson found that Russell knew how to "reason out and come to logical conclusions on problems." Senator Lister Hill of Alabama said that Russell had a "rare capacity to persuade and cooperate without abandonment of principle."[28]

Because of the respect many persons held for Russell's experience and knowledge of contemporary issues, they invited him to speak at civic clubs, political meetings, commencement exercises, meetings of professional associations, dedication services, and news programs. Each fall, after the Senate adjourned, Russell and his staff set up an office for two or three months in his hometown of Winder, Georgia. During those visits, working from that base of operation, Russell often delivered ten or twelve speeches across the state.[29]

To remain familiar with Georgians' concerns, he depended on "close friends all over the State . . . who kept up fairly regular correspondence with him." He was a "great one for" being "thoroughly prepared before going into any situation." According to Cocke, when the Senator received an invitation to speak, he asked, "Now what in the world am I going to tell those people? . . . Why do I need to go make them a speech?"[30] Russell's staff sought information from persons in the communities where he was to speak. For example, on June 25, 1964, Bates wrote to Charles A. Pannell:

---

[28]Cates's interview with Mudd, March 4, 1971, OH 117, 4, 6; *Atlanta Constitution*, January 31, 1984; Cates's interview with Prouty, 3; Cates's interview with Jackson, 3; Senator Lister Hill, quoted in "Senator Richard B. Russell: An Appreciation by His Colleagues," 1, Russell Memorial Library Speech File. All citations in RRLPRS.

[29]Map of Speaking Schedule, Russell Memorial Library Speech File.

[30]McCormick letter to Logue, September 23, 1981; Freshley interview with Cocke, 17.

Many thanks for the material on the Coosa Valley Commission. I would like to chat with you over the phone to get your ideas of what Senator Russell should include in his remarks to your group next month.[31]

McCormick reported that Russell "liked to be briefed about a setup" before speaking. Then, during his speech and while shaking hands afterward, he could mention specific concerns that citizens had communicated to his Washington office. The Senator was "astute in gauging an audience and in making spontaneous adaptations." Russell used a manuscript mainly to "start his own thinking going." While delivering the speech, he took "flight even from the final prepared text . . . when he got on a point that he could tell his audience was receiving well." Cocke said Russell "hated to read a speech" and "to quote anybody." He wanted everything to be original himself. Finally the staff did "get him to" cite Thomas Jefferson. He "was a perfectionist in speaking," remembered Cocke; "he would spend many hours changing `shall' to `will' and trying to make the most minor changes." Darden felt that the "most effective speeches" Russell presented in the Senate were those delivered "from hastily written notes, key words, and partial sentences" that the Senator "jotted down on the back of an envelope."[32]

Early in his political career, Russell prepared his own speeches, dictating them to Dorothy Shippey and, after 1936, to Margaret Appleby McCormick. McCormick described how the process worked.

---

[31]Letter to Charles A. Panell, June 25, 1964, Russell Memorial Library Speech File.

[32]McCormick letter to Logue, September 23, 1981; Cates's interview with Bates, 12-13; Darden letter to Logue, June 30, 1980; Cates's interview with Leonard, 25; Freshley interview with Cocke, 11-12. Cocke indicated that Russell had some difficulty "with the denture situation . . . . He had a automobile wreck" that caused "injury" to his "teeth." Russell had to "watch" his "S" sounds in "particular." Cocke had Russell "drill" on "She sells sea shells by the shining seashore."

Russell collected "reference books and clippings and pencilled notes, and his brain churning with ideas . . . . When he started dictating he had a sound idea of what he wanted to say." Erle Cocke, Jr. recalled that Russell "did not want to use" a speech prepared for him by others. "I'm using your material . . . . I don't want to do that," the Senator insisted. Cocke described how he and the staff "would talk the speech out with him . . . . And then we researched what he had said" Although disliking having others draft his speeches, as the years passed and his responsibilities in the U. S. Senate increased, Russell depended more upon staff members. The Senator's former speech writers explained how they assisted him. Darden remembered that Russell "might mention orally and briefly some of the topics he wanted to cover." Leonard indicated that Russell "would use your paragraph and dictate six of his, and use one of your sentences and use two, three more paragraphs of his own." The speech writers "attempted to express only views that we thought were in accord with the Senator's own," and to "conform" to his "forms of expression." Leonard found that representing Russell's views was made easier because the Senator was "very consistent on the issues of the day."[33]

The speeches in this volume are distributed among four topics: (1) constitutional principles, (2) agriculture and industry, (3) military preparedness, and (4) civil rights. As background for the speeches in this anthology on those subjects, it is well to consider Russell's stance on each of them.

Constitutional Principles

Senator Russell believed that constitutional government formed the "heart of America." Russell referred to himself as an "old-time fundamentalist in the science of government" loyal to America's

---

[33]McCormick letter to Logue, September 23, 1981; Freshley's interview with Cocke, 12-13; Darden letter to Logue, June 30, 1980; Cates's interview with Leonard, 25; Cates's interview with Leonard, 3, 25.

"priceless heritage." "I don't believe you would call me a soap box orator or a flag waver," he stated. In order, however, for the nation to survive free, citizens must remain "constant" in the "old fashioned ideals" of stability in government, law and order, and patriotism. He insisted that governmental policy should be forged from moral maxims of the nation's founders. Because he believed that it was "human nature" for individuals and governments to seek power, he placed his faith in a government of laws.[34]

Russell contended that the only means available for preserving "rights and freedoms" was to maintain the Constitution "as it was written." Obedience to the "written letter" of the Constitution was the best guarantee of integrity, worship, family, education, health, and prosperity. When interpreting the Constitution, he insisted, one cannot "pick and choose" among ephemeral "slogans" and "novel" views. The Constitution was founded upon concrete principles, and was not to be used like an "accordion . . . stretched" to satisfy "any passing philosophy."[35]

To Russell, the essence of his "Jeffersonian and Jacksonian" philosophy of government was that citizens would manage their affairs locally, as specified in the Tenth Amendment. The Senator abided by a "philosophy of natural rights," with "constitutional government" serving as "a system of restraints on government action

---

[34]St. Andrews Day Speech, November 30, 1959, Savannah, Georgia, 7; Old Warhorse Lawyers Club Speech, November 27, 1964, Atlanta, Georgia, 1, Mercer University Speech, June 3, 1957, Macon, Georgia, 3-10; Jasper, Georgia Speech, July 4, 1963, 7; Association of Attorneys General Speech, December 16, 1952, Sea Island, Georgia, 5; Mercer University Law Day Speech, May 13, 1966, Macon, Georgia, 7. For all these references, see Speech File, RRLPRS. See also Walter B. Russell III, "Political Philosophy of Senator Richard B. Russell," A.B. (Honors Thesis, University of Georgia, 1980), 30.

[35]Old Warhorse Lawyers Club Speech, November 27, 1964, Atlanta, Georgia, 3-4; St. Andrew's Day Speech, November 30, 1959, Savannah, Georgia, 25; Georgia State College of Business Administration Commencement Address, June 7, 1959, Atlanta, 6. See Speech File, RRLPRS.

Introduction 17

and as a means of protecting the rights of the individual." Russell contended that, although powers were distributed among the three branches of government, the proper balance of rule among the executive, legislative, and judicial bodies was one that gave authority to citizens in individual states.[36]

Russell favored a partnership between federal and state governments that provided the means of improving highways, airports, water resources, health care, military weaponry, and welfare, but without lessening the autonomy of the states. Federal and state governments should invest their resources to solve problems in a manner that preserved the rights of both. For the arrangement to operate acceptably, Russell argued for more cooperation and less effort by the federal government to dictate policies.[37]

Russell taught that spiritual and moral guidance should derive from "pillars" of democracy, including church and home. Education was also a foundation of the republic, because an enlightened and concerned citizenry was prerequisite to effective local self-government. For citizens to rule their own lives effectively, he instructed, they must prepare for the task. Citizens should study government and apply that social science to problems confronting society. Using his career as an example, Russell explained that one has to "learn to be a Senator" as one would study for business, medicine, and teaching. To him, the United States system of government depended upon free and

---

[36]University of Alabama Speech (original typed version), October 22, 1954, Tuscaloosa, 11-12, Speech File, RRLPRS; Address by Richard B. Russell on Acceptance of the George Washington Award, *Congressional Record*, 104: 7808, cited in Walter B. Russell III, "Political Philosophy of Senator Richard B. Russell" 29; Draft of States Rights Council Dinner Speech;, February 11, 1959, Atlanta, Georgia, 2, Speech File, RRLPRS.

[37]Mercer University Law Day Speech, May 13, 1966, Macon, Georgia, 9-10, Speech File, RRLPRS

wise choices, individual ability and preparation, personal initiative, and productive work.[38]

Russell believed that too many people took for granted the good life available in the United States. Even when itemizing for audiences the products and opportunities that citizens in the United States enjoyed—including radios, refrigerators, automobiles, telephones, paved roads, railroads, houses, clothes, medical services, and Bill of Rights—Russell stressed how that quality of life could quickly deteriorate. Citing Benjamin Franklin, Russell cautioned that a republic could only survive if citizens "can keep it." When democracy functions well, citizens use their "blood-won-rights" responsibly. They care for the elderly, sick, and underprivileged, he insisted, because "a people without sentiment are poor indeed."[39]

Russell ennobled southerners for personifying American ideals. Although to him traditional American values were not a partisan subject, the Senator identified closely with southern culture. Talking in Alabama, he explained the traits he believed made southerners distinctive. He noted that he and his Alabama audience were "the same kind of folks," devoted to the "same cause" and born from the "same stock." Southerners experienced a "heritage" different from persons from outside the region, giving them a keener awareness and greater appreciation of their hard-won freedoms and rights. He praised the sacrifices made by southerners during the Civil War, Reconstruction, and New South.[40]

---

[38] Georgia State College of Business Administration Commencement Address, June 7, 1959, Atlanta, Georgia, 6; Young Democrats of Alabama Speech, September 27, 1962, Birmingham, Alabama, 3; Old Warhorse Lawyers Club Speech, November 27, 1964, Atlanta, Georgia, 1. See Speech File, RRLPRS.

[39] Speech from "Miscellaneous Speeches by Senator," Folder 1 (1942), carbon copy, 1-2, 4; Christian College of Georgia Speech, July 4, 1948, Athens, Georgia, 1-2, 5-9; American Legion Speech, July 20, 1963, Savannah, Georgia.. See Speech File, RRLPRS.

[40] Mercer University Speech, June 3, 1957, Macon, Georgia, 16; Young Democrats of Alabama Speech, September 27, 1962, Birmingham, Alabama, 1.

Introduction

Although opposed to federal intervention into states' decisions, he sought national funding required to serve Georgians' needs. As governor, Russell had supported tariffs to protect Georgia's cotton economy, and asked for a substantial increase in federal funds with which to build highways in the state, using both skilled and unskilled labor. In the 1930s, joining the majority of southerners who considered themselves to be political "liberals," he advocated expanding federal programs to improve the national and state economies. In the Senate in 1935, he praised the Civilian Conservation Corps (CCC) for "making fine citizens out of young men who had been hopelessly tramping the streets of the cities and living on the dole." Although rejecting the notion that the country could "spend our way out of the depression," he admonished colleagues not to discriminate against the South when distributing federal funds. He complained to a Mutual Radio audience that southerners "did not share in the prosperity" following the Civil War. There had been no Marshall Plan for the defeated South.[41] In 1952, Russell campaigned for the Democratic presidential nomination, hoping to bring his Party's stand on the role of government more in line with his own. He lost the nomination to

---

See Speech File, RRLPRS; Segregation in Armed Forces Speech *Congressional Record: proceedings and Debates of the 81st Congress,* Second Session, Vol. 96, Part 7, June 21, 1950, 8992-8993; United States Senate Speech, *Congressional Record: Proceedings and Debates of the 77th Congress,* Second Session, Vol. 88, Part 7, November 17, 1942, 8900-8905; LaGrange, Georgia Speech, October 22, 1959, 3, Russell Memorial Library Speech File.

[41]Kelly, "Richard B. Russell," 52; Numan V. Bartley, *Rise of Massive Resistance: Race and Politics in the South During the 1950's* (Baton Rouge: Louisiana State University Press, 1969), 28; United States Senate Speech, *Congressional Record: Proceedings and Debate of the 74th Congress,* First Session, Vol. 79, Part 2, February 19, 1935, 2195; Quoted in George Brown Tindall, *Emergence of the New South, 1913-1945* (Baton Rouge: Louisiana State University Press, 1967), 483-84; Mutual Radio Address, March 23, 1948, 4, Speech File, RRLPRS.

Adlai E. Stevenson, who in turn was defeated by war-hero and Republican candidate, General Dwight D. Eisenhower.

Agriculture and Industry

Russell equated farming with values of honesty, hard work, and independence, virtues he idealized as standards by which the nation's citizenry and their achievements should be measured. He praised Georgia's "cotton heritage." The Senator expressed "faith in rural" people. To him agriculture formed the "mudsill of our civilization," for "all wealth comes from soil."[42]

There was a practical side for his concern for farmers. Because of the county unit method of electing candidates, as noted above, early in his career Russell depended upon rural voters to keep him in office. In speeches back home, he continually reminded this constituency of work he did for them. In 1939 he informed a Hart County audience how his "strategic position as Chairman of the Subcommittee on Appropriations" enabled him to administer the Agricultural Appropriation Bill to "provide parity payments for the farmers." In 1964, the Senator told how he "resolved many years ago to do all within my power to improve the lot of the farm and the farm family. . . . If I have succeeded in some small way to achieve this dream then I count my life worthwhile."[43]

Russell backed agricultural interests during a period of significant economic change. William F. Holmes explained how, in the early decades of the twentieth century, Georgians were overly dependent

---

[42]National Cotton Council Convention Speech, February 10, 1959, Atlanta, Georgia, 3-5; Ruritan Clubs Speech, December 5, 1959, Hiram, Georgia, 2; Hartwell, Georgia Speech, dictated April 23, 1939, 5; Cairo, Georgia Speech, October 29, 1953, 6, handwritten version. All speeches in Speech File, RRLPRS.

[43]Hart County Crimson Clover Festival Speech, April 28, 1939, Hartwell, Georgia, 9; Georgia Farm Bureau Federation Speech, November 16, 1964, Jekyll Island, 2. Both in Speech File, RRLPRS.

Introduction 21

upon cotton for their income, a practice that kept prices for the crop low, depleted the soil's nutrients, and required heavy spending on fertilizer. From 1921 to 1923, the boll weevil devastated cotton crops. Between 1920 and 1925, the number of farms decreased from 310,132 to 249,095. With the Great Depression, from 1929 to 1932, farm prices generally fell sixty percent, and cotton decreased to five cents per pound. Income from farm marketing decreased in 1932 to thirty-seven percent of the 1929 receipts. By 1937 it climbed to seventy-four percent, but dropped to fifty-eight percent in 1939. Income from cotton in 1939 was thirty-nine percent of the amount earned in 1929.[44]

In the 1920s research in chemistry and the plant and animal sciences had made available to farmers improved ways of managing crops and livestock. During the 1920s and 1930s, the addition of tractors, cars, and trucks reduced farmers' dependence upon labor. Improved strains and breeds of crops and livestock increased production and threatened the prices that farmers received for their efforts.[45]

Russell was keenly aware of problems confronting farmers, and advocated programs to increase their income. As a member of the Senate's Agriculture Appropriations subcommittee, Russell helped negotiate legislation for the benefit of farmers. In a speech to the Senate, he linked agricultural productivity with national security, arguing that, "If we do not have sufficient food to feed the soldiers, all the other items of equipment will avail nothing." In 1935, he was floor manager in the Senate when the Rural Electrification Act was passed. In 1945, to benefit children and farmers, Russell authored the Federal School Lunch Program. Constantly on guard to defend agriculture, when the House of Representatives acted to reduce

---

[44]William F. Holmes, "Economic Developments 1890-1940," in Kenneth Coleman, *A History of Georgia* (Athens, GA: University of Georgia Press), 257-263; Tindall, *Emergence of the New South*, 365, 409.

[45]Gilbert C. Fite, *American Farmers: The New Minority* (Bloomington: Indiana University Press, 1981), 69-79.

funding for soil-conservation programs by $75,000,000, he admonished colleagues: "It should be unnecessary . . . to address the importance of conserving . . . the fertility of our soil." He argued that the two greatest steps ever taken to preserve American agriculture have been the rural electrification program and the soil-conservation program. The rural electrification program has tended to keep the farmer on the farm. The soil-conservation program has tended to help to preserve the fertility of the soil and to restore soil that has been depleted.[46]

The recurring challenge to farmers and to government was to ensure ample agricultural production without endangering farm income, a predicament that Russell closely monitored. To meet World War II demands, the Roosevelt administration asked farmers to increase production. Farmers agreed, but they wanted assurances of protection for their prices, a policy Russell defended. In 1949 Congress approved a policy of sliding price supports, with Russell holding out for a fixed amount for farmers.

In 1953 Senator Russell accused the Eisenhower administration of abandoning agriculture to a fluctuating "free market." In 1958 Russell complained that policies of Eisenhower and Ezra Taft Benson denied farmers an equitable share of the "consumers' dollar" by "lowering and abolishing price supports." During the early 1960s, the John F. Kennedy administration advocated increased restrictions on farm production and government supports to boost prices for crops.

---

[46]United States Senate Speech, *Congressional Record: Proceedings and Debates of the 80th Congress*, Second Session, Vol. 94, Part 5, May 24, 1948, 6320-6225; Atlanta EMC Speech, November 4, 1964, Lyons, Georgia, 2-3, Speech File, RRLPRS; United States Senate Speech, *Congressional Record: Proceedings and Debates of the 87th Congress,* First Session, Vol. 107, Part 8, June 20, 1961, 10804.

Introduction 23

In 1964, midwestern Republicans and southern Democrats cooperated to pass legislation supportive of planters of cotton and wheat.[47]

Russell promoted research that benefited farmers, manufacturers, and consumers. As governor, he funded research for agriculture. In 1931 he made available from the state's contingent fund $50,000 to Dr. Charles Herty. Russell related how Herty operated "a pilot plant type experimental laboratory to demonstrate that Georgia pine could be used in the manufacture of pulp and paper," the result being a "thriving pulp and paper industry."[48] In the Senate, he helped appropriate funds for agricultural research. For example, in 1961, Senator Homer E. Capehart of Indiana asked: "What proportion of" the seventy-eight million dollars "will go toward the finding of new uses for farm products?" Russell answered:

Oh it goes for all kinds of research—to develop new seeds and new strains, to cope with diseases which attack plants. . . . Through the test tube, we have seen the most spectacular increase in the production of agricultural commodities in this country.[49]

Russell helped obtain federal funding for research laboratories nationally and in Georgia. During his campaign for the presidency in 1952, he reminded a Spokane, Washington, audience that he had "assisted in building worthwhile projects in every one of the seventeen western states." As a member of the powerful Appropriations Committee, he kept a close watch on how and where funds were spent.

---

[47]National Fertilizer Association Speech, Atlanta, Georgia, November 18, 1953. 6-7; Georgia General Assembly Speech, February 17, 1958, Atlanta, 8. Both in Speech File, RRLPRS; Fite, *American Farmers*, 169.

[48]National Association of State Foresters Speech, October 7, 1968, New Orleans, 6-7, Speech File, RRLPRS

[49]United States Senate Speech, *Congressional Record: Proceedings and Debates of the 87th Congress*, First Session, Vol. 107, Part 8, June 20, 1961, 10804.

In 1965 he complained that "fifty-nine percent of all government-sponsored university research money" went to "twenty-five institutions," with none located in the South. This "flagrant discrimination against the South," he insisted, must cease. He pledged to use every "legitimate means . . . to influence the location of desirable Federal activities in Georgia." Among the more than two dozen research facilities he helped fund in his home state were the Poultry Disease Research Center, the Forestry Research Laboratory, the Regional Vocational Rehabilitation Center, the Southeast Water Pollution Laboratory, the Piedmont Soil and Water Conservation Project, and the Coastal Plains Experiment Station.[50]

Aware of the increasing number of citizens moving to towns and cities, Russell supported industry, resources, and services for his state and nation. He advocated wise development of the nation's resources as a means of maintaining a healthy economy and strong military defense. Russell asked that displaced farmers be aided by the creation of more industrial jobs. By 1959, realizing the potential for growth in manufacturing in the South, Russell called for a "balanced agricultural-industrial economy."[51]

The Senator strived to develop Georgia's recreation facilities, hydroelectric power, municipal water supplies, navigation, flood controls, irrigation, game and fish, conservation policies, pollution control, industry, and military bases. Before his retirement in 1965 Congressman Carl Vinson and Russell promoted local economies by helping fund military installations and contracts in Georgia. Russell was instrumental in winning contracts for the Lockheed company. In 1958 Russell told an audience in Columbus, home of Fort Benning,

---

[50]Presidential Campaign Speech, June 19, 1952, Spokane, Washington, 3; Georgia Press Association Speech, July 9, 1965, Jekyll Island, Georgia, 15-16; County Commissioners Speech, April 6, 1964, Jekyll Island, Georgia, 7. All three speeches in Speech File, RRLPRS.

[51]Ruritan Clubs Speech, December 5, 1959, Georgia, 6; Gray Civics Clubs Speech, October 28, 1959, Georgia, 6. Both speeches in Speech File, RRLPRS.

Introduction 25

that Georgia ranked fifth nationally in combined military and civilian payrolls of the Department of Defense, a sum of $424 million a year. In 1965 he informed a Kiwanis Club convention that Georgia enjoyed a federal expenditure of two billion dollars a year, four times the amount of the state's budget. In 1970, although ill, the Senator advocated before the Senate continued authorization of $200 million for the C-5A Aircraft Program, concluding: "I am proud to say this airplane was conceived and designed and is assembled by men and women of Georgia, and I cannot deny that I am vitally concerned about their well-being."[52]

When the Senator spoke in communities back home, he told how he obtained funding for projects of local interest. At Chatsworth, Georgia in 1964, Russell explained:

> I sweat a great deal of blood over the Carters Dam Project. . . . There wasn't any money in the Budget in 1962 for the purpose; I finally prevailed on the Senate Sub-Committee [of] which I'm a member . . . to appropriate a substantial amount to get started."[53]

The *Congressional Record* indicates that, along with major projects in agriculture and the military, Russell used his influence to address the following concerns: water conservation, school lunch programs, communicable diseases, federal work programs, labor, airports,

---

[52]Ruritan Clubs Speech, December 5, 1967, Hiram Georgia, 12; Association of United States Army Speech, November 12, 1958, Columbus, Georgia, 2, typed carbon; Kiwanis Club Convention Speech, September 28, 1965, Jekyll Island, Georgia, 12-13. All speeches in Speech File, RRLPRS. See also United States Senate Speech, *Congressional Record: Proceedings and Debates of the 91st Congress,* Second Session, Vol. 116, Part 18, July 16, 1970, 24718.

[53]Gray Civics Clubs Speech, October 28, 1959, Georgia, 8; Carters Dam Speech, November 14, 1964, 2, both in Speech File, RRLPRS.

banking, atomic energy, flood control, highways, work relief, small producers, weed control, rodents, rayon, bridges, liquor, funerals, civil aeronautics, gasoline, medicine, and veterans issues.

Military Preparedness

Russell was a chief advocate for the nation's military defense. He was introduced to the military at an early age, graduating from the Gordon Institute, a private military preparatory school in Barnesville, Georgia in 1915. Russell recognized the lasting influence Gordon Institute had upon him. As a student at the University of Georgia, Russell served in the United States Naval Reserves prior to the Armistice, continuing on inactive duty from 1919 to 1921. This tour of duty enabled Russell to join the American Legion, an organization that provided a base of statewide support for political campaigns. When criticized by Gene Talmadge for his limited military service, Russell answered that he served as his country "told me."[54]

Born on November 2, 1897, Russell's early views on the nation's defense were influenced by stories of the South. In a speech before the United Daughters of the Confederacy in 1931, Russell cherished the "Old South" as a "land of culture, of honor and of chivalry." The "Southern response" to calls to duty and the region's "devotion to principle," he praised, make "our section the bulwark of our democratic institutions to-day." In that early address, Russell warned of the threats of communism and socialism to the country's national defense. In an Armistice Day Speech in 1928, Russell cautioned how even "a land as rich and favored as ours would be more helpless than

---

[54]Kelly, "Richard B. Russell," 48, 50-53; Armistice Day Speech, November 11, 1928, Barnesville, Georgia, 10-11, Speech File, RRLPRS; Lincolntown speech, *Atlanta Constitution*, July 30, 1936; Cartersville speech, *Atlanta Constitution*, August 9, 1936.

Introduction

a lamb in a pack of wolves if we were without means of adequate self defense."⁵⁵

Like most Americans and their elected representatives, initially Russell opposed American involvement in World War II. He resisted participation in international conflict unless the security of the United States was endangered. In a speech at the Hart County Crimson Clover Festival in Georgia in 1939, the Senator promised not to vote "for any measure that will take the sons of one Georgia mother to settle the quarrels of Europe." While recognizing that "the clouds of war are hovering ominously low over Europe," he warned against the "effects of the propaganda" that led the United States "into the last great European war." He advised the nation to "keep our heads and attend strictly to our own business," reminding the audience that "we are blessed with geographical isolation."⁵⁶

By 1941, after Adolph Hitler's German army had invaded Poland and Czechoslovakia, Russell attempted to prepare Georgians for global conflict. At a joint meeting of 4-H Clubs members and their parents and leaders, Russell warned that "Hitler and his satellites in Italy and Japan" threatened the "simple rights of humanity." Sensitive that he had earlier opposed fighting a new war, Russell stated that "it is too late now to debate," for "the Congress and the President have entered into a solemn commitment to aid those fighting Hitler." "We will make" any "sacrifice" required "rather than surrender one jot or tittle of our freedom."⁵⁷ On December 7, 1941, the Japanese attacked the American fleet and military installations at Pearl Harbor, Hawaii.

The Senator then helped ready the nation for war—a nation that lacked planes, guns, and ammunition. In 1942, responding to the

---

⁵⁵United Daughters of the Confederacy Speech, October [?], 1930, locale ?, 1-2, 5; Armistice Day Speech, November 11, 1928, Barnesville, Georgia, 10-11. Both in Speech File, RRLPRS.

⁵⁶Hart County Crimson Clover Festival Speech, April 28, 1939, Hartwell, Georgia, 18-20, Speech File, RRLPRS

⁵⁷4-H Clubs' Speech, ca. 1941, locale ?, 5-7, Speech File, RRLPRS.

Navy's request for aid in recruiting, Russell recorded an announcement to be broadcast over radio stations. In the advertisement, the Senator said the battle lines were drawn, with the enemy's submarines "infesting the waters off our shores." He informed prospective recruits of the forty-nine types of job skills they could learn in the Navy. In 1943, Senator Harry S. Truman asked Russell to chair a committee to visit war theaters and report findings to the Senate. On October 28, 1943, Russell related to the Senate observations made while on that fact-finding trip. He praised the courage of the nation's soldiers, and explained conditions that the Congress must improve. For example, he told how the "problem of transportation involved in the war is so great as to stagger the imagination."[58]

When World War II ended on 8 May 1945, Russell warned the nation not to repeat mistakes of the past and lower its military guard. In a speech to University of Georgia Alumni in 1946, he reminded that "the outbreak of war" in the early 1940s "found us unprepared." Drawing from historical examples, the Senator insisted that "peace cannot be assured merely by winning a war." Russell warned of a new world of atomic warfare when a conflict would "be over in a matter of hours." The human family was now challenged to learn "how to live together in peace or . . . die together in an atomic war." The United States should "exhaust every possibility to come to an understanding with Russia." For America isolationism, he insisted, was "all but dead" and should not be revived. Russell supported the United

---

[58]Robert Dallek, *Franklin D. Roosevelt and American Foreign Policy, 1932-1945* (New York: Oxford University Press, 1979), 222; Navy's Challenge for Service Radio Talk, August [?], 1942, transcribed in Washington, D. C., 1, 5-6, Speech File, RRLPRS; United States Senate Speech, *Congressional Record: Proceedings and Debates of the 78th Congress*, First Session, Vol. 89, Part 7, 8859-8866.

Introduction 29

Nations as an "organization upon which both the weak" and strong nations "may rely for equal justice."[59]

Russell argued that the Korean war was fought "between freedom and slavery." In a speech to an American Legion Convention in 1951, he described how soldiers were assembling once again "for a trial of death," this time in Korea. Only the United States, he insisted, possessed "the resources to stand firm before the threat of global subversion." The country had almost instantly awakened to Communist aggression in Korea. Only "a stockpile of atomic bombs" and the "gallant" soldiers landing on the "peninsula of Korea" allowed "time to correct our costly errors."[60]

Throughout the 1950s and 1960s, with the nation caught up in the Cold War with the Soviet Union, Russell warned that danger from Communism came in the forms of economic competition, internal subversion, and war. In 1959 the Senator used the Soviet Union's launching of a satellite to illustrate the seriousness of the danger of "international communism." Russell contrasted the United States' emphasis upon God and freedom with Communism's Godlessness and slavery. He called for "concrete deeds" from the Soviet Union as proof of their honorable intentions. He demanded that Premier Nikita Khrushchev's words of peace be corroborated with actions, for the Soviet Union respected "only strength and power." In an unusual expression of confidence in the nation's military preparedness, Russell found "a broad public understanding" of the need to maintain a large and well equipped armed forces. He also saw "a few hopeful signs" of improved U. S.-Soviet relations.[61]

---

[59]University of Georgia Alumni Speech, June 13, 1946, Athens, Georgia, 2-16, RRLPRS, Speech File.

[60]American Legion Convention Speech, October 15, 1951, Miami, Florida, 5, 7-11, RRLPRS, Speech File.

[61]Dedication of Federal Building Speech, October 19, 1959, Brunswick, Georgia, 3; Association of Attorneys General Speech, December 16, 1952, Sea Island, Georgia, 9-10; Ruritan Clubs Speech, December 5, 1959, Hiram, Georgia,

Russell addressed the complexity of maintaining a modern military. He maintained that the United State's "salvation" was in the "development of missiles and similar scientific-age weapons." Although straightforward about the need, the Senator explained the difficulty of obtaining "objective advice when a decision must be made . . . by advocates of different types of weapon systems." The "missiles and electronic equipment" employed by the military had become so complex that they required "holders of graduate science degrees to man them." Consequently, he continued, to win the fierce struggle with Communism in the "space age," the nation's education had to advance in "science and production."[62]

Russell divulged the anguish involved in supervising discussions that could determine the destiny of humanity:

> As Chairman of the Senate Armed Services Committee, I have sometimes emerged from a lengthy session when the potential of these great weapons that we possess is outlined . . . wondering if I am not in the midst of a hideous nightmare.

It was now possible, he lamented, that humanity's new weapons might destroy "all that we have known and loved." In 1963 Russell opposed a treaty with the Soviet Union banning nuclear weapons tests in the atmosphere, in outer space, and underwater. During Senate debate, he emphasized the Soviet Union's broken promises. While yielding to

---

16; Douglas Chamber of Commerce Speech, December 8, 1959, Douglas, Georgia, 5, 12-15. All in Speech File, RRLPRS.

[62]Daughters of the American Revolution Speech, April 15, 1957. Washington, D. C., 8-9; Atlanta Chamber of Commerce Speech, December 8, 1959, Georgia, 19; Douglas Chamber of Commerce Speech, December 8, 1959, Douglas, Georgia, 5, 12-15; Dalton High School Speech, December 13, 1962, Dalton, Georgia, 2, 9. All in Speech File, RRLPRS. See also *Citizen News*, Dalton, Georgia, December 14, 1962.

Introduction

no one in his desire for an effective treaty, he opposed "any program of disarmament . . . that did not provide for on-site inspections." When Arkansas Senator William Fulbright retorted that the Joint Chiefs of Staff had endorsed the test ban treaty, Russell answered that he was among those few "independents" remaining who could make "up their own minds," and that he was "not afraid to stand, and to stand alone, if necessary."[63]

Although Russell worried about the evils of the "staggering debt," he was more concerned about the nation's security. "If a majority of the Congress had voted as I have voted over the past ten years," he insisted, "we would have a stronger defense, a balanced budget, and a smaller debt." The Senator counseled that the "stupendous" deficit of more than $285 billion could be abolished by eliminating waste. All suggested expenditures, he advised, should be "measured against the national interest." For example, in the 1960s, the Senator maintained that "scattering" foreign aid "about the earth" was not in the nation's enlightened self-interest and threatened its economy.[64]

Russell opposed the United States entry into the Vietnam war. When President Lyndon B. Johnson accused the North Vietnamese of attacking Americans in the Gulf of Tonkin, however, Congress approved the President's request for authority to protect the nation's interest. By the end of 1967, Johnson had sent 600,000 troops to Vietnam. To mobilize the nation for battle, Johnson depended upon Russell, Chair of the Senate's Armed Service's Committee. Perplexed by the nation's participation in a war many felt it lacked the will to

---

[63] United States Senate Speech, *Congressional Record: Proceedings and Debates of the 88th Congress*, First Session, Vol. 109, Part 13, September 17, 1963, 17154-17167; emphasis added.

[64] Georgia Bankers Association Speech, April 15, 1959, Augusta, 5-6; Georgia Association of County Commissioners Speech, March 24, 1959, Atlanta, 25; Georgia Bankers Association Speech, April 15, 1959, Augusta, Georgia, 30-31; Jasper, Georgia Speech, July 4, 1963, 6; Gordon Military School Speech, Barnesville, Georgia, May 26, 1963, 9-16. All in Speech File, RRLPRS.

win, he admonished leaders never to send "a single American boy" into "combat unless the entire civilian population and total wealth of our country" were to be employed to afford "him the fullest support and protection." Once a president committed troops to the battlefield, Russell believed, the time "for hindsight" was over. The citizenry must "deal with the situation as it exists," with "nineteen thousand American lives" already lost.[65]

On 20 March 1969, speaking on the occasion of the Admiral James Forrestal Memorial celebration, Russell advised that only through cooperation between government and industry could the nation properly equip the military. "With power comes responsibility," he stated. Perhaps recalling his early advocacy of Roosevelt's New Deal programs to provide economic relief for many Georgians, the Senator envisioned a time when the nation could invest the billions of dollars being spent on the Vietnam war for "urbanization programs, education, job-training, poverty, and other similar measures." But, as indicated by the Soviet Union's invasion of Czechoslovakia in 1968, he cautioned, the nation must first satisfy the "increasing demands of our defense establishment."[66]

Civil Rights

In 1936 Russell ran for reelection to the United States Senate on a platform embracing President Franklin D. Roosevelt's New Deal programs. Eugene Talmadge, having won three statewide elections for Commissioner of Agriculture and two for governor, was confident that he could defeat Russell. In hundreds of stump talks, Talmadge

---

[65]Dewey W. Grantham, *United States Since 1945: The Ordeal of Power* (New York: McGraw-Hill Book Co., 1976), 39, 214-222; Veterans of Foreign Wars Congressional Dinner Speech, March 12, 1968, Washington, D.C., 4-7, Speech File, RRLPRS.

[66]Admiral James Forrestal Memorial Award Speech, March 20, 1969, Washington, D.C., 6-14, Speech File, RRLPRS.

charged Russell with betraying the faith of the founders and his own campaign promises of prudence in federal spending. Throughout Georgia Talmadge placed Russell on public trial before the voters for advocating increased federal spending and the integration of African Americans and whites in the workplace. In a speech at LaGrange, Talmadge proclaimed that Georgians would choose his willingness to fight for affordable expenditures over Russell's rubber stamp for New Deal extravagance. Misjudging the attitude of voters, Talmadge predicted that Roosevelt and Russell would be defeated because the "real American people" wanted "less interference with business" and an end to "this crazy orgy of spending."[67]

More in tune with the attitudes of Georgia voters, Russell defended himself against Talmadge's verbal assaults by linking his candidacy with Roosevelt's New Deal programs. Roosevelt, after all, enjoyed great popularity among Georgians. Being a part-time resident of Warm Springs, and having expressed some understanding of the South's problems, Roosevelt proved an asset to Russell's 1936 campaign, a factor the Senator exploited in speeches. In Columbus, Russell praised Roosevelt as a fellow Georgian.[68] Before large and receptive audiences, Russell contrasted cruel conditions confronted during his first campaign for the Senate in 1932, with improvements brought about by New Deal policies. He insisted:

> Four years ago no farm house had a coat of paint, there were no repairs. We saw the women and children of this state working in the sun picking cotton and yet they were not able to get enough for it to buy clothes to wear.[69]

---

[67]LaGrange, Georgia speech, *Atlanta Constitution*, August 13, 1936; Interview in New York City, *Atlanta Constitution*, May 18, 1935.
[68]Columbus, Georgia speech, *Atlanta Constitution*, September 8, 1936.
[69]Marietta, Georgia speech, *Atlanta Constitution*, September 4, 1936.

Because of government support, Russell argued, farmers now were paid twelve cents for cotton rather than five. Creating agencies for national recovery provided Georgians an opportunity to earn a livelihood. Russell backed the Citizens Conservation Corps so that "boys of Georgia" could "learn how to work" and be able to "send parents some money."[70]

Unlike Talmadge's opponents in former elections, incumbent Senator Russell refused to be backed into a defensive campaign stance. Russell cornered Talmadge on the stump. A skillful and fearless campaigner, Russell adapted his speaking style to achieve particular ends. When explaining a position on a key issue, he spoke in a slow, deliberate manner. But when assessing Talmadge's platform in 1936, Russell issued a "devastating fire."[71]

Realizing he was losing the senatorial campaign, Talmadge introduced race into the debate, charging that Roosevelt and Russell "heavily taxed" whites to provide elderly blacks with "huge pension" payments. To defuse Talmadge's potentially explosive charges, Russell recited the regional loyalty oath that "this is a white man's country" and pledged to keep it that way. To demonstrate the absurdity of Talmadge's claims, Russell compared his opponent's argument against pensions for the elderly to ending highway construction "because a negro [sic] might ride on one."[72]

Talmadge's persistent accusations concerning racial desegregation heightened Russell's awareness of the precariousness of a southerner's elected office. There were other reminders. As early as 1934 Russell

---

[70] Macon, Georgia speech, *Atlanta Constitution*, September 5, 1936; Statesboro, Georgia speech, *Atlanta Constitution*, July 5, 1935; Eatonton, Georgia speech, *Atlanta Constitution*, August 22, 1936.

[71] Macon, Georgia speech, *Atlanta Constitution*, September 5, 1936; WSB radio speech, Atlanta, Georgia, *Atlanta Constitution*, July 21, 1936.

[72] Arlington, Georgia speech, *Atlanta Constitution*, August 29, 1936; Omega, Georgia speech, *Atlanta Constitution*, July 24, 1935; Cartersville, Georgia speech, *Atlanta Constitution*, August 9, 1936.

received letters from white Georgians complaining how New Deal policies promoted racial equality by paying the two races equally and by allowing blacks to supervise whites. Russell responded to many individual charges, but disagreed that segregation of the races was threatened. However, after the unruly campaign of 1936 in which Talmadge had introduced the topic of race, Russell returned to the United States Senate resolved to avoid even the appearance of favoring policies that integrated the races.[73]

When Russell entered the Senate in 1932, racial segregation in southern society was enforced by local and state laws. C. Vann Woodward explained how, in 1887, when the two races competed for wages, poor whites demanded that Jim Crow laws be passed to maintain their economic advantage. Local and state laws were approved, separating the races in trains, courtrooms, schools, libraries, hotels, theaters, and residential areas. In 1896, in *Plessy v. Ferguson*, the Supreme Court upheld laws providing for alleged separate but equal arrangements in society.[74]

Although insisting that he did "not like to deal with the racial aspect" of issues and that he was "often misunderstood," after being attacked by Talmadge and receiving criticism from constituents, he opposed proposals that fostered desegregation, explaining that he was "keeping faith with the people" whom he was "proud to represent." Russell argued that court decisions and legislation that ignored existing laws to protect the civil rights of a particular group were unconstitutional. For example, in 1944 he supported an amendment in the Senate that denied transfer of power from Congress to the executive branch to create bureaus and departments of government, hoping to thwart the expansion of the Federal Employment Practices Commission's assistance in the South. In 1946 Russell told Senators

---

[73]Kelly, "Richard B. Russell," 141-142; Fite, 169.
[74]C. Vann Woodward, *Origins of the New South, 1877-1913* (Baton Rouge: Louisiana State University Press, 1971), 211-212; Tindall, *Emergence of the New South*, 143-146, 712.

that southerners had not "made progress toward absolute social equality, and we will resist it." By 1950 Russell was distinguishing between economic and social relationships between the races. "In any official" task, he maintained, blacks and whites could work "side by side," but in any personal arrangement there must be a "different pattern."[75]

In 1954, in *Brown v. Board of Education*, the Supreme Court ruled that desegregating public schools on the basis of race was unconstitutional. In arguing that the Court was attempting to make law rather than interpret it, Russell joined an ongoing debate concerning the proper function of the Supreme Court. Russell concurred with persons who said that judges should render judgments that mirrored reliably the intentions of the authors of the Constitution. Another view was that the meaning of the Constitution must be continuously reinterpreted through new laws regulating contemporary life. Russell maintained that the Supreme Court abandoned "law and precedent." The Senator called for social change through "evolution and not . . . revolution." He opposed the use of politics for deciding constitutional issues. During the 1950s and 1960s, in concert with Republicans in the Senate, Russell led a small group of "Southern Constitutionalists" in opposing civil rights legislation. Unlike a number of political leaders in the South, however, once a civil rights bill was passed, Russell accepted the new legislation as law under the Constitution. In 1964, in a speech at Berry College in Rome, Georgia, that drew wide attention, Russell demanded that the newly-

---

[75]Mercer University Speech, June 3, 1957, Macon, Georgia, 15; County Commissioners Speech, April 6, 1964, Jekyll Island, Georgia, 23;"Segregation In Armed Forces" folder, ca. 1950, 2. All in Speech File, RRLPRS. See also United States Senate Speech, *Congressional Record: Proceedings and Debates of the 85th Congress*, First Session, Vol. 103, Part 9, July 22, 1957, 11152; United States Senate Speech, *Congressional Record: Proceedings and Debates of the 78th Congress*, Second Session, Vol. 90, Part 3, March 24, 1944, 3059-3066; United States Senate Speech, *Congressional Record: Proceedings and Debates of the 79th Congress*, Second Session, Vol. 92, Part 1, January 25, 1946, 379-380.

enacted civil rights bill "must be obeyed and no ifs, ands, or buts about it." The *Rome News-Tribune* of Georgia judged the politically powerful Senator's endorsement of the law to be of "major significance." The *Macon Telegraph* editorialized that, of the "thousands of speeches" Senator Russell has made "this decade," the one at Berry College "stands out as one of the best." "If Senator Russell . . . argues obedience and condemns defiance," the editor continued, "who in this country has standing to suggest otherwise."[76]

The Speeches in this Anthology

Below the editors reprint thirty-seven speeches Senator Russell delivered between 1928 and 1969. In selecting texts, the editors reviewed different drafts of all the speech manuscripts housed in the Richard B. Russell Library for Political Research and Studies at the University of Georgia, as well as those published in the *Congressional Record*. One text below came from the *Atlanta Constitution*. We chose the version of a text that the Senator appeared to have used while delivering each speech; often he amended these manuscripts in his own handwriting. To avoid unnecessary repetition, we cut some segments of a particular speech, when that material was covered in a different text in this anthology. Those deletions are indicated. At the same time, to provide insight into how Russell spoke to live audiences, we transcribed two speeches verbatim from audio recordings: the Presidential Campaign Speech, 19 June 1952, and the Carters Dam Speech, 14 November 1964.

---

[76]LaGrange Chamber of Commerce Speech, October 22, 1959, LaGrange, Georgia, 2; Georgia General Assembly Speech, February 17, 1958, Atlanta, Georgia, 21; University of Alabama Speech, October 22, 1954, Tuscaloosa, 4, 13; County Commissioners Association Speech, April 26, 1966, Atlanta, Georgia, 6. All in Speech File, RRLPRS. See also *Macon News*, July 17, 1964; *Atlanta Constitution*, July 16, July 16, 1964; *Rome News-Tribune*, July 15 and 16, 1964; *Macon Telegraph*, July 17, 1964.

We included texts we judged to be representative of Senator Russell's initiatives during different periods of his career in government. In these speeches, one observes him in face-to-face struggles with issues confronting Georgia, the nation, and the world. One finds Russell expressing strong convictions on issues of vital interest to the citizenry. The texts are organized chronologically to demonstrate the Senator's views over time on constitutional principles, agriculture and industry, military preparedness, and civil rights.[77]

The editors appreciate the assistance provided by the personnel of the Richard B. Russell Library for Political Research and Studies at the University of Georgia, Athens, including Director Max Gilstrap (1975-1978) and Director Sheryl B. Vogt (1979-present), Orlean Castronis, Glen McAninch, Ann Billups, James Cross, Pam Hackbart-Dean, and Pam Ward. The Russell Library is an invaluable resource for study of twentieth-century American politics, society, and culture. We also acknowledge support received from the faculty and staff of the University of Georgia Library. The editors are grateful to Elise Allen Hawkins, Brenda Adams, Jeanette Reid, and Angela Partain for helping prepare the manuscript for publication, and to the editors and staff of Mercer University Press for their support. The editors appreciate the support provided by the Speech Communication Department, University of Georgia, and the University Research Foundation for preparing the manuscript for publication.

---

[77]Note: Writing before the civil rights revolution led to terminological shifts from Negro to black to Afro-American to African American, Russell typically used the term "Negro." As these speeches are historical documents we have, of course, left the Senator's usage intact. Our own introductory materials, however, will use the designation "African American."

I.

Speeches on Constitutional Principles

United States Senate
WASHINGTON, D.C.

religion and neighborliness — a manifestation of religion, on farms & in small communities — than in cities —

I am one of those who believe that future strength & preservation of America depends on maintaining a strong, prosperous & independent farm population — Farmer lives close to nature & knows nature's God. Sees his work in the seasons & in plant life — Farming develops independence of thought and individualism so essential to preservation of our form of government. It needs a love of the land and a fierce willingness to defend it — We have many breeds of Communists & fellow travellers — & subversive groups today in America — I have never heard of a farmer among them —

Did not profit by history of past civilizations

Handwritten notes, speech at a Rural Ministers meeting, Emory University, Atlanta, Georgia, ca. 1942.

United Daughters of the Confederacy
October 1930

In this address to a statewide meeting of the United Daughters of the Confederacy, delivered at the time Russell was elected governor of Georgia, he supported home, church, and school as "pillars of our civilization."[1] As a remedy for false "cults" that threatened to gain a foothold in society, Russell prescribed the patriotism he found to be pervasive in the Old and New South. In a theme repeated throughout his long career in government, Russell stressed the potential for developing Georgia's plentiful "natural resources." The locale for this speech is not known.

* * * * * * * * *

It is a distinct privilege to be permitted to address you this evening. The United Daughters of the Confederacy are entitled to the profound thanks of every true Southerner. Down through the years it has kept the faith and discharged the sacred obligation it voluntarily assumed of preserving to the New South the priceless heritage of the true story of the Old South. To your organization properly goes the credit for keeping the record straight and preserving for this generation the full legacy of devotion to honor and ideals which we of the New South enjoy. Yours is the sacred duty of implanting in the hearts and minds of those who will come after the last here who followed the stars and bars has departed the proper appreciation and conception of Southern birthright, and the true history of the sacrifices made that we might enjoy it.

---

[1]Text of speech from Speech File, Speech and Media Series, Richard B. Russell collection, Richard B. Russell Library for Political Research and Studies [hereinafter cited as RRLPRS], University of Georgia, Athens, Georgia.

A people without sentiment are poor indeed. I like to consider the figures and the epochal events of the [Eighteen] Sixties as a page of thrilling romance founded on facts. No finer service can be rendered the present generation than in keeping fresh before them the splendid achievements and lofty ideals of the Old South. The Old South was a land of culture, of honor and of chivalry. Her sons and daughters brought knighthood into flower on this continent. Through a long four years' night of sacrifice they demonstrated that war could be waged with desperate bravery, without cruelty, and when finally overpowered by sheer force of numbers they accepted the terms of the victors in good faith and without hate.

The Southern response to the two calls to follow the stars and stripes which have come since the last Confederate battle flag was folded should convince the most skeptical that our love of the memories of the stars and bars does not mean disloyalty to the stars and stripes.

The Southern devotion to principle makes our section the bulwark of our democratic institutions today. The future hope of this republic rests in the natural conservatism and loyalty of the Anglo-Saxon South.

In but a little while the last surviving paladin of the lost cause will join his comrades on the other shore. It has been our privilege to hear from the lips of the survivors of the conflict the true story of deeds of knightly valor and cheerful sacrifice for the "storm cradled nation that fell." The duty will soon be ours to keep the record straight and preserve to posterity the true story of the heroism of the true hearted knights of the Southern Cross and the unequalled devotion of the Southern womanhood.

I trust that in another generation we will be able to celebrate the demise of the last waver of the bloody shirt of sectional hate. When the calm and dispassionate judgment of America reaches a true verdict of the Civil War, all sections of this reunited nation will seek to share the glory which hallows the achievements of the Old South. The epic story of the devotion to principle which inspired the four years' fight against overwhelming odds will be the brightest page of American history and the proudest tradition of our national life.

This organization has preserved the glorious heritage of the Southland, a heritage of honor, chivalry and devotion to ideals. A heritage of great achievement which is without parallel in all of the annals of history. The deathless spirit of the Old South hovers over the New South; at once a benediction and a battle cry, calling the descendants of a great past to the building of a greater future.

As the gentle hand of woman has ever sought to heal the cruel wounds of war, so there has been deposed to woman's keeping the sacred duty of keeping green the graves and fresh the memories that hallow the lost cause. Through the efforts of your organization this task has been well performed. In the years that have gone since Appomattox the United Daughters of the Confederacy has sought to preserve the true history of the bloody fratricidal strife of the Sixties and to inculcate in the hearts and minds of all of us the heritage we possess in the fadeless glory of our Southern sires.

Poor is that country which has no heroes,
But beggared that country which having them forgets.

Heaven forbid that Southern womanhood shall ever cease to emulate the gentle modesty, the sweet refinement and the devoted courage of their mothers. May we never see the time when the young manhood of the South will not have the same devotion to principle and the courage of conviction which inspired the paladins of Lee. If we ever cease to revere those who reared the greater and more progressive South from the ashes of the old, and if Southern hearts do not beat faster when the stirring strains of Dixie are wafted on the Southern breeze, then we will have indeed come to evil days.

In your hands rests a greater responsibility than you perhaps realize in directing the future destinies of all the people, and the call comes to this great patriotic organization to not content itself with preserving the memories of the Old South but to be a militant factor in our national life, and to combat the insidious doctrines that would destroy the very institutions and ideals which are sanctified by the flood of the peerless men of the Confederacy, and the sacrifices and suffering of Southern womanhood.

Leaders of the Old South gave their all in the cause of local self-government and home rule and defence of country, home and liberty. There are today at work within our country those who would spread doctrines and theories of government which are abhorrent to the ideals of the Old South and contrary to the fundamental principles of democratic institutions. Within the last few years we have seen the birth of strange cults and groups, the result of the work of communism and socialism. These influences are at work in this reunited republic and are seeking to overthrow and destroy every means of national defence our nation enjoys with the apparent hope that our nation may be placed in the position of absolute helplessness. In spreading these doctrines, which are so inimical to our institutions, these forces are seeking to enlist the aid of those institutions and organizations which have ever been considered the true pillars of our civilization: such as the churches, the schools and the universities, and organizations of women.

Under the guise of preaching pacifism and working to prevent war, they would worm their way into the confidence of these most worthy institutions and organizations and use them and the confidence in them imposed, as a means of disseminating propaganda which has no proper place in our national life.

We should be most careful before introducing any new fad or doctrine of government for many of those that are apparently fair are wolves in sheep's clothing and would fasten themselves in the very vitals of our national existence. I would not be misunderstood when I say that the time is not yet ripe for America to disarm. But nothing could be more disastrous than for our country to be rendered helpless and incapable of national defence in view of the present unsettled world conditions. I am opposed to war as much as any man, and favor cultivating the good will of all the peoples of the earth, but we will do well to bear in mind that "eternal vigilance is the price of liberty."

This organization can be a tremendous factor in the proper solution of the many grave and perplexing problems which confront our beloved Georgia today. I invite and bespeak the sympathetic cooperation of the United Daughters of the Confederacy in my administration as Governor of Georgia. One of our problems involves a matter I know is dear to your heart; that is the prompt payment of monthly pensions to the remaining Confederate fathers and their widows entitled to draw them. I shall commit my best efforts and energies to see that this is done. I cannot do it alone, just as I cannot solve other great problems of our state alone. You who come from every section of Georgia can materially contribute to the success of my administration by interesting yourselves in the affairs of our state government. Georgia is facing economic questions today that will require the best thought of all of our people and I call on the members of this organization, as true hearted patriots who have the welfare of our state at heart, to help hold up my hands and to lend helpful suggestions and encouragement to your representatives in the General Assembly in the solution of Georgia's problems. The times and the condition of our state government demands that all who have the welfare of Georgia at heart reconsecrate themselves to the duties of citizenship.

Georgia is great in natural resources. We have eight of the nine climatic zones known to this continent. We also have practically every type of soil, adapted to the growth of all known plant life, save that which is purely tropical. From the mountains to the north of us down through the sweep of the costal plains to our coast with its great natural harbors, the state offers an ideal typography. We have unlimited water power which has been harnessed in part and supplies the current which moves the wheels in the nearly four thousand manufacturing plants within our state. Our hills have almost every known clay and mineral, and there is unlimited room for future developments in all lines of endeavor.

No state is richer in history and traditions than is ours. But at last it takes a great people to make a great state. The hospitality of our people is proverbial and we in Georgia can boast of the purest Anglo-Saxon stock, and of the fact that only seven-tenths of one percent of our people are foreign-born. The traditions, the history, the genus of our people are too splendid for us to permit Georgia to lag longer. We must devote ourselves to the common cause in laboring to carry our state forward and make it the brightest star in the constellation of states.

The fires of patriotism must be kept burning on the altars of the hearts of our citizens. We do well to seek to catch the spirit of sacrifice and unselfish devotion that animated the heroes of Dixie. We of today are nurtured at the same warm breast of the mother South; we breathe the same southern air; the same pure Anglo-Saxon blood flows through our veins, the same mountains look down upon us, and the same waters lave the same shores. Standing on the peaceful civilization wrought in our forefathers' sweat and blood, and with the inspiration of their deeds before us, we of the New South will be unworthy sons of noble sires if we do not build here in our fair Southland an empire more magnificent and resplendent than the world has ever seen.

May we of Georgia have the strength and vision to lead the way.

Campaign for Re-election, United States Senate
4 July 1936

As governor from 1931 to 1933, faced with a state economy devastated by the Great Depression, Russell reorganized the many agencies of government. When elected to the United States Senate in 1933, he supported President Franklin D. Roosevelt's New Deal programs as the best means available for restoring prosperity to Georgians. In 1936, when campaigning for reelection to the United States Senate, Russell was opposed by Governor Eugene Talmadge. Talmadge charged that Russell merely "rubber stamped" Roosevelt's extravagant policies, and broke his promise to cut government expenses.[2] Arguing that government should help people in need, Russell defeated Talmadge. In the speech below, broadcast over WSB Radio in Atlanta, Russell warned that Talmadge would deny Georgians the benefit of federal programs.[3]

* * * * * * * * * *

The people of Georgia and the United States celebrate Independence Day today. The day is supposed to commemorate the establishment of a real popular government of, by, and for the people for the first time. Out of the blood and sacrifices of thousands of men, poured out lavishly over hundreds of years on this continent has been reared a structure of government dedicated to the proposition that the people are capable of governing themselves. That eternal vigilance is the price of liberty is as true today as it was when Jefferson made that statement.

The people of Georgia were treated today to some amazing spectacles which are rather incongruous on July 4.

In the first place, they have seen those entrusted with power take the position that the most important business of the people, that of

---

[2]Kingsland, Georgia speech, in *Atlanta Constitution*, August 13, 1936.
[3]Text of speech from *Atlanta Constitution*, July 5, 1936.

selecting their public officials, should not be handled open and above board, but was subject to the whim and caprice of one man, who took to himself the right to manipulate one of the most important functions of government in a manner which is without precedent in any land which has any pretense of democracy. How drunk with power one must be to use the machinery of the people to choose those who will represent them merely to exercise his own ego and build up a crowd! Failing to let the people know who the candidates were may be good showmanship, but it is poor democracy.

Another amazing spectacle is to see a man entering a democratic primary seeking a democratic nomination upon a Republican platform. Despite the many assertions to the contrary, I seriously doubt whether anyone in Washington heard the speech from McRae today, but if they did, they listened for a moment, then with the thought that either Hoover or Ogden Mills had changed their campaign style considerably but were sticking to their sentiments, turned the dial to a more agreeable station.

Despite all of the attempts at mystery, I do not think anyone is at all surprised that Governor Talmadge announced against me for the Senate. I have been convinced for months that this issue would be joined. Everyone knows that the enemies of the President, the representatives of entrenched greed, in their desperate efforts again to recapture the government from the hands of the people, are resorting to every known device to confuse and becloud the public mind. They doubt being able to defeat the democratic party, the people's party, by direction, and are therefore determined to sap and undermine from within. They are scheming to send their champions of reaction and predatory wealth to the senate of the United States, to attempt to bushwhack the party and tie the hands of the President. They know that the Senate is their only chance, and that they cannot enter it other than as a wolf in sheep's clothing.

While Governor Talmadge was conducting his abortive and ridiculous campaign for national prominence, and was seeking to get on the national ticket of either the democratic, the Republican, or any other party, he did a great deal of gallivanting around the country, making speeches. In these speeches he was much more bitter and vitriolic in his attacks on the President of the United States than the deepest dyed Republican had ever dared to be. Not even the most partisan one of them was so intemperate as to chide the President with his physical infirmities.

Naturally, this course caused him to be greeted like a long-lost brother by the misnamed Liberty Leaguers. He was formally adopted as the fair-haired child by those super-Roosevelt-haters, Messrs. Renee du Pont and John J. Raskob. Every time he abused the President they patted him on the back and told him what a great boy he was. They furnished the funds to call a convention at Macon, to rally the enemies of the President and the democratic party, and Governor Talmadge, out of his vanity and ego blandly promised that Georgia and many other democratic states would go against the President in November. They called it the "grass roots convention." I do not know why, unless it was because the roots extended all the way to Wall Street and New York City, to syphon money from the pockets of Raskob and du Pont to attempt to deceive the unthinking into selling themselves and their children into bondage. These men, to protect their financial banditry and brigandage, would buy any political opportunist in the country who might be for sale. They are having a hue and cry raised all over the country in mock defense of a constitution that they know nothing and care less about, until it was invoked and put into effect to protect the masses of the people from the ravages of these men and their cohorts.

I do not claim that all the world is hanging in the balance to catch my utterances here tonight, but I am sure that the monarchs of Wall Street are just as interested in what is happening in this senatorial campaign in Georgia as is anyone in Washington. If some of the planks of the platform announced by the Governor today at McRae had been penned by the hand of Hoover, Shouse, Raskob or du Pont, it could not have more completely stated the ideals of government held by that sanctimonious and hypocritical gang.

Time will not permit me to deal with this platform as fully as I shall from time to time during the campaign. I will merely touch a few high points of the platform that the Governor should have investigated as to their effect on Georgia before he so rashly embraced them.

For example, the Governor declared in favor of returning to every state on a per capita basis the amount of taxes paid by the people of that state, and no more, and pledges to see that the amount of federal funds expended in any state are equal to the amount of taxes paid by that state. Such a program sounds good to the big income taxpayers of the wealthy states, but this democratic administration is justly and rightfully compelling to bear the burdens of government.

Such a program would almost ruin Georgia, for our state receives between six and seven dollars from the federal treasury for every dollar which we pay into the treasury in taxes. If the Governor's policy had been adopted, the many millions sent from Washington [to] build roads in Georgia would be reduced to almost nothing. Aid for vocational education of the country boys and girls of Georgia would be withdrawn; not a farmer could receive a single penny in benefit payments from the federal treasury. Despite drouth, cyclone or any other disaster, the federal government would be powerless to lend aid. Federal contributions for old-age assistance would be impossible in the poorer states. The federal government would be unable to assist in combating the screw worm, the boll weevil and other insects. Federal health work would stop, and many other services of the federal government would have to be dispensed with. When Georgia had paid for operating the federal courts and the support of the military establishments at Forts Benning, McPherson, Screven and Oglethorpe, it would just about cover our contribution to the national government.

No, Governor, you should have investigated this plank handpicked by the Liberty League, before you adopted it. When you look into this matter, you will doubtless try to trim and hedge, and forget this plank, but the people will not forget. If by some fortuitous circumstance you were sent to Washington on this platform, I imagine that you would also have some difficulty in persuading the representatives and senators from the 41 or 42 other states who get more out of the federal treasury than they pay into it to adopt this plank. Such a proposition can benefit only the wealthy states, like New York, who have drained us of all produced by our toil for years

Campaign for Re-election, United States Senate 51

and who under the Governor's system would receive the lion's share of all the federal tax money.

The kindred plank on financing in the Governor's platform was a constitutional amendment to prevent the issuance of federal bonds of any kind unless approved by the people of every state. That there has been some extravagance in the relief program, I would be the last to deny. However, if such a policy were written into the Constitution, it would mean that in a time of great depression, the government would be compelled to stand by handcuffed and see citizens starve without being able to lend them any assistance. It would mean that there could be no Home Owners' Loan Corporation and that the thousands of homes saved by that institution would have passed under the sheriff's hammer into the hands of financial interests. The Federal Land Bank would have been powerless to save a single Georgia farm. Not a single bankrupt farmer could have secured a seed loan or a commodity credit loan. The Reconstruction Finance Corporation could not have saved the deposits of a single Georgia citizen, nor would it have been possible to have insured deposits of banks. Every farmer would have been left at the tender mercy of bankers too terrified to extend any credit, and could not have secured a dime anywhere with which to make a crop.

I will have more to say about this plank in the platform from time to time in the campaign. Check up on it, Governor, and see whether you want to try to carry this plank during the remainder of the campaign. No one likes to use the government's credit, but saving the homes and the rights of a livelihood of the people is very important to the preservation of a democratic government.

Governor Talmadge's plank against the government in business was evidently designed to please the power trust, and was aimed at the Tennessee Valley Authority, the creation of which, along with the policy of loans to farmers, home owners and businessmen who could secure credit nowhere else, is the chief so-called business activity of the government, of which the Republicans usually complain.

I will not in the limited time at my disposal attempt to deal with this issue, and the other planks of the governor's platform in detail. I will reserve this for later in the campaign.

In making his many rash promises today, however, the Governor overlooked the fact that he will not be permitted to carry the National Guard to Washington with him. If his statement about how he twice terrified the President into doing things against his will is true, his presence in Washington in such close proximity to the President would doubtless give the President the jitters so badly that he would be as incompetent as the Liberty Leaguers claim he is. Besides his promise to kick cabinet officers halfway across the continent, force the President and every agency of government immediately and without the slightest delay to obey his every command, cram legislation through Congress, whether the representatives of 47 other states wish it or not, the Governor was very temperate in his promises today.

If he really approached the enormous job he has cut out for himself in the manner he promised his spellbound worshippers today, he would be speedily committed to the room recently vacated by Representative Zioncheck of Washington, in a mental institution. There is however, no occasion to worry—the people of Georgia will save the Governor this embarrassment on September 9.

At McRae today the Governor did not come out as flatly as he did before the millionaire clubs in Philadelphia and New York in favor of his favorite idea, that of repealing the federal income tax. The Governor loved that plank in Philadelphia and New York, and to his credit, be it said that he stood by it in a modified form today. Naturally, Republican millionaires, assembled in marble clubrooms, wildly applauded this proposal to strike down one of the sacred fundamentals of the democratic party. In and out of season our party has always stood for the doctrine of taxation in accordance with ability to pay.

A graduated income tax was first suggested by Thomas Jefferson. It was first written into a national platform by the hand of Thomas E. Watson, when he penned the famous Ocala platform. A proposal to repeal it and permit the unbridled concentration of wealth in this country might be applauded by the millionaire clubs of New York and Philadelphia. But it is an amazing spectacle to have the Governor of a state still impoverished by the ravages of the War Between the

Campaign for Re-election, United States Senate 53

States, advocate a policy of exempting the great wealth of this country from its proper share of taxation.

I predict here and now that this is another plank in the Governor's platform that he will try to forget, even though he advocated it months ago in his political newspaper. Call it the *Statesman*? God save such abuse of the word! May the ashes of Thomas Jefferson, of Bob Toombs and Tom Watson rest in peace as the Governor in his over-weaning ego generously compares himself to them!

The Governor complains of increased income taxes. I voted to increase the income taxes of those who have net incomes of over $50,000 per year, after all the generous exemptions have been allowed. For this vote I have no apologies to make, and this issue is one of those which will be fully discussed later.

This campaign gives the people of Georgia an opportunity to settle forever the policies of Roosevelt, in his efforts to serve all the people, or are so blind, as to be led into the camp of reaction.

I stand for the rights of the average man; the democracy of Thomas Jefferson and Franklin Roosevelt. I believe in a government which affords equality of opportunity, which guarantees the right of every man who is willing to work the opportunity to earn his daily bread. I am willing to work for and hope to see that glad day when every American citizen has an opportunity to own his own home, and to be able to buy clothes and shoes for his wife and children, without being considered fair game for predator interests. I am opposed to a government which shields and protects the malefactors of great wealth or one which will permit a concentration of the great wealth with which God has blessed America, in the hands of a privileged few.

Opposed to this school of thought not only in Georgia, but all over America, we find the representatives of the du Pont-Talmadge-Raskob group, who believe that the kings of finance have an inherent and divine right to control the government, to exploit the masses, and to destroy any hope of opportunity to the young man or woman not born with a gold spoon in his mouth ever to achieve independence or to accumulate a competency.

We shall go on record in September. We shall stand up then and be counted either among those who believe that America belongs to all of the people or we will put signs over every highway leading into the state: "This state the property of Messrs. du Pont, Raskob, and associates; bought and paid for."

It is a rare privilege for me to be permitted to carry in Georgia this summer the battle flag of human rights and liberties which has been handed down from every great American from Washington to Franklin Roosevelt. Fully aware of the nature and magnitude of the forces with which I shall be compelled to contend, I accept the gauge of battle. Money will be spent like water in this campaign, but the people of Georgia cannot be bought. I shall deal with issues, facts and figures, without regard to billingsgate or whispered falsehoods. The outcome of this campaign is too important to resort to methods of political bally-hoo and buffoonery. I will not try to becloud the unthinking, those who are unable to reason for themselves, by using the dances and songs of Moonshine Kates or the strains of music of Fiddling Johns [John Carson].

The people of Georgia can decide during this campaign whether the Governor's rubber-stamp charges are justified. I have no apologies for having stood with the President of the United States on internal economic questions, which are a greater responsibility of his than anyone else. However, I exercised my own judgment in the part I played in defeating the World Court, the St. Lawrence treaty with Canada, in paying the soldiers' bonus and in many other issues. Despite those differences I am a real democrat and I still cling to the faith of the democratic party. I am still a soldier, loyal and unafraid, in the army of Americans who will overwhelmingly elect Franklin D. Roosevelt in November.

Those who wish to lend aid and comfort to the Republican party and the Liberty Leaguers, those who wish to harass and repudiate the President, those who wish to snipe the President from the rear, and those who are seeking special privilege or political loaves and fishes, those who wish to be on the side of those who have unlimited money to spend on the campaign, those who believe that representative government is a failure, those who are unable to think for themselves, and follow blindly a political hero selected by standards of gourds or galluses, all of these will find welcome and companionship in the Talmadge-Raskob-du Pont camp.

I earnestly invite to join me for this campaign all of those who have pride of the fair name and fame of Georgia and her traditions, those who are democrats in other than pretense and lip-service; those who have faith in the ideals and purposes and integrity of Franklin D. Roosevelt, and are willing to support a man who believes in his sincerity; those who believe that the farm boy on the remote farm or the child in the underprivileged home have an equal opportunity with all other Americans to carve a career by his own efforts, to live, to enjoy the advantages of modern civilization, and to earn an honest livelihood in honest sweat.

When I decide that I cannot [any] longer be a real democrat, I will not undertake to furnish the Republicans with thunder by seeking to embarrass the President in September to influence the November elections. I will not fight him under cover or knife him in the back, but will be man enough openly to join some organization or party which is opposing him.

The Governor will probably attempt to recant during the campaign much of that which he has said today and in the past. But whether he seeks to gain entrance to the Senate by open denunciation and vituperative abuse of the President and the party, or whether he appears in the hypocritical and sanctimonious guise of a counterfeit friend, the answer of the people of Georgia will be the same.

The question which the people must answer in September is whether they will furnish campaign ammunition to a dying party of reactionaries to bolster up its cause in the doubtful states in the heat of the campaign by letting this state, Georgia, the bulwark of democracy and the second home of the President, be the first to repudiate him and his policies. You and I both know what the answer to this question will be.

The descendants of those who died with Pulaski and Jasper at Savannah, who won undying fame at Kettle Creek, who participated in the writing of the Declaration of Independence, and wrung freedom from the hands of tyranny 160 years ago, will not barter the faith of their fathers for a mess of pottage, and fantastic promises. The ark of the covenant of American democracy is safe in the hands of the people of Georgia.

Freedom Train
29 December 1947

In this speech, Senator Russell addressed a retail, industrial, and labor rally in Macon, Georgia, on the occasion of the visitation of the Freedom Train. The Freedom Train was a touring exhibition of historical documents representing milestones in the history of liberty in the United States. With victory in World War II still on the minds of many, Russell celebrated the American heritage. "Liberty," the Senator insisted, "depends upon a government of law rather than a government of men." Departing from his prepared text, Russell branded Henry A. Wallace as "one of the corps of termites" in the United States "who have no real understanding of democracy."[4] Russell advocated a strong United Nations.

* * * * * * * * * *

It has been several years since I was privileged to address a Macon audience, and I appreciate the opportunity to be with you on this significant occasion. I am sure that we have all been thrilled by the patriotic sentiments so splendidly expressed by those who have preceded me on this program. I extend my hearty congratulations to Attorney General Tom Clark for having conceived the idea of the Freedom Train. I congratulate all of those here and in other cities of the land who have contributed of their time and money to make this program succeed. Those who have sponsored the idea of Freedom Train and Rededication Week are good citizens, who recognize the truth in Jefferson's statement, "Eternal vigilance is the price of liberty."

Our country has but recently emerged victoriously from the greatest war of history. It was fought to preserve our way of life. For the second time within this generation the youth of America were called upon to leave their homes for the four corners of the world,

---

[4]*Savannah Morning News,* December 30, 1947; Text from Speech File, Speech/Media Series, Richard B. Russell collection, RRLPRS.

there to dare and die and sacrifice that individual liberty might not perish from the earth. For the second time within a quarter of a century we were called upon to pour out lavishly of our treasure and our national resources to beat back the threatening aggression of power-mad dictators.

The men who won these wars had been called too soft to fight. The civilization and system of Government which produced them was denounced as decadent. What was the source of the courage and determination which inspired these civilian soldiers and sailors to crush the goose-stepping professionals of totalitarian states? Whence came the capacity and knowledge which enabled the less than seven percent of the earth's population who live beneath the American flag to produce the food and fiber and superior tools of war to keep our allies in the fight with us until our enemies were overcome? What generated the strength of character which caused the most competitive economic system of the earth to replace selfishness with selflessness, and to unite a controversial people as one behind our leadership until the victory was achieved?

It was the working of the American heritage. It was the knowledge that our institutions of government had brought us more freedom, more happiness, and more material blessings than any other people have ever enjoyed. We did not propose to see them destroyed. A priceless part of our heritage is the instinctive defense of human freedom and individual rights. Even though we have enjoyed a "milk and honey" civilization as compared with the rest of the world, we have not forgotten the history of that heritage or the sacrifices required to give it life. We have managed to maintain the spirit of Runnymede [English meadow where King John accepted the Magna Carta] and of the authors of the great charter of July 4, 1776—the immortal Declaration of Independence. Any and all threats to the priceless blessings guaranteed by our American Constitution have been met with the same grim courage which inspired those who through the centuries have dared to defy autocratic power in defense of the inherent dignity of man.

Our Government is not perfect, but it is by all odds the best yet devised. It is elastic enough to effect improvements and changes peacefully and through the will of our people instead of through the vagaries of those temporarily in power. The existence of liberty depends upon a government of law rather than a government of men. Our Constitution and our admirable system of checks and balances therein established is the culmination of an age-old fight for freedom and the rights of the individual man. It provides more adequately for a government of law, written and enforced by the governed, than any other in the world.

Arbitrary power in individuals always attacks the rights of others. The ruthless quest for more and more power has always marked the most benign of governments of men. Such governments inevitably result in a totalitarian rule of absolute dictatorship. Dictatorships have ever brought the most cruel of wars, visiting death, devastation, and unspeakable agony upon masses of people who are helpless to express themselves. So long as dictatorships and totalitarian forms of government shall exist and enslave man to the state, the American heritage cannot be enjoyed in full peace and security. In the very nature of things there will always be an irrepressible conflict, either political or economic, between states where the people are slaves and those where they are free. The threat to our way of life was not removed by the surrender ceremonies in the schoolhouse at Rheims [France, where Germany surrendered, 1945] and on the deck of the battleship *Missouri* [where Japan surrendered, 1945]. We must not let the fact that we have destroyed some of the dictators whose schemes of world domination threatened us lull us into a false sense of security. Through all the years of recorded history men have deceived themselves into the belief that victory in a war could bring a permanent peace. The mistaken belief in 1918 that victory had brought us a permanent peace caused the tragic losses in blood and treasure in 1941-1945. These losses should bring us to the realization that it is necessary for us to strive to make vital the newest document on the Freedom Train. If we are to enjoy our heritage in permanent peace and security we must work and sacrifice until the United Nations becomes a strong and vital force, able to enforce the peace of the earth. We must devise a means of settling disputes between nations without resort to war, just as our courts settle disputes between citizens without resort to the law of the jungle. We must strive for the ideal of a world where all men are free to give expression to their talents and their thoughts as free men. Only when we can acclaim the charter of the United Nations as possessing the authority and significance of Magna Carta, the Declaration of Independence, the Constitution of the United States, and the other priceless charters of human liberty, and send it around the world on a World Freedom Train, will we be assured the full enjoyment of the American heritage.

The way to that glad day is hard and difficult. It is beset with many obstacles. The captious use of the veto power on every move for peace and harmony on earth by the Russians has brought discouragement to some of the most ardent advocates of the United States. But we must not become discouraged. The achievement of the ideal of the United Nations is the last hope of peace on earth. We must exhaust every means at our command to make it a reality.

The average citizen may wonder what he can contribute to the success of the United Nations. He can best contribute by working to make democracy function in these United States. Even an iron curtain cannot forever repel democracy if we improve and perfect its forces in the greatest and most powerful nation of the earth.

The responsibility of citizenship in our own beloved country is therefore very real. The bomb which all but obliterated the city of Hiroshima ushered in the Atomic Age. If we would be worthy of our heritage we must discharge our duties of citizenship every day in the year. We must unite in defense of this heritage. We must see to it that politics stop at the water's edge. Without regard to partisan considerations we must hold up the hands of our representatives in all international councils.

We are guaranteed freedom of speech by our Constitution, but we must not abuse that right by impugning the motives of the men of good will who speak the voice of the American people. They who, whether Republicans or Democrats, desire nothing of the rest of the earth but an era of permanent peace.

It is not an easy task. Great countries of the earth are directed by small groups of fanatical men who will resort to any means to attain their purpose. Even here in our own country we are afflicted by a corps of termites who undertake to undermine the foundations of our Government. The fact that some of them either hold or have held positions of trust and responsibility in our Government has caused most of the confusion in the United Nations. It has caused those who have prevented the United Nations from working to believe that there is great dissension at home. When a former high official of the United States assails the Government which has honored him as being imperialistic, and charges that our Government is seeking to impose its will upon the rest of the world for selfish aims, it is understandable that the Russian representatives in the United Nations would believe that he voices the sentiment of a large part of the people in this country, and that if they will but persist in their course of obstruction they will eventually gain all of their ends with our aid. [This is] particularly defensible in view of our unselfish attitude—[The United States] even spent billions to keep Germans from starving.

Before we can teach democracy to the rest of the world we must teach it to all of our own people. We must educate them to the realization of the basic difference between the spurious democracy proclaimed by the Politburo [executive committee of the Communist Party in the Soviet Union] and the real democracy we enjoy as citizens of the United States. In our wartime zeal we attributed a democratic Government to Russia as a fighting ally. Everyone will do well to recognize now the cold fact that in Russia a handful of masters dominate the masses in an absolute slave state. Mr. [Vyacheslav M.] Molotov [foreign minister, Soviet Union] prates of democracy in his speeches, but he would not recognize our brand of true democracy if he met it in the road. It may be possible to forgive Mr. Molotov, but it is unforgivable for any intelligent American to defend as democratic the form of government imposed by Russia on the satellite states, and which they seek to impose upon the rest of the world.

The very nature of our institutions prevents us from imposing on others by force the establishment of systems of government embodying the principles of ours. We do know, however, that the peoples of oppressed nations everywhere have long strained their eyes to receive a beam from our uplifted torch. By keeping it alight here, we may hope to give them the strength, the wisdom, and the courage to find their own way. The brightness of the beacon which burns here depends upon the strength of patriotism of our citizens and our willingness to sacrifice in time of peace to save that for which so many men have given their lives in time of war. We do not know just what form these demands for sacrifice may take. We have learned, however, the folly of disarming completely until world peace is assured. We must maintain large military establishments until the United Nations is able to walk. Indeed, we cannot discharge our obligations under the United Nations charter unless we do stay strong. It may be necessary to establish a form of universal military training to prepare us against a sneak attack and to give our young men the knowledge which would enable them to survive if thrown into war without warning. We may be required to further assist with our material resources other people who are struggling to save some elements of a free government from impending threat of statism and communism.

For my part, however, I do not believe that mere giving of material assistance to all nations will save them for the cause of democracy. It has ever required effort and sacrifice on the part of those who would enjoy liberty to gain or retain it. We should help those who are willing to help themselves, but we will never defeat communism in any given country nor truly promote the success of United Nations merely by pouring out our wealth on peoples who are not willing to make substantial sacrifices to assure for themselves the blessings of liberty. Real love of democracy is a thing of the spirit. It must be generated in the minds and hearts of those who seek it. It cannot be forced or purchased from abroad.

The Freedom Train is on its way to this city. In the short time it will be here all of our people cannot view its precious cargo. But we can all seek to understand its sacred documents and comprehend what they mean to us in our everyday life. I especially hope the school children, who are the trustees of tomorrow, may enjoy the inspiration of visiting the Train.

The Freedom Train will be here but a day, then it will move on to another city. We can, however, make each week, indeed each day a Rededication Day. We can resolve to measure up to our responsibilities in time of peace as we have ever done in time of war. Only this will assure that the American heritage will be enjoyed by those who will come after us.

I like the story of a remark made by that great American, Benjamin Franklin, when the Constitution was ratified in Philadelphia. The news had gotten out that the Convention had about completed its momentous labors, and a throng of citizens assembled outside Independence Hall. When Franklin came out the people shouted, "What kind of a government have you given us?" Franklin replied, "We have given you a republic—if you can keep it."

Today we can answer Ben Franklin across the years, "We have kept it. Through these one hundred and sixty years thousands of heroes have shed their blood to defend it. We still believe in that Constitution, and we thank you for the manifold blessings it has brought to us. We pledge ourselves to be eternally vigilant, and to make any sacrifice required of us that our posterity may continue to enjoy the blessings that we have known."

Association of Attorneys General
9 December 1952

In this speech, given at Sea Island, Georgia, Senator Russell addressed 162 delegates attending the 46th Annual Conference of the National Association of Attorneys General. According to the *Atlanta Journal*, in this postelection speech, Russell "called for the naval blockade, stepped up military participation by our allies, and use of Chinese Nationalist troops on Korean battlefronts." Russell praised the nation's lawyers as the prime builders of "today's civilization." Referring to himself as an "old-time fundamentalist in the science of government," Russell criticized the federal government's "reach . . . for greater power."[5]

* * * * * * * * * *

My native state is honored that your distinguished body is meeting within our borders. It is your loss that my distinguished colleague, the senior Senator from Georgia, could not be here to address you tonight as the program promised. But it is a high privilege for me in his place and stead to visit in this presence. [Refer to] Gene Cook.

I live in the hill country of North Georgia. We meet tonight on the edge of our southern boundary. A couple of generations ago those who lived along the Coast looked down their noses at their fellow Georgians of the hills. [Refer to the] Wedemeyer story [probably General Albert C. Wedemeyer].

I am glad that I am able to claim membership in the legal fraternity. I hope that I am a lawyer, for I have remembered throughout my career an oft-repeated saying of my father that "there are thousands of attorneys but precious few lawyers." Any orderly society depends upon precedent, and precedents that have become law, for its existence. It is not invidious to say that no other vocation or profes-

---

[5]Letter from Eugene Cook, Attorney General of Georgia, to Russell, December 22, 1952; in Speech File, *RRLPRS*; *Atlanta Journal*, December 10, 1952; Text from Speech File, Speech/Media Series, Richard B. Russell Collection, RRLPRS.

sion has made a contribution approaching that of the lawyer to the building and maintenance of the orderly society of today's civilization.

The lawyer has been the stabilizing influence. In his mind was born the concept of a government of law rather than of man. He has devised the ways and means of creating and guaranteeing the individual rights and liberties which give dignity to the human being.

The lawyer as an officer of the court stands today as the champion and defender of rights and liberties. In Shakespeare's *Henry VI* we find the first record of which I have any knowledge of a Communist movement in an English speaking land. He quotes Jack Cade, the leader of the historic Cade's Rebellion, as holding out the lure of Communism in the following words:

> Be brave, then; for your captain is brave, and vows reformation. There shall be in England seven halfpenny loaves sold for a penny; the three-hoop'd pot shall have ten hoops, and I will make it felony to drink small beer. All the realm shall be in common, and in Cheapside shall my palfrey go to grass; . . . There shall be no money. All shall eat and drink on my score; and I will apparel them in one livery, that they may agree like brothers.[6]

Dick, his chief lieutenant, then spoke up and unconsciously paid the lawyer one of the greatest tributes of history. Instinctively recognizing that no such scheme could be applied in a land where human rights are protected by law, he said: "The first thing we do, let's kill all the lawyers."

In this year of 1952, the Communist program destroying all property rights, striking down the essential freedoms of speech, of press and to worship according to the dictates of individual conscience—the program which will strip the individual of any pretense of dignity and chain him to the wheel of State—can never succeed in

---

[6]William Shakespeare, *Henry VI*, Part II, Act iv, Scene ii.

a land where lawyers are permitted to measure up to their responsibilities as officers of the court.

We live in an age of increasing complexity. The manner of living and habits of thinking of the human family have undergone greater change since the birth of this republic than in any other 2,000 years of human history. Advances in the fields of science affecting human life have forced great changes in our system of jurisprudence. New problems are presented almost daily. The tendency increases each day to look to government for the cure for every ill, and a law to apply to every adjustment in our way of living.

Human nature is such that those who control any phase of government constantly reach out for greater power. The rapid changes have tended to concentrate the power of government in a central source. With every problem comes a demand that the Federal Congress pass a law.

This tendency threatens to eventually obliterate the States and their subdivisions as units of government.

I may be an old-time fundamentalist in the science of government, but I believe that all of our vaunted freedoms, all of the rights of our citizens which distinguish these United States from any other country as a true land of liberty, all of these depend for their very existence upon maintaining the dual form of government wisely decided by the founding fathers and zealously protecting the rights and powers of the States and people from undue encroachment by Federal power.

The shores of human history are littered with the wreckage of great civilizations which destroyed themselves by an undue concentration of power and authority over their citizens. All men intend to use power wisely. Nine may do so, but the tenth in the name of the public interest will take steps to strike down the rights of the governed.

We are living in a day of great tensions which sorely try our endurance. The temptation is great to take the easy path of surrendering the right to govern ourselves to a super state that will do for us without the individual citizen having to worry to reach the proper solution to many varied problems. If we are to keep faith with our past and reach the proper and reasonable goal of our future, we must maintain the rights of the several States and of the people against the constant threat of encroachment by Federal power in whatever guise.

We must preserve the delicate system of checks and balances between the Executive, the Legislative, and the Judicial branches of the Government which have enabled us to grow great. The curse of Communism can never fasten itself upon a land where men are free and possessed of knowledge.

You gentlemen as the Attorneys General of your states bear a peculiarly heavy duty as those chosen by your people to defend the rights of your states. The duty is yours to preserve and defend in the courts that proper balance between the central government on the one hand and the States and the people on the other, which is essential to the American system. The Attorneys General of this nation have a closer community of interests and a greater need for unity than any other group of State officials. The nation owes the Attorneys General a vote of thanks for the manner in which you have measured up to this responsibility in many cases in the recent past.

There is alive in today's world a new and degrading force which threatens every citadel of human freedom which man has tediously erected through the centuries. We know that this force is bent upon world domination and we have seen it bring countless millions under its vile control.

In this enlightened age the issue is crystal clear—even a wayfaring man can distinguish between God and Godlessness and between freedom and slavery. The question will be resolved by the fortitude, patience, and the willingness to work and sacrifice of this generation. Under the American system we have achieved such great strength, that inexorable fate has thrust upon us the responsibility of world leadership. We did not seek—indeed, we did not desire—this costly responsibility. But we cannot escape it if we are to save ourselves and keep alight the lamp of human liberty on this globe.

We are confronted today by a ruthless foe who understands but one language. To meet the threat of world Communism we are seeking to organize the free peoples of the earth, many of whom are tired and listless, into a force strong enough to deter armed aggression and spare mankind the horrors of an atomic war. We have departed from century-old tradition and committed ourselves to go to the defense of anyone of the signatories to the North Atlantic Pact who might be the victim of aggression.

We have taxed ourselves to a degree unheard of in peacetime to rebuild the economies of peoples on other continents. We have drained our nation of many of its natural resources to furnish the costly weapons of modern war to those associated with us in the cause of freedom. We are engaged in the mightiest peacetime effort of human history to build a bulwark against the evil force of tyranny.

All of these have brought us new problems. Problems which must be met in such a way as to preserve the system which is the source of our future.

The increasing responsibilities of the Federal Government in the field of international relations creates a threat to the rights of States and our dual system of government. We must find ways and means to give the Federal Government power to meet the common danger without vesting all power of government in Washington.

Many new problems of law are created in the treaties which we have found it necessary to negotiate as we seek to unify and solidify those states still outside the Iron Curtain. We find that these treaties might well affect adversely the individual rights and liberties of American citizens under the provision of the Constitution which make a treaty the supreme law of the land.

The lawyers of this nation have already sounded the tocsin of danger and the Congress is moving to strengthen the guarantees of individual rights and liberties of our people from derogation by treaty law.

In our mighty effort to stem the march of Communism, we have found it necessary to come into armed conflict on a small peninsula off the coast of Asia. There is many a mile from here to Korea. We are separated by a continent and the greatest of oceans. But tonight the hearts of millions of Americans are there with the brave men who are defending the cause of human freedom.

The conflict in Korea presents one of the most difficult tests of the fiber of our people. The fighting for freedom is being waged in the name of the United Nations. As a matter of fact, we all know that other than South Koreans, we have contributed ninety percent of the men to the United Nations forces and that we have supplied more than ninety percent of the cost of the war.

The Korean War, if not only trying the patience of the American people, is the first real test of collective security. As the strongest member of the United Nations it is mete and proper that in supplying our proportionate part we would have more forces and furnish more arms than any other nation.

However, if we are to maintain the United Nations as a collective effort, it is high time that the other members of this organization increase their contributions to the Korean War. This is necessary not only in justice to the American people, but to create the proper sense of responsibility on the other free nations of the earth if all of the free world has an equal stake in resisting Communism.

It is true that the British are extended. They have responsibilities in the Suez Canal; in the Middle East; have considerable forces in the NATO [North Atlantic Treaty Organization] armies in Germany, and are waging guerilla war in Malaya. They live so close to the millions of Russians and Communist satellites that it is necessary for them to maintain considerable forces in England.

France is engaged in armed conflict with Communist forces in Indo-China, which is a drain upon their regular Army—but it is noteworthy that they do not send drafted men into conflict there.

Australia, New Zealand, and Canada have only token forces in Korea. They can, and should, supply more troops to the common effort there.

The troops of Chiang Kai Shek on Formosa should be trained and equipped as rapidly as possible. I favor their use in the Korean conflict, or on diversions against the Chinese mainland that they are able to handle on their own.

All are agreed that more South Koreans should be armed and equipped as speedily as possible.

In the long course of the [General Douglas] McArthur hearings, I became tremendously impressed with the importance of an airtight Naval blockade against the Chinese Communists. Our Department of State and our representatives in the United Nations should work ceaselessly to secure the approval of a majority of our associates in that body in imposing this blockade.

We have twice disarmed after victory before world peace was assured. We have paid the price of our folly in blood and treasure. We must show the fortitude necessary to maintain adequate defense and deter aggression until the danger has been dispelled.

In the dark days following June 25, 1950, our safety depended upon our possession of the atomic bomb and the means of delivering it. While we have not completely utilized our time since then, we have greatly strengthened our defenses. We have doubled our Air Force and Navy and tripled our Army. We have produced weapons of war which were desperately short in those dangerous days. While our defense is far from complete, we are now strong enough to take our destiny in our own hands.

The threat to the American way of life, both internal and external, has greatly increased the responsibilities of the legal profession. The basic principles of liberty and freedom are eternal. New ones cannot be formulated, but the legal profession owes it to our country and to the world to preserve those principles and to translate them into understandable form in the light of changing conditions. In an age of vast complexity they can be presented in simple terms that will keep them attractive to the new generations who find them commonplace and do not realize the sacrifices made to obtain them or the great danger of losing them. I am confident that under your leadership we will meet these problems with awareness of our past and faith in our future.

University of Georgia Law Day
1 May 1954

In 1952, Senator Russell campaigned to become the Democratic Party's nominee for president of the United States. He lost to Adlai E. Stevenson. In 1954, the Supreme Court ruled that segregated public schools in the South were unconstitutional. Approximately two weeks prior to that judicial ruling, Russell addressed a capacity crowd in the historic chapel at the University of Georgia. Charles Bloch, prominent Macon attorney, introduced Russell, expressing the desire that the Senator become President.[7] Russell discussed "legal principles," changes in the legal profession, the role of "pressure groups," increased power of the federal government, value of "individual rights," and the importance of studying the "science of government."[8]

* * * * * * * * * *

It is a high privilege to be permitted to meet with you on this significant occasion. It is always good to be in Athens. Many of the happiest recollections of my life center about the days I spent in the hallowed atmosphere of this campus.

We glory in the fact that Georgia was the first state to charter a state university. This year the University of Georgia School of Law celebrates its 95th Anniversary. For almost a century it has made a notable contribution to the life and progress of our state and nation. Thousands of graduates have received their training here. The majority of them have entered the legal profession as practitioners. As officers of our courts they have sought to apply to the administration of justice the knowledge gained during their studies here.

Time will not permit me to call the roll of the graduates of this school who have attained distinction not only at the Bar, but in public and official affairs. In every county of the State the graduates of this

---

[7]*Athens Banner Herald,* May 2, 1954.
[8]Text of speech from Speech File, Richard B. Russell Collection, RRLPRS.

School of Law have taken, as they take today, a prominent position in the life of the community and of the State.

As a graduate of the Law School, I am exceedingly proud of the high standards of ethics and of achievement which have been maintained by these men. The careers of many of them bear evidence that this institution has instilled in its graduates the spirit of the legal profession. This is as essential in the making of the complete lawyer as knowledge of the legal principles.

I often heard my father say that there were many attorneys, but few lawyers. The history of the graduates of this school demonstrates that it has produced many real lawyers.

They have brought honor to the profession. In a public capacity, they have served in every office in the gift of the people of this State.

The age in which we live is the most complex known to human history, largely due to the blessings of free government. Our civilization has seen more change in the past century than in any other thousand years.

Necessity produced an age of specialization, even within the old professions and vocations. In the field of medicine, there are specialists who devote their talents solely to some one organ of the human anatomy. Along with all others, many members of the legal profession have been compelled by the tide of events to specialize in some one branch of the law. In Washington, we not only have specialists in tax law, corporation law, admiralty law, and criminal law—but there is a radio bar, a transportation bar, a fair trade bar, a television bar, and others too numerous to mention.

Government has spread its activities into every field of human life.

New legislation, particularly in what is called the field of "government service," has followed the increase of our population, the growth of our nation, and the progress of our civilization. Recent years have brought the enactment of a vast mass of new laws. This has been particularly marked in the field of social security—the regulation of business, such as public utilities—and in methods of taxation. Some of these laws were unknown to the English common law which had served as our guide for so many centuries.

Those who have responsibility for making our laws—whether in city councils, state assemblies, or in the Congress—are caught up in this sweep. Their task has become increasingly complicated.

Almost 16,000 bills were introduced in both branches of the last Congress. It would have been an impossibility for one to read them all—much less study them—and discharge any other duties. After having been sifted through the committee process, only about a thousand passed both bodies. A majority of these are private bills.

The volume of legislation is so great that Members of the Congress tend to specialize in the measures which come before the committees of which they are members.

To add to the problems confronting the lawmaker in any field, he is subjected to special pleading from pressure groups which were either unimportant or non-existent only a few decades ago. In every state house as well and in the nation's capital there are representatives of farm organizations, labor organizations, business organizations, veterans organizations, and racial and religious groups. I venture to predict that every conceivable line of business in which as many as a few hundred people are engaged has a representative on guard to watch every piece of legislation which could even remotely affect the group he represents.

There are times when these organizations are very helpful in bringing information in regard to legislation to the attention of Members of Congress, or to the committees.

However, there are other instances where witnesses before committees elaborate upon the large number of citizens whose voice they claim to speak, with the clear inference that if a member of the committee does not see matters aright, retribution is likely to be visited upon him at the ballot box in the next election.

The founders of our government never intended that public questions should be decided solely on the basis of the number of people involved. They devised our system of divided powers and checks and balances to avoid any action that smacked of mob rule.

Government by pressure groups is one of the real dangers which confront us.

These pressures are not only applied to the members of the Legislative branch. We have seen instances where the Executive Department has found it expedient to bow to such demands.

The founders sought to insulate the Federal Judiciary against any form of pressure from any source, but all of you who are members of the Bar are familiar with decisions of our highest court which would indicate that a political formula had been applied to reach decisions on constitutional and legal questions.

In the very nature of our institutions there is a constant struggle for power between the Legislative and Executive branches of the government. As government expands, this struggle has become more intense. Strong Presidents often impose their wills on the national legislature. There are also times when the Congress clearly usurps powers which belong to the Executive.

The Judiciary was created to decide ordinary cases. It refereed some of the clashes for power between the Executive and Legislative departments. Here of late we have seen a new trend. Some of the recent decisions of our Supreme Court are clearly legislative in character.

Instead of discharging its proper function as umpire, these decisions, particularly in cases where the Executive branch through the Attorney General has intervened, would indicate that the Supreme Court is about to lose its identity as a co-equal branch to become an arm of the Executive branch of our government.

Some of the briefs filed by the Attorney General would indicate that he believes it is the mission of the Court to strike down the rights of the States and of the people reserved in the Tenth Amendment and to transfer them to the central government.

The extended period of cold war in which we are now engaged accentuates our present problems. In a time of national danger it is always necessary to vest the central government with more power in order that it may mobilize the strength necessary to defend our land from foreign enemies.

The Federal Government has vast responsibilities today in the field of international relations, and the safety of us all depends upon its ability to meet these responsibilities. The great challenge is to find

University of Georgia Law Day 75

the ways and means to empower the Federal Government to meet the common danger from abroad without—in our necessity—concentrating too much power in Washington. That concentration is already excessive.

We must not only stop the further encroachment of the Federal power, but we must devise a program which restore[s] to the States and to the people any powers of which they may have been deprived, when the danger has passed.

Representative government is not only threatened in our own land. The whole philosophy of government by law rather than by men is on trial throughout the world. We have seen tired people succumb to the temptation to surrender liberties in exchange for the promise of security. All people everywhere are constantly beguiled to follow the easy way and entrust all power to men who promise to use it wisely.

When men become so indifferent as to be unwilling to fight for their liberties, they resort to the totalitarian state, where one man does the thinking for all. In this atomic age speed in the functioning of government has assumed increasing importance. We cannot, however, afford to accept speed as the only standard. An absolute government—one of men rather than law—can, of course, move much more rapidly than a government reflecting the will of all of the people. But, unfortunately for the governed, those he orders are slaves who know no freedom.

There is a substantial reason for every time-consuming procedure required by our Constitution and by the body of the common law. The founding fathers were not only determined to erect an impregnable bulwark to protect our individual rights and liberties, they were determined that the changes in our forms of government should be a product of evolution and not revolution. Despite—and indeed, because of—the haste and confusion of our everyday life, it is essential for us to know the historic reasons which prompted the building of all of the brakes upon too speedy action by our government.

By virtue of our strength and power, the responsibilities of world leadership have been thrust upon the people of the United States. The less fortunate everywhere look to us for guidance. We must be constantly aware of the effect of our conduct upon the other peoples of the earth—not only those held in slavery behind the Iron Curtain.

Unseemly haste and a quest for sensational headlines will never contribute to the strength of a free government, nor appeal to world opinion. Current happenings in the Congress of the United States would indicate that instead of abolishing old forms we should attempt to strengthen them if we are to avoid making government a hippodrome. Some steps are necessary if we are to not only preserve the dignity of the Legislative branch of our national government—but influence world opinion in the global struggle for the minds and hearts of men.

To my mind, Thomas Jefferson was our greatest lawgiver. He was also a prodigious writer. There is merit in the contention that Jefferson, like the Bible, can be quoted to sustain conflicting viewpoints. Nevertheless, there is one clear thread throughout all of his voluminous writings. It is his belief that government should be kept close to the governed.

He taught that the local sub-divisions should have the fullest possible autonomy; that all police power should remain in the several states; and it was his influence that added to the Constitution the provisions that make our national government one of specific and limited powers.

If there is one thing that is clear from human history, it is the fact that men cannot long maintain the individual rights and liberties which assure the dignity of the individual when all the power of government is concentrated in one pair of hands. Where power is concentrated, freedom is lost.

The shores of human history are littered with the wrecks of civilizations where once free men entrusted their rights and liberties to a wholly centralized government.

Our future depends upon a more enlightened citizenship. This is the only means of producing unselfish leaders of character and ability—leaders described by Woodrow Wilson as, "the deeply human man, quick to know and to do the things that the hour and his nation need."

University of Georgia Law Day

If free self-government is to meet the challenge of the totalitarian state, every citizen must have more familiarity with the science of government. Intensive training and the will to fight and sacrifice are particularly important for those who intend to dedicate themselves to the public service. Edmund Burke spoke truly when he said, "All that is necessary for the triumph of evil is that good men do nothing."

The Law School of the University is keeping pace with the times. Its expanding services will produce that leadership necessary to meet the needs of tomorrow.

I congratulate the Board of Regents and the officials of the University on their foresightedness in establishing this Institute. It is not mere State pride which prompts me to say that our people have shown a much finer appreciation of the meaning of our institutions of government than those from some other areas. Our people are steeped in the traditions of Jefferson and Jackson. We cling to the landmarks our father have set.

Today new and strange philosophies of government which will be destructive to our system are gaining adherents. There is an increasing number of people who regard the fine traditions of the law on which our great civilization is built as out-worn shibboleths.

These theories and philosophies have permeated some of the great educational institutions of our land.

This great Institute of Law and Government will not only counteract dangerous influences from other areas, but give our young people of today—who will administer our government tomorrow—the proper concept of law, ethics, and government.

Nothing is more vital than that all of our people, and more particularly the public officials and members of our law-making bodies, should understand and adhere to the fundamental traditions of Anglo-Saxon justice which guarantee our liberties.

Through the teachings they will receive here, we will preserve our own great traditions and theories of government. We may hope that the light which will go out from here will place them in proper perspective before those who do not understand these theories and traditions. There could be no higher purpose than to develop the natural genius of our people in the field of government and thereby refute the calumnies of those who mistake for backwardness our adherence to fundamentals.

All of the complexities which pose a threat to the American way of life, either by internal subversion or external aggression, have greatly increased the responsibilities of our schools of law and the legal profession.

The basic principles of liberty and freedom are eternal. No man can improve upon them.

However, the changes wrought by our civilization require that they be adapted to altered conditions. The legal profession has done much to gain and preserve these principles. Its leaders owe it to our country to translate them into understandable form to meet changing conditions.

However complicated our civilization may become, these fundamentals must be presented in simple terms so that new generations will understand and appreciate them. Without a realization of the sacrifices made to obtain them, or the effect of their loss, those who come after us are likely to be deceived by the spurious arguments that seek to lead men to exchange their freedoms for the mirage of absolute security. Under the leadership of such institutions as this, we will strive to meet these problems with awareness of the importance of our past and with complete faith in our future.

George Washington Award
30 April 1958

In 1958, the American Good Government Society presented the George Washington Award to two United States Senators, Richard B. Russell of Georgia and William F. Knowland of California. In accepting the award at the Statler Hotel, in Washington, D.C., Russell explained why he considered himself to be a "political fundamentalist."[9]

* * * * * * * * * *

It is not possible for me to express the depth of my appreciation for the meaningful honors awarded me here tonight. They are accepted with the utmost humility. An awareness of my own limitations bars the inclination to vanity that the praise and honors of this evening would otherwise evoke. Had my recommendations been requested, I would have chosen others for this award.

To the society, and particularly to those responsible for initiating the honors tendered, I can only say a deeply felt "thank you." The fact that you feel that my activities through the years have contributed to good government as we would define it is adequate compensation for many hours of toil. The special recognition extended me this evening is indelibly impressed on my memory and will serve as an inspiration to me for the remainder of my life.

It is pleasing to have so many of my friends here to share this experience. Many have traveled from Georgia to do so. But for the friendship and the confidence you have so freely given and expressed, this significant honor could not have come to me. I am deeply grateful for your many manifestations of loyalty throughout the years and particularly for your presence this evening.

---

[9]Text of speech from *United States of America Congressional Record Proceedings and Debates of the 85th Congress.* Second Session, Vol. 104, Part 6, May 1, 1958, 78-8-7809.

I think it safe to assume that most of us here tonight are political fundamentalists. The religious fundamentalists like to emphasize the words of the Holy Writ. Political fundamentalists stress the importance of supporting the Constitution as it is written.

George Washington was a political fundamentalist. He believed that the Constitution meant exactly what it said. Summing up his views in his Farewell Address to the American people, he said:

> If, in the opinion of the people, the distribution or modification of the constitutional power be in any particular wrong, let it be corrected by an amendment in the way which the Constitution designates. But let there be no change by usurpation; for though this, in one instance, may be the instrument of good, it is the customary weapon by which free governments are destroyed.

With prophetic vision, he thus rebuked those who might ever assume that the ends justify the means and warned us against them.

By adhering to constitutional government, in a relatively short period of time we have achieved world leadership. We have builded the greatest civilization in all of human history. We have developed what we call the American way of life in which all of our people not only maintain their liberties but enjoy the highest standards of living that the world has ever known.

For many years now, we have heard the voices of those who insist that the American Constitution is outmoded. Others take the position that this sacred document is a sort of political accordion, to be expanded or contracted with the changing moods of men who temporarily hold power. Time will not permit us to conjecture on what would have resulted if we had accepted these views. But the lessons of history clearly depict the fate of other great civilizations who placed their trust in a government of men rather than adhering to written laws.

It is evident that the effectiveness of constitutional law as a system of restraints on governmental action and as a means of protecting the rights of the individual depends entirely on the recognition and application of those basic doctrines which find their origin in our national charter.

Two of the most important of these doctrines are federalism and the separation of powers.

The doctrine of federalism includes many elements. For the purpose of my brief comments tonight, the element I have primarily in mind is the division of the sovereign power between the National Government and the States. This division was long controlled by the simple rule that the National Government is one of delegated power for enumerated purposes while the residual or undelegated powers remain in the States or the people.

To my mind, a primary test of good government involves an awareness of the importance of maintaining the balance between national and State legislative power intended by the framers of the Constitution.

Various pressure groups are constantly working in behalf of national legislation which violates the intended division of legislative functions between the National and State governments. As we have observed over the last quarter of a century, legislative encroachment by the National Congress is particularly aggressive in times of economic distress. Emergencies of a temporary nature have caused the States to permanently lose many powers that are properly theirs. The lessons of past experience should be borne in mind today.

I am a disciple of the Jeffersonian school. The more that I study government, the more confirmed I become in the faith that the best and most economical government is that which is locally conceived and locally administered.

As a devout believer in the rights of the States and of local self-government, I have deplored and opposed the constant widening of national power in fields which properly belong to the States and their subdivisions.

The other constitutional doctrine that has become distorted is the doctrine of separation of powers. The Founding Fathers were determined to prevent the corrupting and tyrannous effects of undue concentration of power. They sought to safeguard against one big government. They were familiar with the axiom which history had proved before Lord Acton that "all power corrupts and absolute power corrupts absolutely."

They knew that the personal liberties of the individual could not be protected in a government of men. They therefore wisely sought to assure that their descendants would forever live under a government of law. Thomas Jefferson expressed this determination when he declared: "In questions of power, let no more be said of confidence in man, but bind him down from mischief by the chains of the Constitution."

The very genius of our system of government is found in the careful division of power to govern the people. These powers were distributed between the executive, the legislative, and the judicial branches of the Central Government. To assure the perpetuity of the American system, the founders established the most marvelous system of checks and balances ever devised by the minds of men.

This sound concept has been seriously impaired in recent years.

Too often, the Congress has been content merely to consider legislation initiated in the executive branch of the Government.

The willingness to delegate too much of Congressional responsibility to executive agencies, quasi-judicial commissions and boards has also contributed to the erosion of legislative power.

It is needless to say that any segment of the executive branch is all too willing to expand any powers that are delegated.

I freely concede that in the complex society of today the Congress cannot legislate with the preciseness and particularity that was formerly attainable. However, it is possible to establish more definite and precise statutory standards to delegated power. A great benefit from clearer standards would be a reduction in the number of employees of Government who are now doing battle with our citizens as to the effect and scope of delegated powers.

Even more serious than legislative deviations has been the recent encroachments on the rights of the States and on the prerogatives of the legislative branch of the Government by the judicial branch of the Government. Recent decisions of our highest court have contributed more to demeaning the rights of the several States and to centralizing the power of Government than has legislation by the National Congress.

A series of decisions have wiped out a number of rights and privileges which the States have exercised since the birth of our Republic. Under the cloak of judicial interpretation, the judiciary has assumed powers which undoubtedly belong to the legislative branch of the Government. The personal predilections of those enjoying life tenure on the Federal bench have taken supremacy over precedent as established by the decisions of learned and able lawyers and judges.

The tendency of the Supreme Court to rely upon psychology rather than legal precedents and to legislate rather than interpret is a cause of great concern. Judge Learned Hand has long been recognized as one of the ablest of our judges. He has had more judicial experience than all of the members of the present Supreme Court combined had had to the time of their respective appointments. No one could view any judicial situation more objectively. Judge Hand recently referred to the trend to make the Supreme Court a third legislative chamber. If the Founding Fathers had ever believed that the Court would undertake to exercise legislative power, they would certainly have required the members of that body to go before the voters for periodic review as in the case of the members of the legislative branch.

The continuing practice of unrestrained judicial review not only establishes judicial supremacy over the other two divisions of Government; unchecked, it creates a judicial tyranny. The 9th and 10th amendments to our Federal Constitution, designed to limit the powers of the Federal Government and protect the rights of the States and of the people, were once the keystone of our system. The series of decisions to which I refer would cause one to believe that these provisions were no longer valid and binding parts of the Constitution.

The whittling process on the powers of the States by these decisions has gone so far as to threaten to reduce the several States to mere geographical boundaries of administrative areas of Federal departments.

There is at least a partial remedy for this situation. The appellate jurisdiction of the Supreme Court is subject to regulation by the Congress. An informed electorate does not pass upon the selection of

Federal judges, but they can choose representatives who will consider the wisdom of limiting the jurisdiction of the court.

A great organization such as the American Good Government Society can serve as an anchor to windward in these trying times. While pressure groups seek to strike down precedents and traditional concepts and the clamor is loud for change for the mere sake of change, this organization remains dedicated to a Government of law rather than the rule of men.

I shall long remember and be grateful that my efforts have merited your approval.

On the United Nations
4 April 1962

In this speech on the United States Senate Floor, Russell discussed a United Nations Bond Purchase Bill under consideration by the United States Senate that would authorize the President of the United States to lend the United Nations up to $100,000,000.[10] The same day that Russell proposed major changes in the bill, President John F. Kennedy mailed a letter to Senator John Sparkman of Alabama urging passage of the legislation. Kennedy warned "how harmful it would be to repudiate" the United Nations, the "arm of American foreign relations."[11] While offering qualified support for the United Nations as an institution, Russell opposed the legislation because he believed it gave the President unchecked power, and cost "too much money." He insisted that tax dollars and soldiers should only be used when approved by the Congress.

* * * * * * * * * *

Madam President, I have examined very carefully the alleged compromise substitute that has been proposed for the committee bill. I have noted that it is sponsored by the leaders on both sides of the aisle. I realize that such sponsorship means that the so-called compromise substitute has very substantial support on both sides of the aisle. But to me the compromise is no more palatable than the original bill. . . .

It would delegate to the President powers that were not delegated so completely in the original proposal and, overall, in my opinion it would give to the United Nations entirely too much money.

---

[10]Text of speech is from *Congressional Record: Proceedings and Debates of the 87th Congress*, April 4, 1962, Second Session, pp. 5886-5897.

[11]*Atlanta Constitution*, April 5 and 6, 1962; *New York Times*, April 5, 1962; *Washington Post*, April 5, 1962.

I have been urged to support the original legislative proposal or the substitute on the ground that the $100 million involved is a very small sum of money. I still have a great deal of respect for $100 million. I am well aware of the fact that it is not a large amount if it is measured against the amount that we appropriate for the defense of the United States. I am well aware that it is a relatively small amount when it is compared with the amount that the Congress appropriates each year, either for grants or for soft loans to other nations of the earth in what we euphemistically call our mutual assistance program. Because I think it carries too much money, and involves inherent danger to the future policy of this country, I am opposed to the substitute.

As is often the case, in order to deter opposition and full and free discussion and examination of the measure, an effort has been made to paint any person who might question the wisdom of the proposal in any respect as being the enemy of the United Nations seeking to destroy the United Nations.

I was greatly impressed by the able and courageous speech of the majority leader, the Senator from Montana [Mike Mansfield], in opening the debate on this question, when he expressed his belief in what was, of course, the original reason for the creation of Congress—that men should be entitled to express fully and freely their views on issues that are vital to this country without being castigated as ignoramuses or charged with being inspired by some ulterior purpose.

I have a great deal more confidence in the integrity of one who freely concedes the right of disagreement than I have for those who would paint black motives with a broad brush on any person who does not agree with their position. I compliment the majority leader on the speech that he made. I think it is a landmark in this Congress. It measures up to the very best traditions of the Senate. I hope it will do something to clear the atmosphere and permit objective discussion of these questions without immediately impugning the character of those who do not agree with everything that is proposed from any source—the White House, the State Department, the United

On the United Nations

Nations, or even in either House of the Congress of the United States.

I can say with complete truthfulness that I do not favor the abolition of the United Nations. I am not out to destroy the United Nations, and I would not impair any of its functions as contemplated in its original charter.

Recent events have made our membership in that organization of considerably less value than was the case at the time of our original ratification of the United Nations Charter. I bitterly disapprove of the precipitate and callous use of overwhelming military force, as was done in the state of Katanga last year, before all efforts at mediation between the parties had been exhausted. When we think about the length of time—running over weeks and into months—that we met and discussed with elements of the Communist world events in Korea and in Vietnam, it appears shameful that an organization that was created for mediation, negotiation, and the peaceful settlement of disputes should launch a military attack after the very limited effort that had been made to settle peacefully the difficulties in that troubled area.

In spite of my condemnation of that attack, I would not destroy the United Nations through bankruptcy or through inability to meet its bills. The purpose of my amendment is to enable it to carry on, though not in as lush a fashion as is provided in the substitute to which I referred.

I would be less than frank if I did not say that I do not agree with many of my correspondents who have written me hailing the United Nations as "a great bulwark for the peace and security of the United States." I have received resolutions from groups of intelligent people saying that the United Nations is the last hope of peace and the maintenance of our security. I cannot accept that thesis. I regard the United Nations as a useful institution. It is a place where men representing the conflicting ideologies of government that exist in the world today may meet and talk and seek the peaceful solution of problems.

I have been somewhat concerned that so many Americans in high places have made statements calculated to create in the minds of the

American people such great faith in the United Nations that they would be willing to risk the future destiny of this country in the hands of the United Nations.

Madam President, anyone who undertakes to convince the American people today that we can safely depend on the United Nations as a bulwark against the enduring threat of world enslavement by communism is doing the people of this country a great disservice.

I hear comparisons made of the amount that we spend to support the United Nations and the cost of maintaining our Military Establishment. The inference is that we ought to abandon military spending and put that money in the United Nations.

If that day ever comes, we will indeed be undone in this country, and our identity as a great people will vanish.

I can honestly disclaim any desire to destroy the United Nations without being willing to surrender my even greater interest, and indeed my sworn duty as a Senator of the United States, to see that the people of the United States, so far as I can prevent it, are not misled into placing the perpetuity of our institutions and the maintenance of our freedoms in the hands of the United Nations and to rely upon it solely for our protection.

Despite the very eloquent remarks made in its support by those who envision the United Nations as having much more vitality than I attribute to it, I must say that I regard the United Nations as a very frail reed on which to rest in the hope of deterring aggression by any medium-size power, much less by a great power.

Madam President, while I do not wish to destroy the United Nations but wish to see it continue, and wish that it could have increased vitality and strength, I believe that we are a long way and many years, even decades, from the time when we can afford to put the protection of American institutions, and the individual rights and liberties that are enjoyed by the American citizens, in trusteeship to the United Nations.

As I have said, my principal concern about the proposed legislation is the amount of money that is involved. I am concerned because of the oft stated purpose, as restated no later than last week in an editorial in a newspaper in Washington, that the United Nations should have a substantial reserve of funds available in order that it might launch, without any delay whatsoever, the application of military sanctions such as it applied in the Congo.

I do not agree with that philosophy. I regard the attack that was made in the Congo, without exhausting mediation, as sheer aggression and unnecessary aggression. I disapprove of it. Whatever one can say about Russia suffering a defeat by that action, it was aggression, and military aggression, and the use of force which had the Soviet Union as its primary advocate in the United Nations. I do not mean by that to say that the fact that the Soviet Union was leading the stampede to apply military force in Katanga influenced our position. I do say that our position was taken apparently out of the demand of some of the so-called newly emerging nations, such as Ghana, that the last white man had to be driven from the Congo or, indeed, from the soil of Africa, as some rulers in Africa demand, even if such person is a third or fourth generation citizen of the state in Africa in which he resides. I do not propose to put into the hands of Mr. U Thant, the Acting Secretary General, or anyone else serving as Secretary General of the United Nations, a large reserve of money in order that the machinery of the United Nations can again set in force an overwhelming military force against any other state or people of this earth before exhausting negotiation and mediation.

I opposed the war that ended in the conquest of Katanga. I oppose committing American boys and American equipment to that war, or tax money extracted from American citizens into any such reckless military attacks, without approval of Congress—approval that is expressly required and spelled out in what is called the United Nations Participation Act.

I am not trying to destroy the United Nations. I believe my amendment preserves it. It will avoid such precipitate and brutal action in the future. In addition, my amendment undertakes to preserve the law enacted by Congress in 1945, which stipulates the limitations of our participation in this organization.

From reports that have been circulating in the press about the alleged compromise, the distinguished Senator from Vermont [George David Aiken] has apparently changed his view somewhat as to the necessary financial arrangements which must be made to keep the United Nations in operation.

However, on March 15 this distinguished Senator, in an able discussion of his original substitute, laid before us in detail the current financial situation of the United Nations. He pointed out and sustained with figures the assertion that the United Nations is not presently anywhere near the verge of bankruptcy as proponents of this proposed legislation have so stridently proclaimed. . . .

The adoption of my substitute will release the United Nations from all of its indebtedness to the United States, its largest creditor. It has been exceedingly difficult to arrive at a precise figure of this indebtedness, but it is not less than $31,826,000 and it may amount to more than $40 million.

In addition, it will alleviate the financial crisis of the United Nations. So the U.N. evidently is adequately financed at the present time; unless they wish to start another military action, such as was launched in the case of Katanga.

The Senator from Vermont is one of the best informed men in the Congress on the question of international affairs and has represented us as a delegate at the United Nations, and he convinced me completely that the United Nations can maintain its financial integrity until the Court renders its opinion, even if Congress takes no action. It might just be a good lesson to some of our associates in the United Nations and prevent them from taking such precipitate action in the future.

I may say in passing that precipitate action by the United Nations and the abandonment of its declared role as mediator and peacemaker has been responsible for the largest part of its expenditures.

I would like to see it have time to plan and function as a peace-seeking body within the spirit of its charter rather than to look at a substantial bank balance largely extracted from the pockets of the American taxpayer and devise new military operations as a means of expending it.

My amendment is entirely adequate to bail out the United Nations and keep it from failing, but it does seek to deny that body the means of financing additional attacks against nations with

Christian institutions of government and strongly opposed to communism such as that launched against Katanga.

My amendment also renews the provisions of the act of 1945 which would prevent this Nation's being brought into any armed conflict or war without the knowledge and approval of the Congress of the United States. . . .

Before one American boy in uniform may be deployed by the United Nations, and before any assistance may be given to the United Nations in keeping international peace by military force, this action must have been a part of such agreements made between this Government and the Security Council, and must have been ratified by the Congress of the United States. . . .

It now comes to pass that when some of us are in disagreement over any detail in certain areas, and when the role of Government is challenged on some matter, our words are criticized as those of an irresponsible individual who has no knowledge of the subject, or else as words of one who is undertaking to destroy the last best hope of peace on earth.

Madam President, for my part, I resent government by smear, which is getting to be all too frequent. I refer to attempts to intimidate Members of the Senate, to keep them from saying what they honestly believe—in other words, from living up to the oath they take on the rostrum in this Chamber when they are inducted into membership into this body. . . .

The use in any manner whatever of any U.S. military personnel by the United Nations, except in a noncombatant capacity, without the approval of the Congress is completely illegal, ultra vires, and is specifically prohibited by law, in addition to being specifically prohibited by one of the provisions of the Constitution of the United States.

Of course, I know I sometimes irritate some of my friends by referring to that great document, because so many now regard it as outmoded and as being completely outworn and of no value today. But, Madam President, despite that, I remind them that the Constitution of the United States states that only the Congress shall have the power to declare war.

Madam President, if, when I suggest, as I am doing by means of this amendment, that we clarify this matter and restate the fact that the Congress is permitted to participate in these matters, it is said that such a suggestion is unconstitutional because it places limitations on the Commander in Chief, let me point out that those who say it is unconstitutional are about 17 years too late, insofar as this statute is concerned, and about 175 years too late insofar as the Constitution is concerned, for the original act placed no such limitations on the Commander in Chief; and, furthermore, the Commander in Chief then serving said he was perfectly willing to accept it. So my amendment does not contemplate any unconstitutional action.

Madam President, I believe this amendment will bring strength and vitality to the United Nations, because it will clarify the situations under which the United States may participate in keeping the peace around the world; and, as I stated a while ago, the amendment is, overall, in accord with article I, section 8, of the U.S. Constitution, which deals with the powers of Congress, and which declares in paragraph 11 that only Congress has the power to declare war, and provides in paragraph 16 that Congress has the power "to provide for governing such part" of the Armed Forces "as may be employed in the service of the United States. . . ."

We have gone so far from our act in 1948 in abdicating our powers and seeking to flee from our sworn responsibilities that a simple restatement of something that is already the law in the United Nations Enabling Act, passed only seventeen years ago, stirs up a great commotion in the press and in the Congress.

That is how far we have gone in seventeen years by fleeing from our responsibilities and minimizing the position of the Senate and of the Congress of the United States in our scheme of government.

No wonder, Madam President, that the President can use so much equanimity to increase the powers of the executive and the judicial branches of the Government, when the Congress contributes so much to its own depreciation at every opportunity.

I am frank to say that my original opposition to forcing the taxpayers of the United States to pay the largest share of the costs of the military action in the Congo sprang from my conviction that that military action was launched prematurely, before it was necessary, and was carried out with unnecessary brutality after it was once initiated.

I also have a grave question as to the real motives of some of those who have been most active in pressing to have this action.

I fear, Madam President, we have not been very consistent in our approach to world problems. Both the President and the Secretary of State, and the preceding President and Secretary of State, and others in high position, have made many eloquent speeches, almost every time we have been visited by an official from one of the newly emerging nations, pointing out that this country is the child of a revolution, and therefore we have something in common with all newly emerging countries, and for that reason we are opposed to colonialism, even of the most benign type, practiced by our very best friends. Every visiting official has been met with that as a statement of policy. . . .

It is notable that until now the United Nations has, as in that case, enforced its resolutions and edicts against the weak and the helpless, such as those in Katanga, with great speed and energy and, as I have stated, with unnecessary brutality. However, the United Nations can be as silent as a sphinx and can act like a sphinx looking the other way when a strong and powerful nation flouts the provisions of the Charter of the United Nations.

Without regard to any action that we may take in the way of pumping American tax dollars into the United Nations, it is eventually doomed to failure if it continues to follow a policy of one law for the weak and no law whatever for the strong and powerful.

I regret that we were associated in the tragedy of Katanga with the men who perpetrated and still defend the rape of Hungary and Poland by the armored divisions of Soviet Russia by joining them in voting for the immediate military action to subdue Katanga. When the Soviet tanks crushed the lives out of the Hungarians who were seeking to find a way to freedom on the streets of their capital city of Budapest, the United Nations contented itself with a slight slap on the wrist.

When the sanctimonious Mr. Nehru launched overwhelming military forces against little Portuguese Goa without exhausting efforts at mediation or even the offices of the United Nations, not even a resolution of condemnation was forthcoming.

When Red China moved into Tibet and killed the people of that country, destroyed their religion, and forced them to come under Communist control, we expressed sympathy in the United Nations for the Tibetan people. But that was the extent of United Nations action when that hapless land was ravaged by the Communist Reds with all the savagery that was perpetrated by Genghis Khan.

Mr. Khrushchev has felt that he could safely flout the opinion of the United Nations and, indeed, the opinion of mankind everywhere. His most recent expression of contempt was the resumption of nuclear testing in the atmosphere, which was a clear breach of faith and implied agreement. Where, then, was the United Nations, even to give an expression of strong disapproval to his act?

In my view, in all candor, and it is a sincere view, and is not expressed in an effort to destroy the United Nations—if the United Nations is to be of any value to the human family on this globe, it must be prepared to denounce wrong-doing on the part of the strong, and it cannot content itself by launching military action against a weak and impotent state whose major sin was the desire to be free and independent. . . .

Madam President, as I said a moment ago, I wish to discuss the question of one state—one vote in the United Nations Assembly. Within the past week, the Supreme Court of the United States handed down a momentous decision. This decision undertakes to establish a national policy of permitting the Federal courts to redistrict and otherwise reapportion States in order to, as some of the press said in hailing the decision, "make one man's vote equal to any other's." It follows, of course, that if this is true within a State, the Federal courts have a right to redraw the lines of wards, and even precincts, within the cities of the States.

I readily admit that all of the apportionments laws prevailing in the 50 States do not appeal to my sense of fairness. Indeed, I have vigorously supported proposed constitutional amendments to change the method of selecting members of the electoral college in the interests of fair play, because it has seemed to me that that change would be in the interest of fairness and equality. However, I deem it unnecessary for me to state that, under my concept of the Constitution, the Federal courts do not have the right or authority to put a State or city in a receivership and substitute some petty auditor, receiver, or other appointee of the Federal court for duly elected Governors, legislators, and other State officials. Life tenure for Federal judges is the only fragmentary semblance of the long-discarded doctrine of the divine right of kings found in our Federal Constitution. Some of the Founding Fathers were opposed to life tenure by appointment, but even the most ardent advocates of life tenure by appointment for Federal judges in the first 100 years of this Nation's life would have hotly denounced any contention that a petty appointee of a Federal judge could oust the officials of States and rule the people through one-man edicts and ukases that the Supreme Court says have the force of law in the matter of exercising the right of suffrage. . . .

Madam President, I was discussing the Court decision in the light of inequities and unequal representation in the United Nations. It is all the more necessary to consider how the character and appearance of the United Nations have changed since it was first created. The U.N. now has more than twice as many members as it had originally, and it is generally agreed that there will be approximately 20 new members in the near future. The protection once afforded by a permanent seat on the Security Council and the veto power has been greatly diluted, if not nullified, by the greatly increased power lodged in the General Assembly. Of course, that situation grew out of the unconscionable abuse by the Soviet Union of the veto power.

The United Nations has carried to the World Court, for an advisory opinion, the question of whether member nations must pay assessments for extra operations of the United Nations. The new nations which have changed the character and complexion of the United Nations do not have, between them, as many people as the largest member nation.

Indeed that is an understatement in the light of the statement made by my colleague from Georgia [Herman Talmadge]. I had not calculated it, but I know that two-thirds of them do not have as large a population as the single largest member nation.

However, by a two-thirds majority in the General Assembly, this body can change the basis of assessment and assess against the United States, on the grounds that we are the largest and wealthiest country on earth, assessments running into the billions of dollars to be expended on programs of which the majority of the people of the United States might bitterly disapprove.

This new group of so-called emerging nations were in a great hurry to bring military force to bear against Katanga. It is completely conceivable that they might order military action against some other nation that is friendly to us, opposed to Communism, and inclined to the principles of Christianity, as was Katanga. Even though such a nation might be not only one of our closest friends, but could also be an ally that we are bound by treaty to defend, the General Assembly would have the power to assess against us the greatest portion of the cost of carrying out a military attack on such a nation, if the General Assembly declared that necessary in order to maintain world peace, as was declared of the attack on Katanga.

These crusaders against disproportionate voting might well turn their attention to the General Assembly of the United Nations.

During the years I have served in this body, I have seen a great many tables and figures showing the alleged inequities which exist under some elective systems of States of the Union. Let us examine, for a moment, the disproportionate representation in the General Assembly of the United Nations.

Only three members of the United Nations have populations exceeding 100 million people. The United States is one of those nations; yet, we have but one vote in the General Assembly. However, I am sure Senators will recall that before Russia would approve the Charter, Russia was wise enough to demand three votes in the General Assembly, and has them there today.

Our one vote represents a nation of 183 million people. Sitting with equal rights and equal power in the General Assembly is a representative, let us say, of Gabon. When a vote is had in the United Nations, each citizen of Gabon exercises 433 times the power that is exercised by the vote of a representative of the United States of behalf of one of its citizens. In other words, in the General Assembly the voting power of 433 Americans is equaled by that of 1 Gabonese. . . .

Mr. President, I feel that our country is making a great mistake in being guided so often by expediency, instead of adopting, in its foreign policy, a definite principle to guide us in the United Nations and, indeed, in our foreign policy generally throughout the world. To be guided by expediency is incompatible with the role we should play as the greatest, most powerful, and most progressive civilization of the earth. Some of our representatives may feel that they are justified in abandoning their ideas of right and propriety in an effort to woo the votes of the newly emerging nations. Time and again we are told that people of color predominate numerically on this globe, and that at any cost we must maintain their friendship and their approval.

Mr. President, I desire to maintain the good will, the approval, and the friendship of every people of every race or creed throughout the world; but the shortcuts in which we have been participating, in proceeding in line with the spirit that the ends justify the means, will not, in the long run, serve our country well. Such a course will eventually subject us to blackmail in many forms that the American people will be unwilling to pay. Indeed, they are already paying blackmail in greater amounts than they should be called upon to pay.

We are living in a hectic and fast-moving world, Mr. President. Katanga may soon become a forgotten episode. But the fact that this great Nation has not had a specific foreign policy of its own, but can be bulldozed and blackmailed into supporting positions which, in our heart, we know to be wrong, will not be forgotten. It can only cause us to be looked upon with contempt and will eventually destroy our already decreasing prestige throughout the world.

Power is one element respected in every state and among every race and tribe upon this globe. If a nation has great power, but weakness of character to exercise it fairly and impartially, it will eventually lose the new friends for which we have sacrificed close friendships which have lasted over many decades and which have been sealed in blood in two world wars.

I have been very happy to see that so many men of wisdom and influence throughout this Nation are recognizing the need for a reexamination of the role of the United States in the United Nations. I repeat that I do not believe we should leave the United Nations or in any wise lessen our support of the original concept of this world organization. The United Nations was conceived originally as an instrument of negotiation and mediation for the settlement of differences on this earth by peaceful means, rather than by war. War was to be the last, final resort, after every other means had been exhausted. Every time the United States agrees to approve armed attacks instead of negotiation before all hope of peaceful settlement has been exhausted, we demean ourselves and weaken our influence throughout the globe.

I, of course, freely confess that we find ourselves in a new position within the United Nations. The fact that so many nations have been admitted to full membership before they were ready for self-government or before their economies were capable of supporting them has changed the whole complexion of this body. We have been, in a way, responsible for this by our denunciation of colonialism and by our urging the colonial powers to leave areas before the people of those areas were prepared for self-government.

Instead of a democratic or republican form of government, we find that many of these lands have already lapsed into a dictatorship. Unfortunately, any discrimination that we have shown between rulers who are endeavoring to maintain representative government and those who have established absolute dictatorships seems to be in favor of the dictators. . . .

Mr. President, instead of constantly increasing our program of shipping our dollars abroad, it is time for us to consider the interest and welfare of the American people. Under the bankruptcy laws of this country, as they existed at the time I was practicing law—which was a good while ago—if the same rule were applied to the Federal Government as is applied to an individual, this country would be hopelessly insolvent and could be forced into involuntary bankruptcy.

We have given away our assets at a time when we do not have sufficient gold to meet the dollar credits in foreign hands, and to assure the gold reserve of our currency at the 25 percent required by law. It would be impossible for us to meet the demands of our creditors for gold if they were all presented simultaneously.

I realize that there are many who think that a large national debt such as the one we have is a good thing for the country, and therefore they have no concern about having it increased from year to year. I have also heard able men make a strong case to prove that gold is a wholly unnecessary commodity to help sustain a stable economy in this country.

For my part, I cannot accept either thesis. To me it is the height of folly to increase continually our foreign spending program, particularly to Communist countries or neutralists who have no use whatever for us. I cannot refrain from feeling that to increase foreign aid and other foreign spending from year to year will make inevitable a day of accounting; and even if it is postponed for several years, it will present to the next generation problems that will be well nigh insoluble. When our economy feels the full impact of the shortsighted policy that we have pursued for the past 10 or 12 years, our institutions will be shaken to their very foundations; and, indeed, a complete change in our form of government could be brought about.

Mr. President, we defray almost one-half of all the expenses and assessments of the United Nations. Many other nations that are the recipients of our aid program are put in a position to pay their assessments because we have assumed the cost of so many of their domestic projects as to give them free money for this purpose.

I would be the first to oppose any suggestion that our country seek to impose its will by force upon any people, particularly a weak and new state with all of the problems of establishing government and building a viable economy. I do believe, however, Mr. President, that we have made a great mistake, which is being repeated year after year, of not giving specific recognition in our aid program to those nations who respect us and who, through a community of interests or of aims for our respective peoples, support us in and out of season in the United Nations and in other associations of states to which we are a party. If a country proclaims itself as a neutralist, we apparently accept the statement without question, even though it may consistently oppose us in every field of international relations and show strong friendship for the Soviet and never see anything wrong with Soviet behavior. In my view, those who are quick to suspect the United States and to close their eyes to the many untoward actions of Soviet Russia, in my judgment, are not true neutralists, whatever they may call themselves.

If we do not adopt a policy of recognizing our friends before we recognize our enemies before our dollars are exhausted and the last bar of gold has been taken from Fort Knox, we will find ourselves standing alone at some future day when we are confronted with the dire peril to our institutions and our people being overrun or destroyed by the Soviet Union.

In my judgment it would be a very healthy development for this country to examine what goes on in many of these countries who have posted on their front door the sign "Neutralist." It would be even better and would enhance our position in the United Nations and in all other organizations if we would begin to initiate some selectivity in our foreign relations which favors our friends. Every other country on earth measures its relations with the world in concrete and concise terms of its own national interest.

The hour is late. In my opinion we have already wasted many billions of dollars, but it is not too late to reconsider the course we have pursued to date and to initiate a program of our own, conceived in America and directed to the promotion of our own enlightened self-interest.

Coming down to the immediate issue, I submit that the substitute I have proposed is adequate to see the United Nations through its present financial difficulties. It will not put the stamp of approval upon precipitate military action which resulted in the conquest of Katanga and the death or maiming of so many of the men, women, and children of that tortured state.

It will be notice to the nations of the world that we expect other peoples to contribute more, not only to the operating costs of the United Nations, but, when they are able to do so, also to the stability and the development of the emerging nations.

It will avoid the danger, which to me is very clear and real, of providing the United Nations with a financial reserve for any future military action at a time when unstable forces are exercising undue influence in that body.

Above all, Mr. President, it restates the authority of the Congress of the United States to be consulted and to take action before our sons may be ordered to foreign lands to die in battle, perhaps, over issues that could be settled peaceably by a proper exercise of patience and persistence.

I believe it will help to restore our own self-respect and national dignity, and will help regain the respect of other nations of the earth. It will manifest our intention to continue to contribute to the peaceful settlement of disputes everywhere in the world, but will reaffirm our determination not to permit our sons, some of whom have been called into military service against their desires, to be used as gladiators in the arena of the whole world, unless such action has been found necessary in the manner prescribed by our Constitution.

Georgia Jaycees Breakfast
6 February 1966

Addressing a theme suggested by the Jaycees, "God in Government," Senator Russell stressed the positive influence of religion upon people's "moral behavior."[12] He reminded the audience that "responsibility for good government rests with the people." Russell advocated "freedom of worship" and "religious tolerance" as precepts worthy of defending. The speech was given in Macon, Georgia.

* * * * * * * * * *

I am highly privileged to participate in this program today. Although I wish to make clear from the outset that I am woefully inadequate to cope with the formidable and awesome subject you have suggested: "God in Government."

In approaching this task, I cannot help but recall something the great English statesman, Disraeli, said when as Prime Minister, he was asked by a new and quite inexperienced member of Commons if he, the new member, should participate actively in the parliamentary debates. The Prime Minister wisely replied: "No, I don't think you had better. I think it would be better if the House were to wonder why you didn't talk, rather than why you did."

But in the knowledge that you, in the words of one of the ancient prophets, are of "wise and understanding heart,"[13] I shall attempt as best I can to share with you a few brief thoughts on the religious perspective of government.

It is, of course, a truism that hardly bears restating that religion has been the single most powerful force and influence over the course of mankind from the very earliest stirrings of our civilization.

---

[12]Text of speech from Speech File, Speech and Media Series, Richard B. Russell Collection, RRLPRS.

[13]1 Kings 3:12.

Our concepts of morality and our ideal of the universal brotherhood of man are deeply rooted in the teachings of Judeo-Christian philosophy. From this wellspring flows much of our ethical thinking, the origins of our learning and culture, and our belief in the inherent dignity of man. Here, too, is the source of our great democratic institutions of self-government, free institutions and individual liberty.

I long have believed that one of the fundamental and enduring strengths of America lies in the essential religious character of our people. This country was built by men and women who were steeped in the tradition and the beliefs of the Bible. Their reliance on a religious credo became an essential part of our American heritage. It remains so today.

It is, I think, fair to say that one of the most significant and beneficial aspects of our religious heritage is its demand for a high code of moral behavior among those who are entrusted with public office—from the lowest to the highest.

So long as human frailty is a fact of life, there will always be those in positions of public trust who fall short of the high standards that morality demands. I fear there will always be the dishonest office holder or bureaucrat who is susceptible to corruption, just as there always will be the private citizen who is willing to contribute to his corruption. We have seen rather gross examples of this in high places in recent times.

But I think it is a mark of tribute to the essential integrity and morality of the great majority of American people—yes, and to the great majority of public officials—that our government in most instances is conducted without taint or trace of corruption and wrongdoing.

It is important to remember that the question of morality and honesty—or the lack of it—in government is not confined exclusively to those holding office. It addresses itself to the entire body politic—for in our democratic republic, the responsibility for good government rests with the people themselves as well as with the peoples' representatives.

Someone has likened our system of government to a pump: what the system pumps up is pretty much a reflection of what we actually are—a fair sample of the intellect, morals, and ethics of the people—not much better and not much worse. George Bernard Shaw put it more bluntly and more cynically. He said democracy is a device that insures that we shall be governed no better than we deserve.

I do not wish to be understood to be condoning even the most minute deviation from the highest standards of conduct among public officials. One dishonest and corrupt office holder is one too many. Let he who dares betray the public trust be severed from the public purse without equivocation or qualification, and let him be prosecuted in the criminal courts to the fullest limit of the law.

But I do wish to make the point that morality in government is inescapably linked with the morality of the people, and this is as it should be in a government that belongs to the people. I hope this concept will not unduly shock that forty percent of the American public who, according to a recent Gallup poll, gave as their opinion that corruption is on the rise in government.

If it is true that our religious heritage has helped to imbue the American people with a high sense of morality, there is a way to be reasonably certain that these ideals are reflected in our government. The means for doing this is for all our citizens to take an enlightened and active interest in governmental affairs and to participate fully and responsibly in the conduct of these affairs.

As Jaycees, you are keenly aware that good government, honest government, responsible government is hard to come by if too many otherwise good people become too lazy or apathetic to discharge their responsibilities as citizens. I have always believed that of all the worthwhile activities for which Jaycees are noted, among the most valuable are your efforts to get people to register and vote. I encourage and urge you to redouble your activities in these pursuits.

Apart from its impact on public morality, the central thrust of the American religious tradition from the earliest origins of the nation has been the insistence on freedom of worship according to the dictates of one's own heart and conscience.

Georgia Jaycees Breakfast

The tradition was brought to our shores by the earliest settlers from the old world. Many of the hardy pioneers who braved the unknown to hack out a new civilization on the American mainland did so either to escape persecution for their religious principles or to seek wider latitude to worship as they believed.

Thus the Eastern seaboard was peopled by such diverse groups as Puritans and pilgrims in New England, Quakers in Pennsylvania, Catholics in Maryland, and Saltzbergers in Georgia.

Then, as now, religious tolerance in America fell something short of perfection. Dissent from Puritan orthodoxy often met harsh retribution. In Maryland, although the colony was founded as a haven for Catholics, there was a period of Protestant persecution of those of the Roman faith. And here in Georgia the doors to General [James E.] Oglethorpe's hoped-for Utopia between the Savannah and the Altamaha were for a time closed to both Catholics and Jews.

But despite some blemishes, the new American nation was founded in an atmosphere remarkable in its time for both its religious nature and its religious freedom. Among the prominent signers of the Declaration of Independence was one of the leading lay Catholics in the country—Charles Carroll of Maryland. This patriot enjoys a footnote in history for signing himself as Charles Carroll of Carrollton, the name of his Maryland manor. He did so in order that King George's agents would know which Charles Carroll stood ready to hang for independence.

And in Georgia, as anyone familiar with our distinguished old families knows, the bars to Jews and Catholics were soon lowered and both groups joined their Protestant brethren in building a proud and progressive state. Indeed, even before the formal Declaration of Independence, members of the Jewish religion held public office in Savannah and a member of that faith—David Emanuel—became one of the state's early governors. He was, incidentally, the first governor of Jewish faith in this country.

The deep and abiding faith of the founding fathers in God is recorded indelibly in the pages of American history. The great document of independence itself contains no fewer than four direct references to the Supreme Power. And to this good day, no more powerful expression of religious freedom and tolerance is to be found than Thomas Jefferson's Act of Religious Freedom adopted by Virginia in 1786.

This mighty document proclaimed in words clear and emphatic that: "No man shall be compelled to frequent or support any religious worship, place or ministry whatsoever . . . [and] shall be free to profess and by argument to maintain, their opinions in matters of religion."[14]

This act was the forerunner and the model for the First Amendment to our Constitution that proclaims for all Americans for all time that there shall be no requirements or constrains over man's right to worship as his conscience dictates.

I am persuaded that in the long view of history, this may well prove to be the greatest of all the human rights and individual freedoms that we Americans possess.

Do our institutions of freedom—our blessings of individual liberty—flow from God? We may differ on the narrow point of this question. Yet, I am deeply and irrevocably convinced that our concepts of freedom and self-government are certainly God-inspired.

The great principles upon which our nation is based, if they did not indeed spring from divine inspiration, do have their roots in basic religious awareness of the fundamental rights which we know God intended man to enjoy.

This nation today stands as the most powerful nation on earth.

It is not the most powerful because it has the most numbers, because our population is not even one tenth of the population of the world. China alone has four times our numbers.

It is not because we have the greatest natural resources, because there are other areas of the world that are fertile and rich in raw materials.

It is not because our nation has become wise with age, because we are not yet 200 years old.

---

[14]Paul L. Ford, ed., *Works of Thomas Jefferson*, Vol. II (New York: G.P. Putnam's Sons, 1904), 441.

I believe our nation is strong because the United States of America has come closer than perhaps any other society in establishing a step—though not a very long one—toward what God must have meant his people to be, and to achieve.

Throughout much of the world, the wealth, the manpower, and the spiritual strength of the United States today is committed to help the other nations of the earth share in the material blessings of life and—more importantly—in the freedom that makes all of life worthwhile.

In our leadership of free man's struggle against the Godless forces of communist tyranny—and I need not remind you that this struggle is now joined on the field of combat in Vietnam—we can draw strength and faith from the knowledge that we are striving to safeguard the God-given gift of freedom.

Let us, on this Sabbath morning, give thanks to Divine Providence that through accident of birth we are a part of the greatest and most blessed society that man has yet achieved on this mortal sod.

Let us remind ourselves that the great heritage of religious freedom we enjoy does not exist for the one billion persons who live under the bondage of communism. For the communist concept categorically denies God's very existence, and those who dare to worship him do so only at their peril.

That is the despotic and Godless nature of our adversaries who day in and day out—in a hundred unseen ways—seek to extend their dominion and their philosophy of the anti-God over every inch of this globe.

That, too, is the nature of the enemy against whom at this moment 200,000 of our best and finest young men are fighting and sacrificing so that naked and wanton aggression shall not go unpunished.

II.

Speeches on Agriculture and Industry

in spring — harvesting in fall —
Like other facets of modern life
successful ag. has become complex
and highly specialized undertaking.
It, too, has been overtaken by technological
revolution of our scientific &
nuclear age.

Farmers have done outstanding job
Have been so efficient in increasing
production have displaced millions.

When I went to Cong. Natl pop
was about 130 million — about 29%
lived on farms & farmed — Today
with 180 million — only 12% live
on farms — 10 million fewer farm
people are now feeding population
increased by 50 million since 1930.

Entire period one of abundance —
over abundance despite 2 wars &
greatest depression —

Handwritten notes, speech at a meeting of the Turner County Chamber of Commerce, 15 October 1959.

Jute, the Arch Competitor of Cotton
5 June 1936

During his long career in the United States Senate, Senator Russell represented agricultural interests effectively. For example, during the Great Depression, when the price for cotton dropped to five cents per pound, and many lost their farms, Russell supported the New Deal.[1] He reminded voters that the Congress and President had "broken the back of the depression," and he was proud of his part in it.[2] In 1936, when the Senate considered legislation to provide revenue and equalize taxation—to protect Georgia's cotton farmers' income—Russell introduced a bill to tax jute, the cotton farmer's "most dangerous competitor." In the speech below, Russell defended his amendment to legislation that would have taxed unmanufactured jute and jute butts, jute waste bagging, jute yarn, burlaps, and other manufactured articles.[3] Russell's proposal failed.

* * * * * * * * * *

... The charge was made that if Democratic Senators voted for the items presented by the amendment of the Senator from North Carolina we were confessing that the Smoot-Hawley Tariff Act was sound and that we were out-Heroding Herod. I agree with the view that the passage of the Smoot-Hawley Tariff Act did more to demoralize the commerce of the world than any other single act which has ever been passed by the Congress of the United States and signed by the President of the United States. It not only dried up our foreign

---

[1]William F. Holmes, "Economic Developments, 1890-1940," in Kenneth Coleman, General Editor, *A History of Georgia* (Athens: University of Georgia Press, 1977), 257-263.
[2]*Atlanta Constitution*, September 4, 1936.
[3]Text of speech from *Congressional Record: Proceedings and Debates of the Seventy-Fourth Congress of the United States of America*, June 5, 1936, Vol. 80, Part 8, 9080-9084.

market for agricultural commodities but it eventually paralyzed industrial production in this country. By reason of its passage there grew up all over the world a complicated system of quotas, embargoes, trade agreements, and restrictions which obstructed all of the normal channels of commerce, and largely caused the deplorable plight in which the American farmer found himself in 1933, and from which he is suffering today. This act caused the conditions which confront the Congress today in the consideration of measures for the protection of American agriculture, which are wholly different from those which existed at the time of the passage of the Smoot-Hawley tariff.

I think that they were all caused largely by the prohibitive duties levied in that act. We cannot, however, restore our world trade today merely by repealing the Smoot-Hawley Tariff Act. Under the system of embargoes and quotas to which I have referred it would be impossible to secure any great increase in our foreign trade and such action would merely serve to make this Nation the dumping ground for the products of the underpaid labor of all the foreign nations of the world. We are pursuing the only course which is open to us to restore world trade, and that is by seeking through reciprocal tariff agreements to remove the many obstructions to trade and commerce which have caused such a great shrinkage in our foreign trade.

During the course of these negotiations, it is necessary to protect not only American agriculture but American industry from dumping from abroad. The press today carries the news that under the countervailing duty provisions of the 1930 Tariff Act, additional rates ranging from 22½ to 56 percent have been imposed on a number of manufactured articles imported from Germany.

Many products from the same nation have already been assessed higher duties under the nondumping provisions of that act. No action of the Congress in reducing the duties which have increased the prices of plow points, tools, shoes, and hats, and practically everything else which the farmer is compelled to buy is proposed. I doubt if it would be very effective were such action taken. Therefore, during this period of adjustment of tariff matters, I favor the fullest measure of protection for the farmers of this country in the retention of the great market afforded him domestically by the 130 million people of the United States.

The cotton farmer cannot be afforded any measure of protection without the imposition of a tax on his greatest and most dangerous competitor. This amendment proposes to impose that tax on jute. Jute is a vegetable fiber, even as cotton is a vegetable fiber. Jute is a somewhat coarser fiber than cotton, but recent developments in methods of processing and manufacturing have placed it in direct competition with cotton produced by the American farmer in practically every form or use to which either can be put.

The fact that jute is in direct competition with cotton was recognized by the United States Department of Agriculture. Under the provisions of the Agricultural Adjustment Act, providing for the levy of a compensatory tax on jute, such tax in the sum of more than 2 cents per pound was levied. This was done when it became apparent that the increased price of cotton resulting from the processing taxes was causing a shift in consumption to jute. As a matter of fact, I do not know of any commodity produced from jute today in this country which is not directly in competition with a commodity manufactured from cotton, designed for the same purpose. Jute in its raw form enters this country tax free, despite the fact that it is in direct competition with cotton, and articles manufactured from the two are almost interchangeable. . . .

The tax on jute was repealed as to a specific type of bag, which was largely used by the potato growers of this country, and when the compensatory tax on jute was removed to show that the competition did exist, the Department of Agriculture relieved cotton bags of the same type, manufactured for the same purposes, from the processing tax on cotton, so both could compete on the same basis. That tax was removed solely, almost completely, I will say, at the demands of the potato producers of this country, and it did not establish the fact that jute and cotton were not in competition. Quite the contrary. It established the fact that they were in competition, because the tax on the cotton bags of the same type was removed at the same time that the Department of Agriculture removed the tax imposed on jute bags.

Mr. [James P.] POPE: The Senator has referred to the fact that burlap bags are used for potatoes. Does not the Senator also know that they are used for wheat, and that as a matter of fact there is no competition between cotton bags and burlap bags, either as to potatoes or wheat or many other products produced in the West?

Mr. RUSSELL: Mr. President, that argument has been raised by those opposed to a compensatory tax on this product of slave labor in India every time an effort is made to secure justice for the cotton farmer in this matter. I contend that every fact that can possibly be gathered shows that these two commodities are in direct competition, and that cotton can be used to supplant jute in the manufacture of any package material for any commodity. This tax must be imposed if the cotton farmer is not to be forced down further in the direction he has been gradually driven in the past few years toward the same standard of living as those who work in India in the production of jute....

Do not talk to me about defeating this amendment on the ground that jute and cotton are not competitive commodities.

The Senate has already voted into this bill a tax on whale oil to protect dairy farmers in the sale of products of cows. Senators voted for that item, protecting the products of cows from the products of whales and then have said that this amendment should be defeated because jute and cotton are not in competition. There is much more kinship between these two vegetable fibers, jute and cotton, than there can possibly be between whales and cows, and the same thing is true of many other articles which were taxed the other day, in part by my vote, to protect the American farmer from the importation of oils which are substituted one for the other....

I have in my hand a statement furnished by the Department of Agriculture showing the wages paid to the jute farmers: the female wage ranges from 7.9 cents to 9.1 cents a day, and the male wage ranges from 12.1 cents to 15.2 cents a day. That product, produced by that low-paid labor, comes into this country duty free. Is it any wonder that you see burlap and jute bags instead of cotton bags, when you take this domestic market of the cotton farmer away from him and give it to the product of slave labor in India? Afford him the

Jute, the Arch Competitor of Cotton   115

protection everyone else has, and the situation will be reversed. The cotton farmer will have a market here for one and one-half million additional bales of cotton.

I have here reports from the United States Tariff Commission showing the increase in the importation of this commodity. They show that it has been steadily climbing since 1933, as we have made efforts to increase the price of cotton. As cotton goes up slightly in this country, importation of this low-wage product also increases. For the year 1933, there was imported into this country, 517,793,555 pounds of jute, every pound of it in direct competition with the cotton farmer. In 1934, there was a slight reduction to 487,792,815 pounds. When we come to the year 1935, we find that it has climbed to 716,520,742 pounds. Is there any wonder that the cotton farmer is further from parity than any other producer in the country?

The other day I heard a Senator representing a great farm State in the Northwest, when speaking on the commodity exchange bill, say he wanted to vote for an amendment which would benefit the southern cotton farmer, because he had been through that section of the country and observed the living conditions, and also how the cotton farmer was housed, and that of all the farmers in the country, the cotton farmer was in more dire need of Government aid than any other producer. Not a Senator from the cotton States would deny the charge. We all knew it was absolutely true, and lack of protection against jute is largely the reason for this condition.

The cotton farmer gets less income than any other producer in the country and has contributed more to the wealth of the Nation than any other single line of endeavor. For over 100 years he has been exporting 50 percent of his crop. Subtract the total exports of cotton from the total exports of the United States and see where the United States would have been in the matter of favorable trade balances had it not been for the wealth accumulated for others out of the toil of the cotton farmers.

During all of this time the cotton farmer has borne more of the burden of the tariff than any other class of our citizens. Out of his toil and sweat has been builded the favorable balance of trade which through all the years has caused our country to prosper and has made it the greatest commercial nation of the earth. Despite this contribution to the building of America and the prosperity of all sections, he today is penalized by exorbitant tariffs on commodities he buys and is denied any protection on that which he produces.

The fact that the income of the cotton farmer is lower than that of any other farmer of the Nation is no reproach to him. No one toils harder. I have seen the workers in the cotton fields toiling from break of day to long after sunset. They work almost unbelievably long hours. The entire family—man, woman, and children; those just out of the cradle, as well as the aged tottering on the brink of the grave—ply themselves at the back-breaking labor necessary to produce this great commodity so absolutely essential to the human family. The farmer's crops are subject to all of the whims of Nature. Even when fortunate, and producing a good crop, the result is discouraging. Often after he has marketed his crop and paid his debts, he faces the winter with his pockets emptied, with himself and children clad in rags, and with scant supplies in his smokehouse.

No, this is no reproach to the farmers. I have lived among them, and, as in other lines of endeavor, the great majority do their best with the means at their command. But this condition is a reflection on the Congress of the United States, which has within its hands the power of some relief. . . .

There is no article produced from jute that cannot be produced from cotton. But representatives of the cotton State who vote for the many taxes on various kinds of oil from different products, submitted in the hope of aiding the dairy industry, and other lines of agriculture, are now told that it ill becomes anyone to say jute is competitive with cotton. . . .

Mr. President, I have pointed out that as the price of cotton has increased the production of jute has greatly increased and, therefore, unless the cotton farmer is to be permanently denied any approach whatever to parity, it will be necessary for the Congress to take some step to protect this industry.

Not only is this a question which affects the cotton farmer, but it is a question which affects the manufacturer and textile worker.

We have heard many complaints here from the representatives of the Eastern States that it has been found necessary to dismantle many cotton mills in New England. The drift of the mills to sites nearer the cotton fields is not the only cause of the loss of these industries. If cotton could be afforded this protection and devoted to the uses to which jute processed in India is now put, I thoroughly believe it would go a long way toward making the spindles in the New England mills hum again.

On this question the interest of the cotton manufacturer, the cotton textile worker, and the cotton producer are identical. All should unite in a common cause for protection against this slave product. The largest part of it is spun and processed in India. One great combine controls most of the trade in jute. Mills have been dismantled in this country to ship the machinery abroad in order that the mills might be reestablished in India to get cheap labor, thereby denying employment and forcing on the relief rolls mill operatives in this country. . . .

Mr. President, this is in no sense a threat, but it might be accepted in the nature of a warning. I do not like to assume the role of prophet. I desire to point out something, however, which may be of interest to those representing lines of agriculture other than cotton. If my amendment be not adopted, the cotton farmer for a season will continue to endure discrimination and hardship, but he will not starve. He is trained in adversity and reared on hardships. However, he lives in a land on which God has smiled and which has unlimited possibilities in lines other than cotton. Senators are helping the dairy industry in this bill and therefore are making dairying more attractive. If they do not help cotton, this very fact will redound to the disadvantage of the dairy industry, because in the South ten and twelve months' grazing is possible. We have caught new visions down there. It will not be long until the South will have dairy herds and the products of these herds will be invading the markets of this Nation which Senators are seeking to protect. We have started producing wheat in the South and if the farmer is forced out of cotton it will increase competition within this country from those not subject to the forty-two cents per bushel tariff. We have started producing cattle to such an extent that some of the great packers of the Nation are even this year opening packing houses in the South.

There are few agricultural commodities which cannot be produced in the South; and while our people by instinct and inheritance are cotton producers, we will not be forced into bondage, or to the standard of living which prevails in India. When the cotton farmer prospers, he is also the greatest market for the manufacturers of this Nation, for he spends that which he earns.

In my judgment, the adoption of this amendment will not only benefit the cotton farmer and the cotton-producing section, but will benefit all sections. Not only will justice be served, but the development of all lines of agriculture will be benefitted by the adoption of the amendment.

Hart County Crimson Clover Festival
28 April 1939

As chairman of the Agricultural Appropriations subcommittee, Senator Russell guarded the interests of southern farmers. In this speech, for example, he argued for a more equitable income for farmers. The Senator reminded his Hartwell, Georgia, audience of his role in making available to farmers farm loans, parity payments, and rural electrification. While advocating that the Nation maintain a strong military force, he advised caution in committing soldiers and resources to war. Unconvinced that world conflicts could ever be settled, Russell opposed employing American troops in Europe at this time.[4]

* * * * * * * * * *

In 1890, not fifty years ago, fifty-seven percent of the population of the United States were dependent upon farming for a livelihood. Then came the great industrial era which brought about a tremendous shift from the farm to the factory, until today less than twenty-five percent of our people are dependent directly upon agriculture, and are engaged in the production of what we eat and wear.

Despite the decrease in the number of people living on the farm, agriculture is still the mudsill of our civilization. We have learned from bitter experience that no matter how highly industrialized this nation may become, agriculture is still our basic resource. The great economic dislocation which commenced in 1929 and which we commonly refer to as the depression started on the farm. We will never be able to bring about any permanent prosperity or any balanced economy until the farmer is permitted a fair share of our national income and his purchasing power is restored.

---

[4]Text of speech from Speech File, Speech and Media Series, Richard B. Russell Collection, RRLPRS.

This is the primary problem of Government in the United States today. In my opinion every other plan for remedying inequalities and increasing the national income depends upon the successful solution of our farm problem and putting purchasing power in the hands of our farmers, which will enable them to buy the products of industries.

I am so firmly convinced of the truth of this statement that I have devoted the greater part of my time and efforts since I have been a member of the Senate to working toward increasing the farmer's income and bettering the living conditions of the farmer, and equalizing the opportunities of our rural people with the opportunities enjoyed by the industrial workers and those who live in the centers of population where the blessings of our modern-day civilization are easily obtainable.

The objective which has been fixed is to assure the farmer what is known as parity income. This simply means to increase the income of the farmer until it will bear the same relation to the income of those engaged in other lines of work that existed in the normal years from 1909 to 1914. As our national income increased to the high level of almost 80 billions of dollars in 1929, the farmer did not get his fair share. In addition to the burdens of the tariff, which has been a millstone around the neck of the farmer for so many years, the increased wages of labor and profits of capital tremendously increased the cost of that which the farmer buys, without giving him an income from his own products which would enable him to purchase. When the farmer's income reached the low level where his purchasing power was destroyed, the effect was felt by industry and every other line of business, and resulted in the great collapse of 1929 to 1933.

Despite all of the efforts at legislation and the cooperation of the farmers, it must be admitted that we are still far from a solution of the farm problem. The parity price of cotton today is approximately sixteen cents a pound, when we all know that cotton is selling in the markets for about eight and a half cents. Parity for wheat is $1.12 per bushel. Wheat is selling today for fifty-four cents. The parity price for corn is about eighty cents a bushel, whereas corn on the farm today is only bringing a little more than half this amount.

The benefit payments from the National Treasury have brought the total income of the farmer to about seventy-five percent of parity, but much yet remains to be done, and other steps must be taken if those who produce food and clothing for the world are to be placed on an equal basis with these of other vocations.

Cotton occupies a peculiar position among our agricultural products, and in all fairness should be accorded special consideration and treatment. It is our great export crop, and through the years has been the one commodity which year after year has brought into this country money from abroad, which has maintained the favorable trade balance that has made America the richest nation of the world. However, due to local considerations, it has been very difficult to secure fair treatment for the cotton farmer. As a matter of fact, frankness demands the statement that he has been discriminated against in our farm laws and our national policies affecting agriculture. This has not been due to any lack of effort on the part of representatives from the States producing cotton, but to the fact that those States have not had sufficient votes in Congress to secure justice in the face of the combined opposition of those representing States producing predominantly dairy products, wheat, and corn.

For example, we have been preaching diversification as the salvation of the agricultural South as long as I can remember. Those who did not understand the reasons therefore have condemned us for clinging to the one-crop system and producing only cotton, while purchasing other commodities which we could produce as well as any other section of the world. Nevertheless, when the Farm Act of 1938 was under consideration, the representatives of other agricultural interests, in the face of the fact that the cotton farmer alone was required to make a great reduction of his acreage planted to cotton in 1938 offered, and after a bitter fight, voted into the bill a provision which restricted the use of the lands that were taken out of cotton so as to avoid competition with their farmers in an increased production of dairy products, hogs, wheat, and corn in the South. My sense of justice was so outraged at this very unfair attitude that I felt constrained to vote against the entire bill after this provision was inserted.

We are plagued today with another burdensome surplus of cotton amounting to more than sixteen million bales. Due to the reduction of acreage in this country, other lands have started large-scale production of cotton, and our exports have fallen from a long-time average of seven million bales to approximately three and a half million, or about half of the normal amount. This has resulted in placing cotton in a worse position than any other agricultural commodity, and necessarily working a hardship on the cotton farmer.

In an effort to recapture our foreign markets, we hope soon to be able to embark upon an export program which will move a part of the surplus which is depressing prices.

In my opinion we have reduced the acreage devoted to cotton just about as far as it is possible to go without permanent injury to the cotton industry. We have undoubtedly encouraged production in foreign lands, and our loan policy has made it profitable for foreign producers to produce cotton at their standards of living while keeping our American producers of cotton on the lowest standard of living of any people in the United States, including those who are employed on W.P.A. [Works Progress Administration].

The income of the cotton farmer has been cut from both ends. He has been compelled to reduce his acreage and his production without securing an increase in price, with a loan figure fixed at the lowest amount allowed under the law, with prices at distressingly low levels and production cut to an almost irreducible minimum. I have been able to see no solution to the cotton farmer's problems and no way for him and his family to exist except by appropriating funds from the National Treasury for parity or price adjustment payments to supplement the amount he receives from the sale of his commodity. I am proud of the fact that I offered and fought to a successful conclusion the amendment which provided the first parity payments to farmers under the present farm bill.

I am glad that I am in a strategic position as Chairman of the Subcommittee on Appropriations handling the Agricultural Appropriation Bill to make the fight again this year to provide parity payments for the farmers in the sum of 250 millions of dollars for next year, in addition to the soil conservation payments. This provision was defeated in the House, but I shall fight with all the power of my being to restore it in the Senate, and to see if we cannot finally prevail upon the members of the House of Representatives to realize the importance of this appropriation to the entire economy of the United States.

Without this appropriation, Government payments to farmers next year will be approximately thirty percent of what they will be for the current year. With the gloomy outlook for farm prices next year, particularly in the case of cotton due to the staggering surplus and world production, I do not believe that the farmers of this country, particularly the cotton farmers, can get along with any such decrease in income.

One of the most ominous trends in our modern-day civilization is the increasing number of farm tenants. We are all familiar with case after case where good farmers have lost their homes, through no fault of their own, by foreclosure and sheriffs' sales, and have been forced either on the relief rolls or to join the increasing number of tenants.

Farm tenancy has been increasing at the rate of approximately 50 thousand families per year for a long period of time, due to the lack of equality in the distribution of our national income. This is a tremendous problem, and despite the enormous expenditures of public funds during the past six years, very little has been done to effect a cure. We have made a modest beginning in setting up the machinery to lend money to selected tenants to enable them to acquire homes. As early as 1935 I offered an amendment to the $4.8 billion relief bill authorizing the use of funds for loans to farmers to acquire lands, and stated on the Floor of the Senate that this was the only way we could hope to solve our unemployment and relief problems permanently. I stated then that it was costing approximately twelve hundred dollars a year to keep a man on W.P.A. rolls, but when the year ended the money was gone and the man was still in need of relief, whereas if he had been enabled to purchase a farm, he would have been in position to become permanently self-sustaining.

Later legislation known as the Bankhead-Jones Act, to which I gave my most earnest support, set up a permanent program of long-time loans to tenant farmers to buy homes. The only trouble about this program is that it does not go far enough really to combat the increasing tide of tenancy. Last year the House only appropriated fifteen millions of dollars for this purpose. When the bill came before my Committee I amended it to increase the amount to 25 millions of dollars, and finally secured this amount. This year the House has only appropriated 25 millions of dollars in the bill which is now before my committee. I shall endeavor to increase this amount to fifty millions of dollars.

Bear in mind that these monies are not given away, but are loaned on the best security in the way of farm lands in the United States. I wish that existing law authorized the appropriation of still larger amounts. We cannot justify insuring four thousand million dollars of mortgages which are evidences of loans to build houses in the cities and towns for borrowers through the Federal Housing Administration and the appropriation of one billion, six hundred millions of dollars for slum clearance and the building of better homes for the underprivileged in our cities by the Housing Authority, while telling tenant farmers, who live in the poorest houses in the United States, that they cannot have a pittance of fifty millions of dollars to grapple with one of the most serious problems facing America today.

Another step in the series of efforts to equalize the opportunities of the farm people with those who live in the towns and cities has been the creation of the Rural Electrification Administration, to lend money to farm cooperatives in order that the farmer might have available that necessity of present-day life, electric current. As a member of the Subcommittee of the Committee on Appropriations handling the Independent Offices Bill, which contains an appropriation for the R.E.A., I offered the amendment which increased this item to forty millions of dollars two years ago when it was reduced by the House. I also fought for the special appropriation of $100 million for these loans.

Georgia has fared exceedingly well in the distribution of these R.E.A. funds, and I hope that the day is not far distant when every farm home in the State of Georgia will have electric lights and electric current for the many uses to which it may be put in the home and on the farm. I must say, however, that in view of the low income of farmers today, many of them are not able to pay even the modest amount of the monthly bills for this service, and I have been giving considerable study to some means of reducing the cost of current to farm families.

The South has been impoverished ever since the Civil War as a result of discriminatory legislation and policies of our national Government. In 1860 the South had thirty percent of the population of the country and possessed thirty-six percent of the wealth. It is estimated today that we have twenty-three percent of the population and eleven percent of the national wealth.

I have not hesitated to condemn the discriminations against the South in the matter of the tariff, freight rates, and the distribution of Federal funds. The great Democratic president of the United States [Franklin D. Roosevelt] has frankly admitted and pointed out that the people of the Southern States have not had a fair chance to share in our national wealth. We are making some progress in rectifying the most manifest of these injustices, but the progress is slow, for those who profit at our expense are naturally very loath to surrender the advantages which have accrued to them as a result of these unfair laws and policies.

Since the Civil War the Southern people have contributed through taxation hundreds of millions of dollars to the National Government for the payment of large pensions to Union veterans. We have been compelled to tax our own impoverished people in addition to take care of the heroes of the sixties. Due to these and other causes which I could enumerate if I had time, the Southern States have not been able to secure their proportionate share of the funds provided by the Federal Government under the Social Security program to match the State payments to the blind, the crippled, and the needy aged. I believe that in order to secure fair treatment to the old people in every section of the country, the Federal Government should assume the entire cost of the payment of old age pensions. I would like to see the Federal Government pay up to $30 per month to each of our needy aged. Realizing that we cannot secure all of this at one time, I have introduced a bill to take the first step by providing that the Federal

Government shall pay $15 per month in addition to such payments as are made by the State to each old age pensioner.

Thus far I have been unable to get favorable action on the bill, but its introduction has helped to bring about a provision in a bill which has been reported favorably to the calendar requiring the Federal Government to pay as much as $10.00 per month to each old age pensioner in the States paying their old age pensioners as much as $5.00 per month, in States having per capita income below the national average. This would mean a total of at least $15.00 per month to each old age pensioner. (Point out impossibility of States having low per capita wealth and low per capita income paying as much to old age pensioners as wealthier States.)

Closely related to our agricultural and unemployment problems is the important matter of immigration. Due to the unsettled conditions in foreign lands and the persecution of minority groups in some countries, there is terrific pressure being exerted in America today to relax our immigration laws to enable these refugees from foreign lands to come into the United States of America. The American people are an idealistic lot. I am sure I am safe in saying that we feel more concern about the sufferings of human beings in foreign lands than do any other people of the globe. I deeply sympathize with those who are being persecuted, or who are suffering from economic causes throughout the world today, but I believe in the old adage that charity begins at home. So long as we have thirteen million American people out of jobs and American farmers producing such a surplus of cotton, wheat, and corn as to bring about starvation prices I am unalterably opposed to opening the doors of America to a tidal wave of immigration from abroad that will make these conditions worse.

There are just so many jobs in the United States. If these people come here it will be necessary for them to live. That means that they will either displace Americans from jobs that they now hold or that they will become a charge to the relief rolls of the various States, cities, and towns, and will force a still greater division of the monies that are available to provide for our own people in distress.

We cannot afford at this trying period in our national existence to throw wide open the doors of immigration. For my part, I would be willing to stop immigration for a period of years, or until we have solved our own internal problems.

The clouds of war are hovering ominously low over Europe today, and a terrible undeclared war is raging in Asia. We are once again feeling the effects of the propaganda which swept us into the last great European war. Many of our people are taking sides in the line-up between the totalitarian states, ruled by dictators, and the so-called democracies of Europe.

We will do well in this world crisis to remember our last experience in settling Europe's troubles, and keep our heads and attend strictly to our own business on this side of the Atlantic Ocean. My sympathies are naturally with the so-called democracies, though I must confess there is very little difference between the Government and the rights allowed the individual in some of the alleged democracies and in the dictator countries. My sympathies, however, do not cause me to be willing to commit this country to any course which might eventually lead us into a foreign war.

The flower of our young manhood poured out their blood in France, and this country incurred obligations which will eventually call for the expenditure of sixty-nine billion dollars in our efforts to settle the affairs of Europe shortly over twenty years ago. This time we demand that Europe settle its own boundary disputes and disagreements, without our aid and intervention.

Some of the European quarrels and disputes are founded on issues and contentions that are over two thousand years old. They have fought war after war to settle them, and they still remain unsettled. We went over in 1918 to help them settle these disputes in the war that was supposed to end all wars. The truth of the matter is that the very nature of these European differences is such that I have little hope they will ever be settled. They will be subjects of contention and strife forever.

We are blessed with geographical isolation. I am in favor of building up our national defenses to a point that will enable us to deter any acts of aggression, but I insist that these armies and navies and fleets in the skies be used solely, wholly, and exclusively to protect the vital interests of the United States, and not to be thrown in the scales to settle any balance of power in a European war. I am not willing to sacrifice the life of one Georgia youth to settle any of Europe's troubles, and so long as I am in the Congress of the United States I shall never vote for any declaration of war or any course or policy which is likely to commit us to a state of war unless the vital interests and the integrity of our own country is threatened or attacked.

4-H Clubs
ca. 1941

When Senator Russell addressed these 4-H Clubs and their guests, German forces had invaded several European countries.[5] Congress had voted Lend-Lease aid for England's initiatives, and United States military personnel in Greenland were alerted to protect the Nation's shipping from German submarines. In this speech, the Senator explained the importance of the "farm home" for free government. If the country would remain free, he argued, "it must guarantee 'equality of opportunity' for all its citizens." Drawing upon his experience on the U.S. Committee on Naval Affairs, he outlined the need for building a powerful Navy. For the war effort, the citizenry would also have to increase food and industrial production. Russell also defined the "essential freedoms" required for a nation to prosper.

* * * * * * * * * *

Young Friends of the 4-H Clubs, Ladies and Gentlemen: I deem it a happy privilege to be permitted to address this fine gathering of young people.

With a wide variety of resources and despite great industrial developments, Georgia is still preponderantly an agricultural State. We are blessed with a fine climate and vital resources. We can produce in Georgia any plant not purely tropical. We have great wealth in and beneath our soil; in our water power; our forests; our minerals and in the throbbing wheels of our factories. We have scarcely scratched the surface in developing these resources, but the greatest wealth in Georgia is found in the hearts, the minds and the bodies of our young

---

[5]Text of speech from Speech File, Speech and Media Series, Richard B. Russell Collection, RRLPRS.

people. Our hope of the future lies in the proper development of this greatest of our natural resources.

No organization has done more to build-up and bring out the best that we have than the 4-H Clubs in every County of our State. The leaders of this movement are entitled to the congratulations and appreciation of our people.

These United States that we all love built its great civilization upon the firm foundation of agriculture. In the early days of the republic the great majority of our people engaged in farming for their livelihood. A farm home and farm life were the most desirable and attractive. Farm life was clothed with a dignity and gave a feeling of independence not found in any other vocation. The institutions of free government were conserved in the minds and hearts of farmers. Our freedom was won largely by the blood and sacrifice of farmers. At the building of our great industrial empire, other groups, highly organized, seized and kept control of the Government. Step by step, slowly but surely, discriminatory laws were enacted which unduly burdened the producers of food and clothing. Life on the farm began to deteriorate; the farmer's very independence became one of the reasons for his downfall. Living far apart from his neighbors, ofttimes unaware of the adverse effect of legislation, he fell a victim to the greed and avarice of smaller but more highly organized selfish groups. Some of those groups became the victims of their own selfishness. In the hard school of experience, we learn the lesson of the interdependents of capital and labor, as well as that the prosperity of agriculture is tied to the prosperity of those groups.

We have come back to the original conception of the founding fathers who held that every American Citizen, no matter where he lives or what he does, is entitled to equal treatment at the hands of big Government, and equality of opportunity in earning a living. The decline of every great civilization of the past has been due to the destruction of farm life. Discrimination against the farm resulting [in] the impoverishment of the soil and the narrowing of opportunities afforded farmers as compared with other vocations, has been a contributing factor in the decline of every great empire this world has known. To save America from the fate of Rome and Greece and

Carthage, we have come to realize that it is necessary to revive the independence of farm life and rebuild the dignity of the farm home. We have made much progress in this direction; laws have been passed by both State and Federal Governments to restore a measure of equality to those who live on the farms; country schools and country roads are being improved; the lines carrying electricity are gradually reaching out to more farms. The Government has realized the necessity to help the better farmer preserve the fertility of his soil and to take steps to more nearly equalize farm income with the incomes of those who do not live on the farm. There is still much to be done to place the roads, the schools and the churches in the country on a par with those in our centers of population. There is a crying need today for more doctors and better health facilities in rural areas. We have made only the first steps towards progress in giving the farm home the conveniences of modern civilization and we are still a long ways from assuring the farmer a fair share of our National income. However, the important thing is that we have recognized the justice of the farmers' claim. To these things we have at least a vision of our goal and a conception of what it will take to reach it. The fact that the young people living on the farms are acclaiming properly proud that they live on the farm and show that pride by their interest in improving life on the farm and farm homes, is a great part of the battle. The realization that the future of our civilization depends upon the fate of our American agriculture is a challenge to them to carry on the fight until victory is won.

The fight would be long and hard if conditions were normal. The odds are increased by the fact that the world today is engaged in the most titanic conflict of all history. Forces are at work in the world today which threaten not only the progress which we have made in affording equality of opportunity, but also endanger the essential liberties which all Americans enjoy and which constitute the American heritage. Every generation has had a measure of blood, sweat and tears. Every generation has felt the defeat of needed reforms and has seen injustice victimize and bear down many of our people. But under the priceless constitutional guarantees of freedom, we have been able to freely discuss ways and means of remedying our troubles on the street corners and in places of assembly; in our homes; in schools; and wherever we meet our neighbors. However much we may have disagreed on political policies of Government, every true American has always agreed that at any cost we must preserve the basic freedoms of free speech; freedom of assembly; a free press and the right to worship in the manner of our choice. To those essential freedoms add a system of public education and you have the very minimum of the essential rights of any peoples' government.

Today in over two-thirds of the world, those simple rights of humanity are being ground into the dust or are gravely threatened by the threat of [Adolf] Hitler [of Germany] and his satellites in Italy and Japan. In Germany today, they know only two "H's," and they are "Heil Hitler." Head, heart, hand and health are important only to equip a human robot to serve in Hitler's machine of destruction. Churches and schools are only permitted to stay open to glorify Hitler and his program of destruction, and enslave all other people. No person can question any act of the government however unjust. Where two or more people talk together, they are afraid to express their thoughts lest they come to the attention of the Gestapo of all education. All of life is devoted to teaching the males to prepare for war and the females to bear more males to fight in more wars. Falsehoods and purgery are glorified if it gives aid to Hitler's policy of enslaving the rest of mankind. If Hitler were content to keep his philosophy and his armed forces within Germany, we would not be greatly disturbed about the form of government and the ideals of the German people, but his every movement has shown his intent and purpose to inflict the German idea upon all of the other peoples of the world and indeed to enslave other peoples for the sole benefit of the Germanic race. You are familiar with the withering march of the Nazi legions across eleven lands once free. You know how Hitler turned without any provocation upon his supposed Ally, Russia. With such an evil being with so much power aloose in the world, America has been forced to turn aside from all other endeavors and prepare to defend ourselves and the Western Hemisphere. We are arming to defend our liberties and our institutes of Government against the ruthless Nazi tyranny and the poisonous Nazi philosophy. We are making every effort to provide for a National Defense.

I have always been a strong advocate of a big Navy for if we dominate the Atlantic and Pacific, no enemy from across the seas can ever land on American soil. We are now building the greatest Navy ever seen. We have called our young men from peaceful pursuits into the Armed Forces and we are building thousands of those vital instruments of warfare, planes and tanks, and teaching them how to use them. We have embarked upon a program costing stupendous sums and requiring a measure of sacrifice of every man, woman and child beneath the Stars and Stripes. We may as well state in all frankness that hard times which will try the souls of the American people are ahead of us. We will be compelled to pay taxes heavier than any we have ever known in order that the Nation may continue this gigantic program of National Defense until we will be so well armed that no foreign aggressor will think of attacking any point in the Western Hemisphere. We have recognized the importance of supplying the tools of war to those nations which are resisting aggression. The Congress and the President have entered into a solemn commitment to aid those fighting Hitler, both to give us time to complete our defense and keep him from seizing more of the resources which are now so essential to the fighting of wars. Our policy of aiding Great Britain and the Democracies is now the first national policy of our Government. It is too late now to debate; it is our duty to support the President in carrying out this policy.

The farmers will have new duties of supplying food and clothing to those we are committed to aid, as well as to build up a greater reserve within this Nation. Those who work in our industries have a high responsibility to produce more than they have ever done before. This is no time for strikes and delays in defense production over trivial causes. No selfish interest should be permitted to hamstring or delay this program because the measures we are taking are to insure the safety and the lives and the liberties of our people. There can be no price on liberty. Patrick Henry, in his immortal cry of "Give me liberty, or give me death," valued liberty more than life itself. Whatever may be the sacrifice required of us we will make it rather than surrender one jot or tittle of our freedom. We have before us the glorious picture of the weak communities moved by a dream of institution and free government daring to defy a great empire—ragged men and brave women suffered and struggled through seven years to gain their independence. With all our faults we have grown and expanded under the process of Democratic Government. To save our constitution and ordinance of free government, we will defy any conqueror. We do it to save America, the America of our fathers in the past, the America our children will make greater in the future. We are not at war, nor engaged in sending an Army abroad. We hope and pray that we will not be engaged in any shooting war. We do not want war. But if we are forced to defend this country, our freedom, and our way of life, I believe that we will do it in a manner worthy of our heritage. If we are forced to fight, I believe that American productive genius, American ingenuity, and American courage will maintain our proud boast that the American Flag has never gone down in defeat.

National Rural Electric Cooperative Association 19 January 1943

Senator Russell delivered this speech to the first National Convention of the Rural Electrification Association (REA).[6] Russell was floor manager in the United States Senate when the Rural Electrification Act was passed.[7] The REA was meeting in St. Louis, Missouri, to help mobilize production of farm commodities needed for World War II. Russell defined the REA as a "power for democracy" and a "mighty weapon of warfare." He praised the delegates' cooperative efforts to make "electricity available to every farm home."

* * * * * * * * * *

Mr. Chairman, Mr. President, Ladies, and Gentlemen: This is a high privilege which I enjoy in being permitted to take part in this significant meeting. I have been gratified to see so many of my constituents from the deep South demonstrate their profound interest in all that pertains to the activities of the Rural Electrification Administration by their presence here today. There are some real farmers in this gathering. The REA has shown for once and all what farmers can do on a cooperative basis.

I recall many years ago hearing of an alleged farm meeting which was called in my State. A large program was planned. Many high-powered speakers were invited. The farmers, as usual, were at a very low ebb, and this meeting was called to solve all the farm problems. After the meeting was under way and the dinner had been consumed, the speaker was up addressing himself to the question of "What is

---

[6]Text of speech from Speech File, Speech and Media Series, Richard B. Russell Collection, RRLPRS. Handwritten notes by Russell on this speech available in Russell Collection.

[7]Russell's EMC Speech, November 4, 1964, Lyons, Georgia, 2-3, in Speech File, Speech and Media Series, Richard B. Russell Collection, RRLPRS.

Wrong with the Farmer." All of a sudden there was a great commotion out at the door. The confusion grew so great the speaker had to desist. It threatened the entire meeting. Finally quiet was restored, and one of those who was sitting near where the commotion started said, "Go ahead, Mr. Speaker, it is all right now. That was just a fool farmer trying to get into this meeting" (Laughter).

This is a real farmer's organization. This is a significant meeting of this great group of representatives of cooperatives sponsored by the Rural Electrification Administration. For the first time you have gathered to combine all the power which under our democratic system of government resides in the members of these cooperatives, in presenting a common front—a common front to retain the gains which you have made heretofore and to close up ranks as we press forward at the very earliest opportunity to our objective of making electricity available to every farm home in the United States, and in assuring the lowest possible rate to every farm consumer (Applause).

In my humble judgment, the historian of the future in covering the events of the past ten years will point to the creation of the Rural Electrification Administration as one of the really great strides which our Nation has made in its entire existence in building a real democracy (Applause). Too high tribute cannot be paid to that great American Progressive, George W. Norris [Senator from Nebraska] (Applause), for his unremitting efforts in bringing this organization into existence.

We who have been interested in this program since its inception realize how fortunate we have been in the caliber of the men who have headed the Rural Electrification Administration. It has been my privilege and pleasure to know each one of them personally, and each and every one of them have been imbued with a love of the work they were doing. They were unafraid of criticism, and they were men of ability and capacity. We have been fortunate in the personnel of the several boards of directors of all the cooperatives with which I am familiar. And the fact that such great strides should have been made by the several cooperatives in forty-five of our States bears tribute to the zeal of each of you who are taking time off from your own private affairs here today in order to make plans for the future.

In peace times we look upon the program of the Rural Electrification Administration as a power for democracy. Private enterprise had grown too timid to venture out on the farm. It had not had the vision to span the mountains and the plains, to go down the valleys and across the rivers to bring electricity to where the farmer lives. This program was founded in that vision. The farmer has been producing food and clothing for us all in the present while compelled to live in the past (Applause). He lived in a world, a world which enjoyed more blessings of science and progress than any had ever imagined or visualized but a few years ago, but by the very force of circumstances he was compelled to live in darkness and in drudgery. Our object is to bring him into the light and leisure that is common to our civilization (Applause).

This program has shown the boys and girls who were seeking a way to leave the farm that life may be pleasant there, that they may enjoy the radio and the leisure to read, to improve themselves, and thereby become better citizens and contribute more to their Government.

Democracy is rooted in the soil. Without a vigorous, a happy rural life, the institutions of democracy cannot survive, and this great program has contributed more than any other thing of which I know to give the rural life the incentive to carry on and to keep agriculture as our fundamental vocation and bulwark of our democracy from perishing from this civilization of ours (Applause).

We have a service now that, as other inventions of science, such as television and others we cannot envision today, can be had in the homes of people everywhere. The boys and girls and the people on the farm will enjoy them even as do their city cousins. One would not have thought a brief period ago the first meeting of the representatives of these cooperatives would be held in response to the call of the country to make plans for contributing to the success and victory in a great war that is vital to our existence as a people.

This war has caused us to temporarily desist from the full culmination of the REA program. That is one of the many sacrifices that is required of us. The pressure of war legislation has caused us to be unable to bring to passage before this time of the Rankin-Russell Bill, of which I am proud to be a co-author with that stout fighter for

Rural Electrification, Congressman John Rankin from Mississippi (Applause). It has been laid aside, of course, temporarily, and I use that word advisedly. At the very first opportunity it is our intention to endeavor to press it to passage.

The splendid record of repayments recited here by Mr. [Harry] Slattery shows that no sounder investment has been made by any of the lending agencies of government than the loans that have been made by the REA, but the Rural Cooperatives are entitled, as a matter of simple right, to a better interest rate and to a longer amortization of these loans (Applause).

A few months ago when men talked of the American way of life we envisioned a new radio, a new automobile, a little larger bank account, a better suit of clothes, a better house, plenty of food. When we consider the dire fate which has overtaken the conquered people of Europe we realize all too well that those things are only incidental in the American way of life. We realize that unless we are willing to forego temporarily some of those luxuries we have enjoyed as the richest people of the earth, we may suffer the humiliation and the debasement of other people, and we are called upon to battle to the very death for the simple rights for Americans and for our posterity to hold up their heads as free men.

The one supreme effort before the American people today is, of course, to win the war at the earliest possible time and with the smallest possible loss of life and of wealth. Every American citizen must dedicate himself to the relentless prosecution of this war until the final victory is achieved. The war effort is paramount, whether on the fighting line, on the production line, on the farm, on the home front. We have no time now for business as usual, politics as usual, strikes as usual, or for, indeed, the accustomed life of this country, until we have been assured that the policy of enslavement by force represented by the Axis thugs and bandits has been forever crushed and forever buried (Applause).

There can be no compromise with the forces of evil which threaten us. One might as well undertake to compromise with a rattlesnake as with either [Adolf] Hitler [of Germany] or Hirohito [Emperor of Japan]. They must be crushed and crushed completely. No sacrifice is too great to enable us to achieve that end. The stake in this contest, as we all know, is whether we shall remain as free men or be slaves.

When we were attacked at Pearl Harbor [December 7, 1941], the first reaction of our people was to seek to get on a war footing. In the haste and confusion of that hour we thought only of machinery. We knew that war had been mechanized, and we discussed war in terms of planes and tanks and motorized infantry and motorized artillery. We thought of it as moving forward propelled by gasoline. We devoted all our time and our talents and our energies to building the machinery, and in our haste we overlooked certain fundamental facts, and we forgot about things to which we were accustomed but which were just as essential to the waging of successful war. This meeting here today is to in part take up that slack. It is to mobilize the leadership represented by you men and women here into a nucleus to carry on the production of farm commodities, that are just as essential to the successful conduct of war as planes or tanks or any other of the modern machinery of warfare.

That great Captain, Napoleon Bonaparte, once stated that an army moved forward on its stomach. And here today, despite the motorization of war, we find that all of the planes and all of the tanks and all of the motorized equipment on earth will avail us nothing unless the men that operate them are properly fed and are properly clothed. That is one essential requirement of waging warfare successfully which has not changed with time.

Little did we realize when we passed the legislation creating the Rural Electrification Administration that we were forging such a mighty weapon of warfare. We are now faced with a real crisis in farm production in this country. The attractive wages of industry have caused a great migration from the farm. The Army and the Navy have taken their toll of farm labor. At this period, when requirements of "Lend-Lease" are greater than before, when it is necessary to secure more food and clothing for our increasing army than ever before in our history, we find that farm labor has been seriously depleted, that farmers are having great difficulty in obtaining the necessary machinery, fertilizer, and other things necessary to make crops, and this critical situation in which our country finds itself is a challenge which the American farmers must meet today.

Food is indeed an offensive weapon of war today. As Mr. Slattery quoted the Secretary of Agriculture [Claude Wickard], food will win the war and food will write the peace. It is known everywhere that the hope of securing food and clothing was a mighty factor in the ease with which our forces took over a great part of French North Africa. The hope of securing food and clothing produced by the farms of the United States keeps alive the spirit of resistance and inspires the flickering light of hope in the hearts of all of the conquered people of Europe today.

With this great handicap of labor, the American farmer will, in my opinion, rise in this emergency and will supply the needs of the nation, and in this great accomplishment power which is furnished by the Rural Electrification Administration will be an important factor. The Department of Agriculture estimates that almost two million active farm laborers have left the farms within the past eighteen months, either for industry or for the Army and Navy. The difficulties are great. But, the stakes are high, and the contribution to the welfare of your country will be inestimable.

The Congress has been somewhat derelict in not taking the proper steps to keep the labor on the farm. Every one of us should have known it was impossible for any farmer to compete with the wages that are being paid in industry today. Some of us have felt that farm prices were too low to furnish an incentive for production as well as to enable the farmer to meet the cost of his production. Those difficulties, to those who love freedom, who are descended from those who were able to wring freedom from the hand of tyranny, will be but an incentive to greater efforts.

The farmer may well be the unsung hero of our victory in this war. No poet will sing hymns to his fortitude and to his unremitting labor. No medals will be pinned on the farmer's breast. They do not even award the farmer an "E" for excellence in production as they do those who work in defense industries, although I think they surely should. There should be some recognition of his superhuman effort (Applause). I made that suggestion to the Secretary of Agriculture some months ago. I was interested in reading the paper today to see where somebody else had made a similar suggestion, but he had coupled with his the idea that we send around stars from Hollywood to the farmers to display these badges and pin the badges on the farmer's chest (Applause). That may meet with the hearty response of the farmer, but all these stars had better look out for the farmer's wife, and I suspect the farmer would rather have the farmer girl with pink cheeks to pin the badge on him (Applause). Whether he secures this honor or not, the farmer will have the consciousness in his own soul of having made a real contribution to the salvation of his nation.

I do not share the optimism of some of those about this war. Our men are performing superhuman feats on many fields of battle. American soldiers are stationed throughout the world, more than one hundred places outside of continental United States, and at thirty or more of those they are at death's grip with the enemy. But we have just now begun to fight, and I fear that the hard road to final victory will be longer than some of the experts think. It will be a great tragedy if the idea is implanted in the minds of the American people that this war is just about over, because if those experts should be wrong, if we should relax in our efforts, considering the character of the foe with which we contend, that relaxation could be fatal.

We know that the American soldier in this war that the Axis leaders said was soft has lived up to the finest traditions of American heroism. They have proved again, on sea and sod, that they could meet their God in a manner that becometh man. We on the home front must be worthy of the courage of those on the battle front (Applause).

Even though the farmer does not have the panoply and the fanfare that may attach to some, he will not in this emergency let his sons or the sons of his neighbor or the sons of any American mother down. He will give his all to furnish the elemental necessities of war. Those of you who have believed in and fought for the Rural Electrification program as a powerful instrument to spread and to entrench democracy are confident that as a weapon of war it will be even more powerful in bringing the final victory to the Flag that we all love. I thank you (Applause).

American Farm Bureau
10 December 1946

In this speech, delivered in San Francisco, California, Senator Russell praised farmers as defenders of the nation's cherished institutions.[8] Concerned about the economic uncertainty the Nation was experiencing at the end of World War II, the Senator called for profits for farmers equal to those of other groups. Despite all the legislation passed, he regretted, farmers still did not enjoy "stability in . . . income." Referring to his efforts on the Senate Appropriations Committee in behalf of farmers, Russell reviewed legislation passed that benefitted agriculture through soil conservation, commodity loans, rural electrification, farm-to-market roads, school lunches, and agricultural research.

* * * * * * * * * *

During the years I have been in the Senate I have devoted most of my time and efforts to legislation dealing with farm life and farmers' problems. I have done this for what I conceive to be sound reasons. In 1933 when I assumed office, the farmers of this country were utterly prostrate. Coming as I did from a farm community, and having spent most of my life with farmers, I well realized that our farm population has always been the lowest income group in our nation.

I have endeavored to promote farm legislation because of the disparity between the farmer and all other groups in this country. The farmer has enjoyed fewer of the blessings of our modern-day civilization in his home, in his schools, and in his everyday life, than has any other group of workers in our country.

---

[8]Text of speech from Speech File, Speech and Media Series, Richard B. Russell Collection, RRLPRS. Handwritten notes by Russell on this speech available in Russell Collection.

As our nation has become industrialized there has been a great movement of our population from the farm to the city. It has not been many years since an overwhelming percentage of our people were rural. Today only twenty percent of our population live on the farm. We have learned from bitter experience, however, that the other eighty percent of the people cannot prosper while the twenty percent who farm are bankrupt. None of us can prosper unless the farmer receives a fair price for his product.

In addition, I am convinced from my study of history that no civilization can long endure unless it is self-sufficient and has a prosperous and contented farm population. It behooves all who love our form of government and its institutions to interest themselves in the welfare of the farmer, because the twenty percent of the people who still till the soil constitute the greatest bulwark of our nation against the subversive influences which work ceaselessly to change our form of government, and indeed plan to overthrow our most cherished institutions.

We hear considerable complaint today about the high price of farm commodities and the admittedly increased income received by the farmers during the war years. It is true that there has been considerable improvement during these past few years. The farm income during the war has been at the highest recorded level. We must bear in mind, however, that the farmer had a long way to go. His income is still below the income of industrial workers. For example, the per capita farm income in 1945 was $585.00, the highest ever known. However, in that same year the average per capita income of all persons in the United States, including the farmer, was $1,294.00. The farmer is only well off in comparison with years past. He is still not well off in comparison with other groups. Our objective and the objective of all true friends of agriculture is to see the farmer get the same pay for the same work as the other fellow receives, all other things being equal.

The increase in the per capita farm income has been considerable. However, it has not enabled the farmer to bridge the gap between the farm income and the average income of other groups. As a matter of fact, the farmer's income has barely kept pace with the increase in the national income. The total national income in 1945 was nearly 162 billions of dollars. The farm net income reached a new high of 16.8 billions of dollars, but the fact remains that the twenty percent of our population who live on the farm only received 10.4 percent of the total income.

It should be pointed out to those who refer to the gross farm income of the nation as a sign of unparalleled prosperity on the farm that during the so-called parity years of 1909-1914 the farmers received 14.9 percent of the total national income—more in proportion. In 1918 the total farm income amounted to 17.9 percent of the total. The farmer has received more dollars during the war years than he has in the past, but his percentage of the total national income has not increased as much as it should, nor enough to close the gap between the farmer and the rest of the nation which has separated him from a fair share of the total national income.

We are passing through a period of confusion and uncertainty. The dislocation of world economy caused by war is never easily corrected. The war from which we emerged victoriously last year was the greatest ever known. It is therefore no cause for surprise that the postwar period should bring us so many perplexing problems and so much unrest and confusion.

This period of adjustment wherein we seek to stabilize our economy is particularly challenging to farmers. He is the first to feel the ill effects of the declining prices which mark the beginning of a depression. He is usually the last to experience the benefits of a prosperous period, for the prices of industrial products and wages usually go up before the farmer benefits from any increase in the value of his raw commodity. The product of his toil is sold as futures on the great exchanges, and is therefore subject to violent up-and-down fluctuations when speculation is heavy.

Agriculture is the most hazardous of all occupations. Not only is the farmer compelled to gamble with the weather and with insects, but he is the only man who works with his hands producing the essentials of life who does not know what he will receive for his product at the time his work is done. His wage is the price of his product in the marketplace, and until recent years the farmer had no idea what he would be paid for his work at the time he pitched, cultivated, and harvested his crops.

The recent antics of the cotton market changed the wage of the cotton producer by as much as twenty-five percent after the farmers' work was done. This disastrous decline is a glaring illustration of the fact that despite all of the legislation of recent years the farmer does not yet have the stability in his income or in the operation of his business which other lines of labor and enterprise enjoy.

The fight for equality for agriculture in our national Congress has been a long, hard one, and it must still be waged in the future. Despite the fact that for many years the farmers were the most numerous group in our country, they were the last to receive any benefits or protection from national legislation. In our country's beginning, our infant industries received the benefits of a tariff, which has grown and been extended through the years. Industry is also protected by patent laws and a mass of other legislation. More recently labor has been the beneficiary of much special legislation enacted by the Congress. Indeed, such sweeping protection has been given to organized labor that some labor leaders have successfully challenged the very power of our national government and officials elected by all the people.

Despite all of these laws for other groups, the first efforts to enact laws for the benefit of the farmer were met with the cry of socialism. Until recent years the farmer's voice was not heard in the clamor which beset our national capital. We had the anomalous situation of a large group of people living and buying in a protected economy while selling the products of their toil in a buyer's market in competition with the entire world. The farmer was slow to seek special legislation. He reluctantly did so when broke and helpless after a long and losing struggle against the impossible odds imposed by the advantages gained by other groups through national legislation.

There are now many laws on the statute books for the protection of the farmer. Not one of them came easily. Hard fighting and ceaseless working were required to secure the enactment of every one of these laws. The farmers fought to get them, and let those who seek their repeal take warning now that the farmers will fight to keep these laws just as long as there are others on the statutes for the benefit and protection of other groups.

The American Farm Bureau Federation has been the greatest single factor in securing the enactment of these helpful laws. This organization has sent some real agricultural statesmen to Washington to protect the farmers' interests. Men like Ed O'Neal, Lynnwood Wingate of Georgia, Walter Randolph of Alabama, and other leaders know their way around Washington. They have given new life to American agriculture, and have rendered a service that cannot be bought with money. They have recognized that in this day of blocs, pressure groups, etc., only through organization can the farmer secure justice in legislation. They have preached the doctrine throughout the land so successfully that the farmers' claims now reach the most reluctant ears. It has been a pleasure to work with the Farm Bureau Federation in the long fight for equality for agriculture.

The efforts of these men and the most disastrous depression of history finally compelled the government to recognize that it had some responsibility toward agriculture. I doubt if even the most ardent advocates of low farm prices would like to go back to the trying days of 1932. Five-cent cotton, eight-cent tobacco, two-cent peanuts, and thirty-cent corn and wheat not only bankrupt the farmer but set in motion a train of events which bankrupt everyone else.

Let those who demand a reduction in the loan rate of agricultural commodities or the withdrawal of all federal aid for agriculture bear this in mind.

Let us briefly review some of the laws which have been enacted by Congress in the effort to secure recognition for the farmer along with other American citizens. Every effort made by the government to assist the farmer in his unequal struggle has paid rich dividends during the war years. Not only was the farmer called upon to feed and clothe our armies and our people at home, but upon these patriotic fighters for victory was imposed the task of providing the food and fiber without which our allies could not have carried on the war. The wisdom of the various Agricultural Adjustment Acts [Triple A] was amply vindicated by the wonderful record of production made during the war years. The soil-building and diversification program was a material contribution to this great record. The increased fertility of our soils enabled us to greatly increase the production per acre of almost every needed commodity.

Every dollar invested in the conservation program under the Triple A has been of as much benefit to those who live in the cities as it has been to the farmers who received it. Every effort to reduce the appropriations for payments for soil conserving practices should be opposed in the national interest. The farmers profit very little from these payments, but the program does enable them to preserve the most priceless asset of America, the fertility of our soil and the capacity to sustain life in our land.

As a member of the Appropriations Committee ever since I have been in the Senate, I have participated in the appropriation of hundreds of billions of dollars for many purposes. I measure my words when I say that I do not believe any federal expenditures have given us as much return, dollar for dollar, both for the present and in the future preservation of our civilization, as have the funds which have been expended to partly compensate the farmers for the soil conserving practices which have been carried out over the country.

The rise and fall of civilizations in the past have been marked by the rate of depreciation of their soils and their dependence upon others for food and clothing. Let us heed the lessons of history. Without regard to which political party may dominate the government for the moment, we must continue these wise investments in preserving this priceless source of life in our country.

Legislation dealing with agricultural problems has never been handled on a partisan basis during my service in the Senate. Both Republicans and Democrats who are friends of agriculture have forgotten party lines and personal or partisan advantage in dealing with these matters. I am sure that despite the fact that our democratic processes have wrought a change in the complexion of the Congress, under the Republican regime Republicans and Democrats will continue to work together to protect and preserve the gains made by agriculture in the past and to see that the farmer does not fall behind other groups in the uncertain days which lie ahead.

The most immediate bulwark against a drastic decline in farm prices is the provision in the Stabilization Act of 1942 making mandatory loans by the Commodity Credit Corporation at 92½ percent of parity on cotton and 90 percent of parity on almost every other major agricultural commodity until two years after the war is officially declared ended. This is the most effective protection for agricultural prices and farm income which the farmers have ever known. If the protection of commodity loans should ever be removed, it is inevitable that ruinous prices will come again. The assurance afforded the farmer by this law that he will not be compelled to sell his products at excessively low prices made possible the production to which I have already referred as being so important in the winning of the war.

It is my view that this legislation should be made permanent, and I shall introduce a bill in the next Congress to bring this about. It is very unlikely that there will be any radical changes in the status of other groups in this country, and there is little probability that any of the economic advantages enjoyed by industry, business, or labor will be taken away from them. The farmer stands to lose considerable ground, and if this protective legislation expires he will not know the minimum he may expect for his product when he plants his crop.

We have heard a great deal of complaint about the so-called losses of the Commodity Credit Corporation. Some of the metropolitan press have opposed the continuance of this organization on the grounds that it was losing too much money. These people either do not know or do not want to know the facts.

The so-called losses by the Commodity Credit Corporation went to keep down prices to the consumers. Hundreds of millions of dollars were paid out as subsidies on milk and other commodities to avoid necessary price increases. This enabled industrial workers, those who live in the cities, or those who do not farm, to secure milk and other necessary food and clothing at a lower price. The farmer has never favored these subsidy programs. He would much prefer to get his fair price in the marketplace. He has always been suspicious of the subsidy program, and there have been cases where subsidies have been used as a device to keep down farm prices.

American Farm Bureau 149

There have been no losses on the commodity loans extended to the farmers by the Commodity Credit Corporation. I had occasion to look into this matter the other day. Since the inception of this Corporation it has loaned more than four billion dollars to farmers on various commodities. Instead of having suffered any loss on these loans, it has made a profit of nearly one hundred and six million dollars on commodities handled in its loan programs.

I fear the truth of the matter is that some of those who are opposing the operations of the Commodity Credit Corporation designed to maintain decent farm prices are more interested in low prices for farm products than they are in the so-called losses to which they refer.

These people talk of a free market for the benefit of the consumer. Those who operate our factories can reduce production at any time the market is glutted. The farmer can only reduce production by not planting at the beginning of a crop year. He cannot do it once his crop is laid.

To those who demand a so-called free market for agricultural commodities, I would point out that neither industry nor labor operates in a free market. Neither of them proposes to do so, and there is no reason why the farmer should be compelled to do so. In the days which lie ahead it may be necessary to have some controls on production under the Agricultural Adjustment Act if we are to maintain a floor under the farmer's product, but such controls would be better than leaving the farmer alone and unprotected in a highly protected economy.

I regard the efforts which have been made by legislation to improve living standards on the farm as a vital part of the farm legislative program. The Rural Electrification program has been a great instrumentality toward bringing about better living conditions on the farm. The hundreds of farm electrification cooperatives throughout the country have been eminently successful. With one or two exceptions all of them are current with their loans. The prophets of gloom who said that all of the money loaned would be lost have been confounded by the splendid record of achievement of these farm cooperatives. Electric current has been carried to thousands of farm homes. We must not desist in our efforts until every farmer who desires to have the blessings of electric lights and the aid to better living which comes with farm electrification has secured this service. We must also continue our efforts to see that this electricity is supplied at a lower rate.

In the enactment of laws providing for a system of public roads, the importance of farm-to-market roads has been recognized. The friends of agriculture in the American Congress have insisted that every bill providing appropriations for highway construction in this country enacted in the past several years must contain funds to help build roads for farmers who do not live upon the main highways.

I feel a sense of personal pride in the laws providing for a school lunch program in our common schools. For years I was compelled to fight each year to provide for this program in the Agricultural Appropriation Bill. The program has now been written into substantive law. It is not only an important part of our school activity in building future citizens by providing them with a good meal at lunchtime, but in the days of surpluses it affords a splendid means of consuming farm commodities which might otherwise have a depressive effect upon the market price of many products.

Not only has provision been made for substantial help in supplying the food, but for the first time we have funds this year to assist in providing the necessary equipment for the poorer schools with which to prepare the lunches.

One of the most important measures enacted by the last Congress was the bill providing for great expansion in agricultural research and marketing, which I was privileged to handle in the Senate. The widest chemical and physical research is now recognized as essential by all great industries. A considerable part of their annual budgets are devoted to this purpose. We are truly living in an age of new discoveries in utilizing practically every material known to man.

No one farmer is able to maintain vast laboratories and conduct comprehensive experiments. Under this bill the government will undertake not only to develop better seeds and plants and methods of cultivation, but to go into the field of finding new uses for farm products.

For many years the farmer has been greatly handicapped in keeping pace with new methods of marketing commodities. Entirely too much of the cost of farm commodities to the consumer has gone to the middle man. Under this bill the government assumes the responsibility of developing better marketing practices, which should enable the farmer to receive a larger percentage of the consumer's dollar than is the case at present.

Hand in hand with this research program belongs the program to strengthen the Extension Service. Through this valuable service all of the latest methods are brought to the farmer, and any well balanced farm program will properly emphasize the improvement of our Extension Service.

In my opinion one of the greatest challenges we face is to work out a revision of the parity formula. The present formula is inadequate. It is based upon conditions which existed from 1909 to 1914. We have undergone a revolution in our manner of living and method of doing business since 1914. We have fought two great wars. Our nation has seen a tremendous increase in shift in our population. Industry is operating upon an entirely different basis. Most important, industrial wages have risen to undreamed-of heights, and with the diffusion of small plants throughout the country there is now direct competition between industry and the farmer for labor.

We have adopted a national policy of high prices and high wages. Indeed, confronted as we are with a staggering public debt of 265 billion dollars we are compelled to maintain high prices and high wage standards. It will require as much money each year to service this debt as the total cost of government in most pre-war years. It is in the interest of the farmer to have high wages for industrial workers. City families must have purchasing power to pay fair prices for the things the farmers raise. In like manner, the farmer must have a fair income if he is to purchase industrial products. In this era when necessity compels us to maintain high prices and high wage standards, common justice demands that the farmer receive some credit for his labor and wages paid for labor in competition with high industrial wages when he comes to market his crop.

The continuing fight for equality for the American farmer is a fight to preserve America. If our country is to endure, the farmer must be admitted to full citizenship with all other American citizens. No civilization can long endure without a strong rural population. The farmer lives close to Nature and Nature's God. Our farm population is the sheet anchor to windward which holds the ship of state firmly against the storms of unrest which might encompass the destruction of individual liberty in our land. The farmer believes in the dignity of the individual. He has no patience with regimentation or suppression of individual rights, whether under the guise of communism or fascism. Wherever he may live, the farmer is inherently democratic.

In an age of self-seeking and cynicism he clings fast to the faith of his fathers. The farm home is the citadel of the Christian religion and belief in spiritual values. The children who come from these farm homes know that there is such a Book as the Bible. They still receive training from their fathers and mothers. Juvenile delinquency is no serious problem in rural areas.

When we strengthen American agriculture we strengthen America. Farm life must be made more attractive to stop the flow of fine girls and sturdy boys from the farms to our cities. When the income of the farmer reaches true parity with that of other groups, when his roads and schools are equal to those which serve other segments of our population, when he has in his home those blessings of modern civilization which all of our other peoples enjoy, we may truly believe that we have created a civilization in these United States which will stand through the centuries.

We cannot—we must not—relax in our efforts until we have redeemed the promise of the covenant of the Constitution that the American farmer shall have true equality of opportunity with every other group in our land.

Tufted Textile
Manufacturing Convention
30 May 1947

In this speech, Senator Russell addressed several hundred persons attending the Second Annual Convention of the Tufted Textile Manufacturing Association in Savannah, Georgia.[9] He spoke of the challenges involved in adjusting from a war-time to a peace-time economy. Admitting the difficulty of cutting government spending, the Senator advised paying off the Nation's "staggering national debt" by "expanding [the] volume of business." Of considerable concern to the delegates was the prospect of the impending Taft-Hartley Bill, legislation approved by the Senate prior to this speech and enacted into law by the Congress the following month. Russell maintained that the Taft-Hartley act would protect the right of American workers to choose whether to join a union, while requiring laborers entering into a contract collectively to honor it.

* * * * * * * * * *

The amazing production records of American industry during the war years are now a part of our history. Those achievements again demonstrated that free men living under a democratic form of government with a system of free enterprise can outproduce as well as outfight even the most highly developed totalitarian states that the world has ever seen.

The speed with which American industry changed from producing for peace to a basis of total war kept our allies in the fight and saved thousands of American lives. The difficulty of operating in a wartime economy was much greater to some segments of our industry than to others. For example, the handicaps of the tufted textile plants during the period of war with its controls and allocations was much greater

---

[9]Text of speech from Speech File, Speech and Media Series, Richard B. Russell Collection, RRLPRS.

than that of a manufacturer of automobiles. I know all of you are happy that Government controls and allocations have practically been eliminated and we are once again functioning in a reasonably free economy.

This transition period from war to peace has again proved the resourcefulness and resiliency of the American system. Every person in this country capable of doing anything at all had some kind of job during the war. Employment reached a new all-time high level. It was freely predicted by eminent economists that within months after V-J [Victory over Japan] Day we would have from seven to ten million unemployed in this country, and that the transition from war to peace would bring us problems that were all but insoluble. We have had our troubles in this period it is true, but the transition from war to peace has brought us surprisingly little friction. The national income has increased rather than decreased, and unemployment has not to date presented any serious problem.

It would be expecting too much not to look for some kind of recession. There is bound to be a leveling-off period here and there. We already have it in some lines of business. But there is certainly no reason for us to be forced to go through a serious depression again any time in the near future. If we can but practice restraint and avoid the temptation to force prices higher on scarce articles in the effort to get all that traffic will bear, there is no reason why this country should not enjoy a long period of relative prosperity.

Indeed, with a staggering national debt of almost 260 billions of dollars, it is essential that we maintain high purchasing power and an expanding volume of business. A reduction of the national income, even to the level of the best of the prewar years, would invite national financial disaster.

For seventeen years we have operated under an unbalanced national budget. Despite the increased taxes and the tremendously increased revenue of the war period, *we barely paid half of the expenses of fighting the war from current income.* The greater part of it was borrowed from the people and became a part of the national debt. This debt must be paid, and there are only two ways to pay it. One is by reducing expenditures of the Government, and the other is by levying taxes. Both are unpleasant and hard to do.

The Congress was presented with an annual budget of 37½ billions of dollars by the Chief Executive for a peacetime year long after the fighting had ceased. At first blush many people would say that it should be cut right half in two. I am one of those who believe in effecting every possible economy in the operations of Government. I had high hopes at the outset that we would be able to reduce the budget by at least four and a half billions of dollars, and that we might apply these savings on the national debt. An examination of the progress of the various appropriation bills through the Congress today leads me regretfully to conclude that we will be fortunate if we save two and a half billions of dollars in actual expenditures.

A brief study of the larger items in the budget shows some of the difficulties which beset the advocates of economy in the Government. Many of the larger items of the budget are irreducible. The interest on the public debt, for example, is five billions of dollars—more than an ordinary budget in most of the prewar years. There is an item of two billion one hundred million dollars in the budget for tax refunds, and though eight hundred million dollars has been reduced from this amount to pad the budget cuts, frankness impels the statement that this item, whatever may be determined to be due the taxpayer by the Courts or the Department of Revenue, must be paid as surely as the interest on the public debt.

Seven billion two hundred million dollars of the total budget is set up for the Veterans Administration.

The Congress is now engaged in what may well prove to be historic legislation, attempting to deal with relations between labor and management. There is probably no other field of legislation which so stirs the emotions of great segments of the American people. The unfortunate legislator who tries to be fair and legislate in the public interest suffers more anguish when bills dealing with labor relations are pending than at any other time. On no other issue is there such a violent difference of opinion.

On the one hand stands the militant groups of trade unions and their sympathizers who insist that our present labor laws are perfect, and that the addition of a comma or a period is a manifestation of enmity and a savage desire to enslave all who toil. On the other hand the unfortunate legislator is confronted with that belligerent group who are so exasperated over the excesses of some segments of labor that they demand the passage of stringent bills to "put labor in its place"—legislation which would have the effect of shackling if not destroying all labor unions.

I have often looked with envy at the members of the Senate who might be considered as accredited to either of these groups. They are spared a great deal of trouble. They know in advance that they are either to vote against any labor bill or to vote for any measure which is designed to regulate labor.

Labor unions have a very definite place in our society today. They have brought great benefits to their members and to all of those who toil. They have helped to build this country. For many years labor in this country was at a disadvantage. Then the pendulum swung to the other side. Organized labor was given tremendous power, but responsibility commensurate with this power was not imposed. A few greedy labor leaders seized upon this situation. They demonstrated a public-be-damned attitude as pronounced as that of the masters of monopolistic finance in the last generation. Some few even went so far as to defy the Government of the United States and set themselves up as being beyond any law. Their actions threatened the health and welfare of all of our people. The wounded pride of one of these would-be dictators has been the occasion of action which threatened to paralyze the entire economy of the nation, and to bring great injury to all of our 140 million people.

It is intolerable in a democracy that any man should set himself up as being greater than the Government. It is still a proper function of Government to protect the welfare of the majority of its citizens. The average American has no desire to destroy trade unionism. Neither does he wish to suffer on account of the actions of any labor czar. Under the American system of fair play it has become necessary to enact laws which would make labor organizations assume responsibilities in connection with the great power which they exercise.

In my opinion the bill recently enacted by the Senate [Taft-Hartley, 23 June 1947] does just that. It does not deny any working man any substantial right as an American citizen. It does provide that when working men combine together in a union they shall be responsible for the contracts into which they enter, just as everyone else in this country is responsible for his contracts. We already had laws on the statute books to prevent the employer from coercing any employee from joining a union. This bill goes further and protects the right of the individual worker by making him free from coercion from anyone who would force him to join or not to join a union against his will. In addition, it undertakes to protect innocent parties who are not in anywise involved in a labor controversy from being damaged by jurisdictional strikes or by secondary boycotts. The Senate bill is as much designed to protect the individual worker from unscrupulous or tyrannical labor bosses as it is to protect both labor and management from unfair practices or the public from unnecessary hardships. There is nothing to the claims that the Senate bill will destroy all of labor's gains. It does undertake to restore the proper balance in our industrial life.

I do not contend that the bill is perfect. Much will depend upon the way the new law is administered. But I do know that in the complex civilization of today some way must be found fair to labor and fair to management which will prevent the paralysis of our national economy and the suffering which comes to all of our people with a general strike in one of our major basic industries. If this bill does not do the job, it is up to the Congress through the process of trial and error to keep enacting laws until we are able to secure fair legislation. . . .

Presidential Campaign
19 June 1952

In 1952, Senator Russell campaigned to become the nominee of the Democratic Party for President of the United States. He lost to Adlai E. Stevenson, who was defeated in the general election by Dwight D. Eisenhower. During the campaign, in a swing through the Northwest, Russell delivered this speech in Spokane, Washington, to delegates to the national Democratic convention from Washington state and Idaho.[10] Other persons from a three-state area heard the speech over radio station KWEW. A reporter mentioned the "refreshing candor" with which Russell addressed questions during a press conference, how he avoided derogatory statements about opponents.[11] In the speech, the Senator detailed his experience working with the economy, natural resources, agriculture, and national defense. He reminded this audience of special projects he helped obtain for the western states. The text of this speech was taken verbatim from an audio recording.

* * * * * * * * * *

Good evening, ladies and gentlemen. I welcome this opportunity to speak to my fellow Americans of the great Northwest from the city of Spokane, Washington.

I"m glad to talk to you who have the good fortune to live in the states of Washington, Oregon, Montana, and Idaho about the vital issues that confront our nation. I'm glad to tell you frankly how I, as a candidate for the Democratic nomination for the presidency of the United States, feel about some of those issues.

---

[10]Text of speech from Speech File, Speech and Media Series, Richard B. Russell Collection, RRLPRS.
[11]*Spokesman Review*, Washington, June 19, 1952; *Spokane Daily Chronicle*, June 20, 1952.

Presidential Campaign

But first I think it would be well to tell you something about myself and the experience that I think fits me to serve in the highest office in our land.

I was born fifty-four years ago in a little agricultural community of Winder, Georgia. I was the fourth of thirteen children. My father was Chief Justice of the Supreme Court [of Georgia] and my mother, now eighty-four, is the nearest thing to a saint that I have ever known on this earth. My father, a staunch Democrat, was once asked why he did not have fourteen children in the family. He replied that he had understood that one out of every fourteen children born in Georgia happened to be a Republican, and he did not want that to happen in his family. It never did.

My father taught me two precepts which I have followed faithfully throughout all of my thirty-two years of public life. The first was that there was no higher career than to serve the public. The second was that every public office should be considered a public trust.

Upon my discharge from the Navy, I was elected at the age of twenty-two to the [Georgia] General Assembly. I subsequently served ten years in that body, four years as Senator, and at the age of thirty-two, I was accorded the honor of being elected governor—the youngest in my State's history.

In nineteen hundred and thirty-two, I was elected to the United States Senate. There I have served the people of my state and my nation for the past nineteen years.

In looking back on my early days, I recall that when I announced my candidacy for governor the politicians of my state all said that I couldn't win. I made them eat their words. Two years later, when I decided to run for the Senate against a veteran member of Congress, the same "he can't win" chorus was offered. The politicians were wrong again.

They were wrong a third time, too. That was in nineteen hundred and thirty-six when Governor Gene Talmadge tried to take my Senate seat away from me. Governor Talmadge got the worst beating of his career in that election, and since then I have had no serious opposition in my state.

Now the politicians, particularly those from the large metropolitan areas, are saying that I can't win the democratic nomination for president because I am a Southerner. This is sheer nonsense. The people of this country, in these critical times, are not interested in where a man was born. They are interested in getting the best man they can to serve as Chief Executive of this nation.

I intend to show those who say I can't win the error of their thinking at the convention in Chicago next month. The odds have been against me before, and I have overcome them. I can and I believe I will do it again. Furthermore, I am confident that I am the one Democrat who can win overwhelmingly in November against any candidate the Republicans nominate, and I do not care whether it is Senator [Robert A.] Taft or General [Dwight D.] Eisenhower.

The two years I served as governor of my state, where I trimmed spending to the bone and brought the state budget into balance, and the nineteen years I have served in the Senate have been among the most critical in American history. When I entered the Senate in nineteen hundred and thirty-three, it was to serve in the Administration of that great American, Franklin D. Roosevelt. The nation then was in the depth of a depression—a depression that is the best remembered gift of the last Republican administration.

Although it was another Roosevelt—the great T.R.—who signed the Reclamation Act just fifty years ago, it was Franklin D. Roosevelt who ushered in the golden era of reclamation. Reclamation during the past twenty years has transformed the west, conserving the natural resources, turning arid lands into rich food-producing areas, and diverting destructive torrents into wealth-producing electrical energy.

Throughout my long career in the Senate, I have supported and fought for reclamation projects. As a member of the Appropriations Committee I have been in a position to give powerful support to these projects when that support was needed to keep them alive. My record will show that I have assisted in building worthwhile projects in every one of the seventeen western states.

I have the conviction that the development and conservation of our natural resources is essential to the maintenance of a strong, stable economy—an economy which will continue to support our rapidly growing population. I know that this development and conservation is needed to assure us the necessary military strength to withstand Communist aggression in all of its insidious forms, for economic strength is necessary to create military strength.

Western development programs have gone far beyond merely stabilizing local economies. They create opportunities in manufacturing, agriculture, business, and mining. They are a fine source of strategic raw materials and these developments have opened up profitable markets for the commodities produced in other sections of the nation. Whatever builds for the West, builds for the nation. The vigorous drive, the determination of the people of the West has felt—has made its presence felt—throughout the entire United States.

The natural resources have made these United States the strongest and most productive and prosperous nation on earth. Without these natural resources we could not have built the great industrial machine that is the wonder of the world. The day we cease the development of our resources will be the day that marks the beginning of our decline. The national government can promote and encourage these great activities, or it can hamper and discourage them.

Let me remind you that it has been Republican leaders in Congress who have dragged their feet with regard to reclamation. These Republicans fail to recognize, or perhaps they do not want to recognize, that these great irrigation and power projects are not just spending for the fun of spending, but investments in the well-being and security of America.

As your President, I assure you that development of the West will move forward progressively in my administration. I would be less than frank if I told you that these developments can be carried on in their entirety as rapidly as you and I would like. We must be realists and recognize the fact that the vast rearmament program must—which we must push forward with all possible speed if we are to avoid the catastrophe of a third world war—that this program must come first. Money, money which in a peaceful world could and should be used for the development of natural resources must in many cases now be allocated to tanks and guns and planes [for the Korean War]. The projects which are capable of contributing the most to the overall good of the nation must take precedent over many others which, though desirable, must be postponed. Nevertheless, I pledge you that there will be no turning back on the programs of development for the West. There will be no standing still. The Democratic party under my leadership would continue to be the party of progress.

Neither will there be any turning back on the farm programs which, hand in hand with many of the public irrigation and power projects, have enabled this country to feed and clothe its people and to develop the economic and military might on a firm and solid basis. The farmer of this country is the vital key to the strength of this nation.

As Chairman of the Senate Committee on Agricultural Appropriations for the past nineteen years, I have never lost a major fight for the American farmer. There have been many of these fights—usually with Republicans, but I have seen that the funds were provided to enable us to encourage and maintain a prosperous agricultural population. I have been in the forefront of the battle to promote the Rural Electrification Administration—that agency which has revolutionized life in thousands of farm homes in all sections of our land by bringing electric current to those homes. I have protected the appropriations for soil conservation against the attacks of those who short-sightedly fail to realize that a productive soil is a necessary asset to any long-lived civilization. I have seen to it that funds were provided for agricultural research and development, for better farm housing to support—for the price support program for the basic farm commodities, and for the school lunch program which has made possible milk and nourishing food for children of all races, colors, and creeds in our schools.

Our farm population has been decreasing, but fortunately the efficiency of those engaged in farming has increased even faster than the population. We have six million fewer people on farms in the United States today than we had in 1940, although the national population is twenty-five million above that of twelve years ago. But these fewer people on farms are producing so well that the American people are eating better today than they were in nineteen hundred and forty!

This marvelous productivity of American agriculture has also provided the raw materials which are vital to the smooth functioning of our industries and to meet the new discoveries of our time. It has likewise made possible the release of badly needed manpower, manpower necessary to operate the tremendous industrial machine required for the rearmament program and to develop a strong and sound economy.

This productive record of the American farmer offers a sharp challenge to all other persons on every job to give their best efforts in this time of crisis. If every other person in the nation will contribute as much in increased productivity to the building of the strength of the United States as the average American farmer has contributed, then we have no fear that we will not meet successfully any test that may come to us. And there will be other tests, severe tests, in the trying years ahead.

It would be most pleasant to be able to tell you tonight that the world was headed for a long era of undisturbed peace, that we could reduce taxes next year and that our economy could be geared to increasing civilian production. I cannot, in good conscience, tell you this. No honest man who has knowledge of all of the facts of today's world can make that statement.

On the contrary, we will have our courage, our determination, our patience, and our economy tested in very severe ways. I have the utmost faith and confidence that the people of these United States will cheerfully meet this challenge. I know that they will make the sacrifices necessary to turn back this godless tyranny of Communism and all of its threats regardless of the form of aggression the Kremlin may choose.

Our first job, our main job, is to rearm America. As Chairman of the Senate Armed Services Committee, having knowledge of the facts and having handled the defense legislation, I believe that we arm for peace and not for war. A third world war is not inevitable. But it will come if we fail to make this country strong. If we falter in this arms program, we are inviting a catastrophic conflict which no one can finally win. Our Communist foes recognize one language and one language only—the language of strength. If we over-night could triple our air strength in Korea you may be sure that we would find on tomorrow a new and more conciliatory attitude on the part of Communist negotiators. If we were stronger in all aspects of our national defense, the Communist-inspired threats, the many crises which are developing in various parts of the world would soon disappear. The Communists move forward only where they find weakness, chaos, and confusion. They do not attempt to move in those areas where they find strength, confidence, and stability.

In conjunction with our rearmament program we must maintain the very closest collaboration with the other free nations of the earth. The Atlantic Pact, and the North Atlantic Treaty Organization erected upon it, are vital to the security of the American people. They are also vital to the security and freedom of the people of Western Europe. It is not just charity which has dictated our foreign aid programs. It is in our own self interest to assist those people who have managed to stay outside the Iron Curtain and who have the will to defend themselves. There is no honorable way we can ignore the responsibility coming down to us through the centuries of man's struggle upward toward freedom and individual dignity. Nevertheless, we must insist that our allies and associates recognize the mutuality of this program. We must insist that they do their utmost, more than they have done to date, to protect and defend themselves. I believe our foreign aid program can be held within reasonable limits, and as President I would constantly review it to insure that these programs are meeting their objectives and at decreasing costs.

There is still another major test which we, the American people, must face up to. It is the test of our ability to keep our economy strong and healthy despite the unprecedented demands which are now being made of it.

We must move to bring our national budget into balance. That cannot be done next year but I believe that it can be done by legislation enacted in the year of nineteen hundred and fifty-four without jeopardizing our national defense program, provided of course, there is no material increase in world tensions. I am of the opinion—from

Presidential Campaign

knowledge based again from my experience as Chairman of the Armed Services Committee—that in nineteen hundred and fifty-four we will be over the hump in many aspects of our rearmament program.

This will permit substantial reductions and, if they are coupled with economies which can be effected in non-essential federal expenditures, we can bring about a balanced budget. A balanced budget is our best weapon against inflation, our best weapon against the further cheapening of the value of the dollar.

We cannot expect either tax reduction, as attractive as that sounds, or new, high-sounding federal spending schemes until we have completed the rearmament program and brought the budget into balance. Between tax reduction and new spending schemes, certainly taxes should be reduced.

But I tell you frankly, it is foolhardy and misleading in view of the actual facts that exist, to talk about an immediate fifteen percent tax cut next year, or to hold out a vision of a thirty or forty billion dollar budget in the immediate future. This Republican propaganda is designed to get votes, but it ignores realities. It will not deceive the American people. I would like to see—and I know that the people would like to see—the actual blueprints of these magicians who promise to perform this fiscal legerdemain.

Now if their purpose is to wreck the arms program, if they wish to isolate this nation from the free peoples of the world, if they want to meat-axe the reclamation and conservation programs as they have tried to do in Congress, why they can effect the quick reductions they talk about in such glib terms. But these reductions would leave the nation defenseless, friendless, and at a standstill. And who, I ask, besides the Masters of the Kremlin, wants an America like that?

I believe that in this critical period of American history, our people are looking for the best leadership in our government that is available. They are looking for ability, integrity, experience in government, patriotism, and devotion to duty. I ask only that my candidacy be measured by this yardstick which should be applied to all who seek your suffrage.

I know that the American people have no intention of trying to turn back the clock and destroying the great gains in social, economic, and conservation legislation which the Democratic party has produced over the past twenty years. That clock would not be turned back under my leadership as your President.

I also believe that the American people recognize the importance of deferring experiments with new and costly federal programs, however attractive, until the first things have been accomplished. We certainly want no new adventure that would lead the nation down the road to socialism. There is plenty of elbow room within the limits of the Constitution to attain legitimate social objectives by cooperation without resorting to bureaucratic centralization and federal compulsion in these times.

I am one of those who believes that the government should be kept as close to the people as possible. I believe in protecting the Constitutional rights of every individual citizen. Every American, regardless of his race, his creed, his national origin, will get fair and equal treatment from my administration as president. I will give the people a clean government, a just government, a middle-of-the-road government devoted to the welfare of all of the people and to protecting our common interest and safety.

The greatest issue before us today is one which rightfully should unite our people, not divide them. The great issue is, in the final analysis, the issue of survival in today's dangerous world. With God's help, with wise leadership, with devotion to country and to our principles, we will survive. We will come through this time of danger, we will press forward, we will keep the light of freedom burning brightly as an inspiration to all of the peoples of the world.

Good night and Godspeed.

Turner County Chamber of Commerce
15 October 1959

In Georgia, Senator Russell delivered many speeches to civic clubs, Chambers of Commerce, and other organizations. In these talks, he complimented leaders for progress made in their communities, and inspired citizens to further strengthen their economies. In this speech, recognizing the shift of population from farm to city, Russell called for a balance between agriculture and industry.[12] The Senator praised residents of Turner County for their success in attracting new industry. In what became a recurring theme in his speeches, Russell stressed the importance of water conservation for economic growth. The Senator reminded the audience of his role in funding the construction of several dams in Georgia and in supporting farmers. He also examined agriculture's contribution to the state's economy. The speech was delivered in Ashburn, Georgia.

* * * * * * * * * *

I am honored to be here tonight as the guest of the Turner County Chamber of Commerce.

This proud and progressive community has a very warm spot in my heart. It is a great pleasure to be able to renew old acquaintances and to visit with my many friends from Ashburn and Turner County.

I regret that I was unable to be with you last week for the dedication of the first stretch of the new Interstate Highway 75. Naturally, there are some understandable fears that this new highway will have an adverse effect on the business of the community. But I hope and pray that in the long run it will be a boon for the entire area that it serves.

It has been an inspiration for me to follow your determined and energetic efforts to bring new industry to your fine community. The

---

[12]Text of speech from Speech File, Speech and Media Series, Richard B. Russell Collection, RRLPRS.

establishment of the Manhattan Shirt Company's Ashburn plant last year is dramatic evidence of your faith and determination.

I know that you can be counted upon to press forward with vigor on the task you have begun. By your actions, you are proving the strength, vitality and ingenuity of our great American system that has brought our people the greatest way of life and the highest standard of living the world has ever known.

Certainly, the task of bringing new industries to the smaller cities and towns of Georgia so as to balance our economy is one of the foremost challenges facing our state today.

It is a widely recognized fact that the rural areas of Georgia are rapidly declining in population. We are told that about 100 of our counties are losing population.

It is less well known, however, that this loss of rural population is being partly offset by a corresponding increase in the size of the towns and cities in the rural counties.

Your own county has experienced this trend. Since 1940, Turner County has dropped from 10,846 to an estimated 10,500 last year. During the same period, the City of Ashburn has grown from 2,266 to an estimated 3,500.

Obviously, this means that many of our people are leaving—or are being forced to leave—the farm in search of a livelihood elsewhere. Not all of these people are moving to the great metropolitan centers as is sometimes supposed. Many of them prefer instead to stay in nearby towns and smaller cities where they are happier than they would be in the overcrowded cities.

I believe this is a healthy trend that should be encouraged. It can prevent our rural counties, which have always been such a source of strength and stability to our state, from withering and dying on the vine.

Since the end of World War II, Georgia has undergone a spectacular era of unprecedented economic growth and expansion that has been due in no small measure to the efforts of groups and organizations such as yours.

The figures and statistics that tell the story of our fantastic growth have been recounted often. But some of them are so exciting and so significant that they need to be repeated in order to inspire us to even greater efforts in the future.

Between 1950 and 1957, Georgia ranked fourth in the nation in the number of new commercial and industrial firms established. Just recently, we have learned that our annual industrial payroll has passed the billion dollar mark and that our total non-farm employment now exceeds a million persons.

The State Department of Commerce reports that almost 200 new plants have been established in Georgia during the first nine months of this year. This is at a rate of almost one new plant daily. The Department estimates that the total investment in new plants that will come to our state this year will amount to $100 million dollars.

It is significant that Georgia's industrial growth is proceeding faster this year than last. This gives the lie to those false prophets who dolefully predicted that new industry would steer clear of Georgia because we are determined to operate our public schools in a manner that is to the best interest of all our people.

Georgia's economic and industrial progress is not accidental. There are many sound and solid reasons for it.

Businessmen know that they can expect fair and just treatment from both our state and local governments. Our tax laws are fair and equitable. Georgia is centrally located in the growing Southeastern market and is served by an excellent land, water and air transportation network.

The people of Georgia themselves are one of the major reasons why industry is attracted to our state. They constitute one of the greatest reservoirs of industrial talent and energy to be found anywhere in the world.

Finally, Georgia is blessed with an adequate supply and potential supply of water that has become a prime essential for all industry today. Without water, there can be no industrial growth and expansion.

Indeed, water has become so important to our everyday life that the future progress of any given area will be measured by the availability and the proper use of its water resources.

Water is so commonplace that it is easy to take this precious, God-given resource for granted. But the fact is that the consumption of water and the future demand for it is increasing faster than the national population.

Fifty years ago, when our population was about 85 million, the daily consumption of water was about 450 gallons per person. Today, with our population in excess of 175 million, the per person water consumption in the nation has increased to 1,500 gallons daily. By 1975, when the population is estimated to be 220 million or more, the daily need for water is expected to reach 2,000 gallons per person.

It is easy to see that in the very near future the availability of water will perhaps be the major determining factor in the future growth of the country. Those areas that exercise the foresight to develop and conserve their real and potential water resources will become the areas of greatest economic promise.

With water an obvious key to future growth and prosperity, Georgia has a priceless opportunity today to guarantee for itself an even brighter and richer tomorrow. We have an abundant rainfall and we have a magnificent system of rivers that flow from the mountains in the north to the Atlantic in the east and to the Gulf of Mexico in the south.

Through the proper development and utilization of these resources, we can bring the benefits and blessings of our bountiful water supply to every city, town and rural community in our state, regardless of where they are.

I am exceedingly proud of the part I have been privileged to play in the development of our rivers. As a member of the Senate Appropriations Committee, I have been successful in fighting for and obtaining funds to finance such projects as the Jim Woodruff, Walter George, Columbia and Buford dams on the Chattahoochee; the Clark Hill and Hartwell dams on the Savannah, the Allatoona on the Etowah, and many other types of development and improvement of other river systems in the state.

In the past, we have been hampered by the lack of an overall plan of coordinated development that will result in the maximum utilization of our water potential. That is now being remedied.

Under a law I sponsored last year, a Federal Commission headed by Jim Woodruff, Jr., of Columbus has now undertaken a study to formulate a plan for the overall development of our entire river and water resources. The plan to be developed will not be limited to the immediate areas near the major rivers, but will encompass the entire state. This is, of course, a long-range undertaking. The Commission is expected to require two years to complete its plan.

In discussing the past, present and future industrial development of Georgia, I do not want to overlook the great importance that agriculture continues to hold in the state's overall economy.

The two million Georgians who still live on farms or in rural towns and communities have a direct and personal interest in the maintenance of a sound and prosperous agricultural economy in our state.

Our goal is to achieve a proper balance between industry and agriculture in Georgia. To achieve this goal, we cannot afford to permit our agriculture progress to lag behind industrial progress. They must go hand-in-hand.

One essential to successful farming today is an adequate program of agricultural research. I have long been convinced of the crucial importance of farm research and have worked through the Senate Agricultural Appropriations Committee, which I have the honor to head, to strengthen the government's present work in this field.

As a result, I secured approval in the past session of Congress for a number of research projects of direct benefit to Georgia farmers.

One of these projects now underway at the Tifton Experiment Station is the development of feed pellets from Coastal Bermuda grass. Because of its extremely high food value, Coastal Bermuda grass converted into concentrated feed form through the pelleting process offers exciting promise for the state's livestock growers —particularly in this area where Coastal Bermuda thrives so well.

Farm experts tell me that this new process will make it possible for Georgia farmers to produce the equivalent food value of 278 bushels of corn from an acre of Bermuda grass. Stated another way, it may be possible to produce 1200 pounds of beef from a acre of this grass through development of the pelleting process.

I was also able to obtain for the Tifton Experiment Station an appropriation of some $500,000 for the construction of a laboratory to develop new scientific methods of controlling the destructive corn borer and other grain insect[s].

Another million dollars was appropriated by Congress under an amendment that I sponsored to conduct an all-out research program to eradicate the boll weevil. We may be at long last on the threshold of stamping out this vicious pest which too long has robbed our farmers of literally billions of dollars. Goodness knows, the cotton farmer makes far too little now to have to share his meager return with the boll weevil.

We were also able in the past session to obtain an increase in the funds for soil and water conservation research in Georgia and to begin a new research program to help our apple growers in North Georgia.

It is nothing less than a national tragedy that our farmers are undergoing severe financial hardship at a time when our nation generally is enjoying boon times and unprecedented prosperity.

Since 1952, the total personal income of the nation has risen almost 40 percent. But during the same period, farm income has dropped 17 percent.

I had the Library of Congress conduct a study of what has happened to Georgia farmers as compared with the non-farm population in our state since Mr. [Ezra Taft] Benson [Secretary of Agriculture] and Company took over in Washington. I was shocked and astounded at the results.

Between 1952 and 1957—the latest information available for comparison—farm income in Georgia declined by $82 million while non-farm income increased by more than a billion dollars. Put on a person-to-person basis, Georgia's per capita farm income dropped from $410 to $324 during the period while the per capita non-farm income rose from $1,099 to $1,351.

The meaning of these figures becomes more appalling when you consider the declining number of farmers. Many simply have been unable to survive the economic wringer and have been driven from the land entirely.

Benson, when confronted with the shocking condition of our farmers, blithely attempts to pass the buck to Congress. This is his means of attempting to cover up the miserable failure of his own farm policies and program.

The Benson program—or what passes for his program—is to drive down farm prices by lowering or abolishing farm price supports. He professes to believe that this will reduce surpluses. But the only thing he has accomplished has been to reduce farm prices and farm income, and to create a long casualty list of farmers driven from the land.

Over my vigorous opposition, Benson has been able to lower the average of all farm price supports by 20 percent since he took office in 1953. But instead of reducing government-held surpluses, they have actually increased by 300 percent under the Benson regime.

And talk about spenders! It now costs more to run the Department of Agriculture than any other activity of the Federal Government except defense and interest on the national debt.

In fact, more tax money has been spent on all federal agricultural activities since Benson took office in 1953 than was spent by all previous secretaries of Agriculture since the Department was created in 1862.

Despite a 13 percent drop in farm prices under the Benson program, food prices in the grocery store have increased five percent since the present administration took office.

Congress has been unable to do anything about the chaos in the farm program because of Benson's strange hold over the President. Efforts to write a sound and sensible price support program have been frustrated by vetoes and threat of veto.

Some major changes will have to be made in the White House and in the Department of Agriculture before we can restore sanity and solvency to our farm program.

I sincerely hope the voters of the country will make those changes in next fall's elections.

I also hope that those elections will make some changes in Congress among those who have built their political careers on baiting, hating and berating the South. . . .

I am now cautiously optimistic that at long last a break is appearing in those clouds of war that so long have cast their ominous shadow over mankind's longing for peace.

The international climate has undergone a profound change as a result of the visit of Premier [Nikita] Khrushchev to this country and of President Eisenhower's impending return visit to Russia.

Certainly, on the surface anyway, there has been a general easing of east-west tensions. It remains to be seen—and for the Communists to determine—whether this easing of tensions is more apparent than real.

Before his arrival, I was gravely apprehensive about the wisdom of the President's decision to invite our acknowledged enemy to visit our country as an honored guest. But on balance, I believe the net result of his visit has been good. . . .

As I told him when he was visiting with the Senate, I think it would be an excellent thing for the Russian people to be able to have decent homes, cars, television sets and all the other things that we consider commonplace in America. Certainly if Russia attains a standard of living approaching our own, both the Russian leaders and the Russian people would be more reluctant to risk it all in the certain devastation that would accompany a nuclear war. . . .

Georgia Crop Improvement Association
18 February 1963

In this speech, Senator Russell addressed the Eighteenth Annual Meeting of the Georgia Crop Improvement Association at the University of Georgia in Athen.[13] The Association presented the Senator a plaque for service to agriculture. In the address, Russell praised the association for its contribution to agricultural research. He explained the reasons for the high yields produced by farmers, and described the success he had in the Senate funding research facilities in Georgia.

* * * * * * * * * *

Mr. President, and my friends of the Georgia Crop Improvement Association, I deeply appreciate the warmth of the welcome that I have received today. It is always a pleasure to be in Athens and on the campus of my alma mater, the University of Georgia. . . .

The Georgia Crop Improvement Association has in a short span of years done a tremendous job for our farmers and Georgia agriculture. In each year since the Association's program began, in 1945, we have seen new evidence of its impact upon our farm production.

It has been said that "he who plants a seed plants life." But this is only true if the seed is good so that when planted under proper conditions, it will germinate. And also from the standpoint of the planter, the seed must be pure and true as to its varietal and other characteristics.

This past year the Association has tagged over 500,000 bags of seed with a value of about eight million dollars for the seed alone. This seed is kept bagged and labeled, guaranteeing to the dealer and the farmer that they are the seeds as labeled and are not mislabeled and the contents do not include noxious weed seed. Your standards are so

---

[13]Text of speech from Speech File, Speech and Media Series, Richard B. Russell Collection, RRLPRS.

high that Georgia seeds are recognized throughout the world as being of the highest quality.

This organization is responsible for making available to the farmer, directly, the beneficial results of the research in agriculture that has been done in Georgia and the Southeast.

In the role as the legal seed certifying agency in Georgia, the Association now sponsors an educational program over television and radio and cooperates with the newspapers and with the county agents in bringing about a better understanding to our farmers of the great value in planting certified seeds of superior varieties.

Your Association knows Georgia's future cannot be greater than the qualifications of its youth and I congratulate you in sponsoring a tuition scholarship here at the College of Agriculture for a student in agronomy.

You have wisely developed an educational program, the Bonus Seed Program I believe it is called, with the Extension Service, as a bonus for farmers planting good seeds.

You have cooperated with Georgia's strong 4-H Clubs in their program for crop improvement.

The motion picture, "As a Man Soweth," is being shown to farmers and seedsmen all over Georgia, visibly comparing the results of planting good seed versus the inferior crops that bad seed produce.

This fine new seed laboratory which has been built here on the campus is a lasting monument to your good work and through its facilities, even greater effort will be made in developing finer seed.

So, I am proud of what you are doing and am glad that I have been able to participate over the years in your activities.

It makes me very humble indeed to be the recipient, not only of the generous words that have been spoken about me here today, but also of this beautiful plaque as a visible reward and honor for what I have endeavored to do throughout the many years of my public service for Georgia agriculture. I have a good many scars on my body from the numerous legislative battles in which I have been engaged in behalf of our number one industry in Georgia and the South, and indeed the nation—agriculture.

It has not been an easy task, for as this great civilization of ours, now the envy of all the worlds, has raced toward ever higher goals of development, production—making possible all of the comforts of life that we know—of economic reward for our people—indeed of all the betterments of the good life as we know it today—the status of our farmer and of agriculture, not only in the Southland, but across the country, has not kept pace with the other areas of our growth. No one knows this better than you.

Of course, our production in agriculture has been one of the most phenomenal accomplishments in this period of world history. Throughout all of human history, mankind has been compelled to wage a constant struggle to produce sufficient food and fiber to insure his existence.

But ours is the only civilization known to man that has been faced over a period of years with the problem of dealing with more food than our people can eat and more fiber than they can wear.

One of the great miracles of the present era has been the record increase of production with fewer hands by American agriculture.

Our production has been so great that we have been the bread basket for hungry people in almost every country, both old and new, in every conceivable corner of the globe. And despite the fact that we have given away or sold for soft currencies many billions of dollars of food and fiber, we are still confronted with the complex problem of tremendous surpluses.

This is not the case in any of the Communist countries, where agriculture has been collectivized and has been stumbling along from one crisis to another. In the Communist bloc of nations shortages of agricultural output are the rule, rather than the exception. This is reflected in the stagnation of agriculture in the Soviet Union, in food rationing in Bulgaria, Romania, East Germany, Cuba, and other satellite countries, and in the starvation and hunger now so widespread throughout Red China.

The Communists pretend that collective farming on large collectives and State Farms is the most advanced and efficient system of farming and the only one which can produce the maximum of agricultural output with a minimum of waste in capital investment and use of labor. However, thirty-five years of collective farming in the Soviet Union and a decade of socialized agriculture in the countries of Eastern and Central Europe and in Red China have demonstrated not only that this is not so but that exactly the opposite is true.

The official Soviet periodical in the field of economics, *Problems of the Economy*, made this admission in its June 1962 issue:

> Our land today produces only one-third to one-half of the basic farming items that the people's economy requires. Also, the material and technical equipment of our agriculture is only one-third to one-half of what it should be in order to achieve the required volume of agricultural produce.

The failure of the collective farms in Communist countries has been the most monumental failure of Communism. In order to enable the people to live, it has been necessary to allow each farmer a free acre or two from which he might sell on his own account anything that he produced. This limited capitalist operation has produced sufficient food, even though sold without price controls, to keep people alive. In Russia, I have seen with my own eyes the scanty provisions in the state stores. Going from there to the marketplace, I have noted the thriving business carried on by farm wives selling the produce of the free acre of land given each farmer.

In the beginning, the Communist system squeezed agriculture to build industry, but the one problem that has been beyond the reach of even the able Mr. [Nikita] Khrushchev [of the Soviet Union] has been an adequate agricultural program. Throughout time, the farmer has been the most independent of men.

Americans pay a smaller part of their income for food than in any other industrialized country and in most others. We pay nineteen percent of our income for food as compared to thirty-six percent of the income of the Japanese or thirty-three percent of the income of a citizen in West Germany, and a whopping fifty-three percent of the income of an average Russian.

Our farm production is a miracle based on the land-grant college system of research and extension with aid from industry in the development of machines, equipment, and pesticides which have combined to make our farm technology the finest in all history.

In this centennial celebration by agriculture, the impact of research done in the colleges, by the Federal agencies, and by private industry to achieve our present day agricultural efficiency has been stated many times.

This abundant production has met the high level of consumer demand growing out of a prosperous and expanding economy.

This great agricultural factory, of which we are so proud and about which we frequently read and hear so much criticism, assures us that we will eat well today and tomorrow, and probably have plenty left over.

This accomplishment has resulted primarily through a series of changes; changes resulting from advances in research, greater efficiency in production and management, the development of better varieties that are more disease and insect resistant and of better quality; new herbicides, fungicides, pesticides, and many other accomplishments which time does not permit me to mention.

There have been changes affecting the seed business and its organization. Changes in the system of seed distribution and financing. In fact, changes have occurred in every segment of business associated with our agricultural economy.

We are all well aware that the total number of farms is decreasing and this trend towards the factory farm has been a source of great sorrow to me. Perhaps the greatest single factor in the debasement of the American character has been the decline and fall of the family farmer.

This is unfortunately an economic fact of life and one that is not likely to be reversed. Centralization and mass production is the order of the day.

In 1862, one farm worker in American supplied enough to support five people. Today one farm worker supplies enough for twenty-seven people. Compare this with only five that one Russian farmer can feed. If we farm with the same techniques and the same seeds and fertilizers used only twenty-three years ago, in 1940, there would be a need today for an additional eight million farm workers.

Some consumers do not have any idea of the tremendous advance that research, which brought about the resulting increased efficiency on the farm, in the seed business and all other enterprises relating to agriculture, has brought directly to them. If our farms today were still using the practices that were available to them only twenty years ago, it would cost thirteen billion dollars more a year just to produce our food and fiber.

That amounts to $288.00 for each American family. This annual savings of thirteen billion dollars in production costs is more than twice the costs of all the agricultural research conducted in this country by the Federal government, by all the States, by all of our industry—in the past 100 years.

While remarkable achievements have been made in improving the efficiency of growing farm products we know that these products would have little or no value if they could not be moved to consumers through the nation.

Our people in Georgia cannot eat all the poultry, peaches or peanuts that we produce or use all the cotton that comes off our farms. For this reason, marketing must be improved in order that products may reach as many consumers as possible at low handling cost and in the best possible condition.

I have secured additional funds to support improved marketing research and in bringing about cooperation of the Agricultural Marketing Service with the Georgia Department of Agriculture in planning the new Atlanta State Farmers Market, one of the finest institutions of its kind in the world.

Through this facility more than forty million dollars worth of products per year are moving. People from all over the United States and from many foreign countries have come to see this testimonial to the interest of Georgia in the marketing of the products of its farms.

We have a Federal Program now underway in cooperation with the University [of Georgia] in conducting research to improve pre-cooling of peaches in order that these products may reach the consumer in better condition.

At my request the Agricultural Marketing Service has extended its packaging and container studies to Georgia peaches. During the 1962 season, these researchers made nineteen test shipments from Georgia to the big markets in and around New York City. The objective of this project is to expand the outlets for peaches by placing high quality, tree-ripened fruit before as many consumers as quickly as possible. Work is also being done to develop better pre-cooling methods for sweet corn and other commodities.

Through close cooperation with the University of Georgia, the Agriculture Marketing Service has developed improved work methods and equipment for eviscerating and packing chickens in Georgia processing plants. Application of the recommendations growing out of this research has already brought large savings. Research is underway to develop equipment for packing chicken parts to an exact weight in pre-marked containers in order to reduce the labor costs and waste involved in present methods.

These examples show the organized effort that is being made to improve the efficiency of growing farm products and moving them to consumers throughout the country. Efficient production and distribution are both essential to the welfare of Georgia farmers, to the success of marketing firms, and to the ability of consumers to maintain a high standard of living.

The fact that the wages from an hour's labor will buy a larger quantity and higher quality of food than ever before in the history of this or any other country is the strongest possible testimonial to the value of the efforts being made to improve the production and distribution of food.

I am exceedingly proud of the part I have been able to play in the past twenty-eight years as Chairman of the Senate Subcommittee on Agricultural Appropriations, in expanding our agricultural research facilities to serve not only our State but the entire nation.

Here in Athens on the University campus, I secured the funds to build a million-dollar Poultry Disease Research Center which will conduct extensive research into poultry diseases, breeding, management problems, husbandry methods, and other matters.

We have built the Forestry Research Lab here which will be engaged in finding ways and means of combating the diseases which are taking such heavy toll of our forests in Georgia and the Southeast, and research to find better methods of utilizing forest products.

Soon, construction will begin on the Southeastern Water Pollution Laboratory on the University campus at a cost of two and one-half million dollars. This magnificent new facility will serve the Southeast in helping to solve the enormous problems of water pollution which have increased with the rapid industrialization of our State and region.

Close by, in Watkinsville, I had established the Piedmont Soil and Water Conservation Experiment Station which received an additional $125,000 in fiscal year 1963 for the addition of a chemical analysis unit to the new soil and water research facilities, for which $425,000 was provided in fiscal 1958.

At the Coastal Plains Experiment Station at Tifton, we now have studies underway in coastal bermuda pelleting. Bermuda grass hay is being used increasingly as a livestock feed all over the Southeast, but farmers have been encountering problems in producing high quality hay which has hindered Bermuda grass from becoming a major source of feed supply in the area. The studies now underway in Tifton will bring about improved breeding and cultural practices; developing effective and economical equipment for feeding Bermuda grass hay as pellets as compared to leaf or baled hay, and equipment for handling, storing and feeding the hay; and evaluating the acceptability and nutritional value of pelleted Bermuda grass hay for different classes of livestock.

Only last year, I obtained a half million dollars to construct a Regional Tree, Fruit, and Nut Research Station to be located at Byron to conduct research into various problems of the peach growers in Georgia and the Southeast. This laboratory will also investigate the potential of producing other tree, fruit, and nut crops in Georgia and the Southeast.

In addition to operating and construction programs for these Georgia Laboratories, I have obtained increased funds for research in

Georgia on improved vegetable crops; for pecan insect control and for apple breeding.

Our agricultural surpluses are so vast that one of our main problems has been developing new uses for farm products. This is the most fertile prospect for agricultural research at the present time, and I have been endeavoring to develop a competent program of utilization development.

I sponsored the legislative directive to the Secretary of Agriculture to initiate a nation-wide hog cholera eradication program and I am pleased that as of the first month of this year, fifty-five counties in Georgia, having about one-half of Georgia's swine population, were participating in the Cooperative State-Federal program. In these counties, approximately 200 outbreaks of hog cholera have been reported in fiscal year 1963. Reports indicate that the number of outbreaks in these counties decreased shortly after the eradication work was begun. In fiscal year 1961, Georgia reported approximately 1,300 outbreaks of hog cholera and in fiscal year 1962, there were 800 reported outbreaks of this disease of much cost and concern to our Georgia hog producers.

The Federal program to assist the States in cooperative agricultural extension work and our experiment stations have helped immeasurably in the development of our Georgia agriculture, its production and efficiency. In the last six years, Georgia has received more than eighteen million dollars for these worthwhile programs and I am glad to say we have been able to increase Georgia's share each of those years with the exception of one. In fiscal year 1963, Georgia will receive more than three million dollars of Federal money for its Experiment Station Service and Extension Service.

Of course, only eleven percent of our population today still lives on farms, and little more than ten percent of our total labor force is actually engaged in farming. Many people seem to feel that Agriculture is not as important as it once was, but the fact is, of course, that agriculture is still our largest industry. It is still the mainstay of our national economy as it is of our national life.

Today about 7.1 million people are employed on our farms and ranches but I have seen statistics which show that this is twelve times as many people as work in the steel industry; nine times as many people as work in the automobile industry; and nearly two times the number of people in our transportation industries and public utilities combined. In fact, there are more workers engaged in farming than in all the industries that manufacture nondurable goods, including processed foods, tobacco products, textiles and wearing apparel, and in a large number of other commodities.

My interest in agriculture has never diminished and I do not foresee the day that it ever shall. This beautiful plaque which you have given me today will serve only as a stimulus for my efforts in the future and you may be assured that wherever in the legislative halls of Congress the battle of the farmer and of agriculture is underway, that I shall be in the front lines fighting as hard as I know how for our Georgia farmer and for his interests.

Thank you so much.

Carters Dam
14 November 1964

Concerned that southern states had not received their fair share of federal funding, Senator Russell used his considerable influence in the United States Senate to finance projects for Georgia. He gave this address at Chatsworth, Georgia, on the occasion of the "Progress Celebration" of the Carters Dam project.[14] In its planning stage, the Carters Dam was to be 1,950 feet long, and 447 feet high, form a reservoir eleven miles in length with a sixty-seven mile shoreline, at a cost of over seventy million dollars. In this speech, Russell emphasized his commitment to preserving water resources. In a relatively humorous narrative, the Senator explained how he negotiated for federal dollars to build the Carters Dam. He envisioned how the dam would make available additional hydroelectric power, recreational facilities for tourists, and improved navigation. The text of the speech was taken verbatim from an audio recording.

* * * * * * * * * *

And hearing this very complimentary and laudatory introduction, I am more assured than ever that the people in the Seventh District did exactly the proper thing in the recent election (laughter and applause). I had been of that opinion—but my service with your distinguished Congressman in the Congress of the United States, [John W. Davis] where his integrity, his hardworking capacity, and his unusual ability is rapidly gaining for him a position of real leadership—but he nailed it down with that introduction this morning. I (laughter) appreciate it very, very much.

This is a very happy occasion for me, and in many respects I'm glad to participate on this program with General [A. C.] Welling. We've had very many fine men in the Division of Engineers in the

---

[14]Text of speech from Speech File, Speech and Media Series, Richard B. Russell Collection, RRLPRS.

30-odd years I've served in the Senate, but we've never had a more dynamic figure than General Welling. I wish we could just revoke the Army rules, and just keep General Welling down here permanently. I think we'd get all of our rivers fixed up with him to press for us in the Engineers . . . [couple of inaudible words]. But unfortunately the Army has a bad habit of moving these people around. But he has certainly contributed mightily to the development, not only in Georgia, but in the entire southeast.

I'm happy to see so many old friends here this morning. Of course there are those who have participated in former occasions and who've had a great interest in this project who have crossed over the river and are taking the last long rest on the other side, and I miss some of them today. I would not undertake to call names because that would require too much time and evoke too much sentiment.

I've been interested in a great many projects of this nature. During my time in the Senate I've contributed to the construction of a number of them, but I had a peculiar interest in this project. And I sweat a great deal of blood over the Carters Dam Project.

About forty years ago, in the Georgia Legislature, I found out about how dangerous it was to ever make a flat promise on what you were going to do (Russell chuckling) in a legislative body. And that's particularly true when it involves the appropriation of money. And I—nothing worse can happen to any member of any legislative body than to make a flat promise to his constituents that the Congress will appropriate money for this project or that project and then find that you can't deliver the money. You can't hardly go home; if you do you can't go to the section where you made the promise.

I well remember up the road here a mile or two where many members of the present gathering were in attendance—that after we'd been up and seen this magnificent site and had whiffed the mountain air, I was carried away to a certain extent that I violated one of my fundamental rules, and I made a flat promise that I'd see that money was appropriated to start this dam. I started worrying about it before I got home (Laughter). And I worried about it (chuckling) for a long time.

Carters Dam 187

There wasn't any money in the Budget in 1962 for the purpose; I finally prevailed on the Senate Sub-Committee which I'm a member, committee in the Senate, to appropriate a substantial amount to get started and we went into conference with the House as you do on bills of that nature.

We walked into the conference and the first announcement made by the Chairman of the House Conferees, the late Clarence Cannon [Senator from Missouri], was that the House Conferees had had a meeting and they had determined that under no circumstances would they approve any appropriation—for that was unbudgeted for a fresh start or a new start—as they call it, anywhere in the United States. Well, I sat there and worried about that for a while and we finally got down to the item, got to discussing it and I tried to show why they ought to make an exception to the House rule in this worthy project—and it is a worthy project—but I didn't get very far. And they allowed me about twenty minutes and then they said, "Let's pass this over and go on to something else." Well, about the second or third day we were going along (chuckling)—the bill—and we got into the question of some transmission lines. [U. S. Representative Phil] Landrum [of the Ninth Congressional District of Georgia]—it was in the House—supporting the Senate Committee report was entirely different on the transmission lines, and Mr. Cannon had an overweening interest in those transmission lines (Laughter). Well, we sat there and discussed the transmission lines for some two or three hours and carried it over to the next day. In the meantime I got to trying to think up a compromise because I found out earlier in life—and I've been in the legislative business now over forty years—that all legislation is a result of compromise—and I tried to figure out a compromise on those power lines and I finally hit upon one that I had a little trouble selling to my own conferees in the Senate. But I finally did, and it suited the House just fine, because it gave the Secretary of the Interior [Stewart L. Udall] almost absolute authority to make determination of the question. Well, I made it a point to waylay Mr. Cannon out in the hall on the way down to the conference the next morning (chuckling); I said, "Mr. Chairman, I think that I've got—about have the Senate Conferees now convinced—the proper solution of these transmission lines." And I said, "I'm going to bring it up in there today. And if the Senate does accept it, I am expecting you to recur to the consideration of the Carter Dam Project (chuckling) and reconsider your problem (chuckling)."

Well (chuckling), my lucky star was still over me; we (chuckling) finally worked it out and therefore I can come up into this section of Georgia again. It looked like once (chuckling) that I was going to have to forego visiting here because all the leading citizens said, "There is that fellow that promised us he'd get that money to start that dam, and they haven't got a dam cent yet (Laughter)."

And so I learned again a lesson that I'd learned in the Georgia Legislature—and I can assure you from henceforth and forever more—that I shall say, "I will do my very best to get the money," not, "I'll get the money," to start with (chuckling).

Now this is a significant occasion not only for this area of Northwest Georgia with all of its lovely scenery, fine people, and unlimited opportunities for growth and progress; it's a significant occasion for the entire state and, of course, for the entire river basin. I notice we have here this morning Mr. [George] Cleere [Executive Vice President of the Coose-Alabama River Improvement Association]. I don't know, he said he's from Montgomery. I don't know when he goes home to get his mail. I think he's walked (chuckling) the banks of every tributary of that entire river. He's walked up and down more branches than any thirty revenue officers combined (laughter) in the course of his (chuckling) service to get the entire river navigable up to Rome and we intend to achieve that before we complete our efforts.

Now the significance of this project is many-fold: First, this project in its own right will provide a new stimulus to the economic growth and development of this entire section and when completed, this—the hydroelectric generators—will add 174 million kilowatt hours a year of electricity to the available power supply for this area. That's an awful lot of electricity. And the need and demand for electricity is increasing almost as fast as the need for pure water in unlimited supply. That'll be an attraction for new industry and we hope will provide many new and better paying jobs.

This project will also provide protection from the floods from the rich farm lands along the Coosawatee and also the Oostanaula. It'll help to guard the downstream communities against the ravages of flood waters that have in times past caused great damage.

But one of the major benefits, and that is surprising—that major benefits that a project of this kind brings—and it's going to be particularly true with respect to Carters Dam—is the unexcelled recreational facilities that this lake will offer. This 450-foot high dam, the highest in the eastern United States, and I've been told if they computed the height from the same formula over the whole country, it'd be the highest in the United States. It will impound one of the most picturesque lakes in the entire world. It'd be almost impossible to have cloudy or muddy water in this lake the way it is situated. And this magnificent body of water will be available not only for the enjoyment of the people of this area who like to fish and boat and swim and camp, but it'll create an entirely new industry in this area by bringing in a stream of visitors; it'll attract them by the millions.

I am not given usually to exaggeration, unless it happens to be up in this section of the country, but I confidently predict that within a few years after its completion, this project will become one of the outstanding tourist playgrounds in the entire eastern United States. And I foresee the rise of a whole new industry in this area to cater to the wants and the needs of the people who'll come here from far and wide to enjoy this scenic wonderland.

Now beyond the immediate benefits of those of you who live in this area, Carters Dam is highly significant for another reason. It is a key link in a comprehensive, long-range development of the river system, the Coosa-Alabama, to which I have already referred, that will stretch from the mountain peaks of Northwest Georgia to the Gulf of Mexico at Mobile.

This project will contribute measurably to the success of the navigation of this river by enabling us to control the stream flow that is a part of the plan to extend a nine-foot navigational channel from Mobile to Rome. This channel will link Rome with the inland waterways of the country and to the sealanes of the seven seas; thus this will add a new and important dimension to the economic and industrial growth of all of Northeast Georgia.

I am very happy indeed that I have had the privilege in my service in the Senate of serving on the Senate Appropriations Committee. I was very fortunate to get on that committee when I first went to the Senate. Since I'm in a reminiscent mood this morning, I'll tell you about that; I don't think I've ever made the statement about it in any remarks I've ever made anywhere in Georgia. But I went to the Senate shortly after Huey Long reached there, and Huey had the whole Senate in a furor and in a turmoil. And he would denounce the leadership—Senator Robinson of Arkansas—and he got mad and resigned from all his committees because he didn't get what he wanted. And I'd had a pretty stout campaign going to the Senate myself and word had got out up there (chuckling) that I was just about as mean as Huey Long (Laughter). So when Senator Robinson called me out and says, "Senator Russell, I want to discuss your committees with you," I said, "Well, I want to be on the Appropriations Committee, Senator." "Oh," he says, "Senator, we have men who've been here for years who are waiting to get on the Appropriations Committee." I said, "Well, Senator, if I can't get on the Appropriations Committee, I don't want to be on any Committee. My people in Georgia expect me to be on the Appropriations Committee." I didn't know (chuckling) about the Huey Long incident at the time; I just had gotten there (Audience laughter). But I told him that and he went off and came back the next day and said, "Well, I worked it out for you Senator Russell (chuckling) where you'd be on the Appropriations Committee." I was one of the few men who ever started out in the Congress of the United States on the Committee on Appropriations.

But I have worked on these various river projects. I've heard this cry about "pork barrel." Of course a "pork barrel" project I found out is a project that couldn't possibly be located in your community (Laughter). If it's a project that could be located in your community, why, here's a very meritorious project that should be developed and contribute mightily to the strength of a state, and of the nation, and of the world. People that get out and fight for billions of dollars for interstate highway systems—and I support that, I think it's one of the—I think it will go down in history as the outstanding contribution of President Eisenhower's eight years in the White House—the interstate highway system. But people who'll fight for that, and spend billions on that—they will quarrel about any river and harbor project unless they happen to have a river or a harbor in their community. It's a "pork barrel."

But these rivers of ours are part of the heritage of all of our people. And it's—they should be developed for the benefit of our people. And I think that the expenditure of a reasonable amount of tax money each year in the development of our natural resources is an entirely proper function of government. We've seen these other great civilizations rise to great heights—the people think they're dominating the whole earth—have all that they desire, and they fall and crumble. And too often it's been because they've been indifferent and careless in dealing with the gifts that a benign Providence had placed at their disposal. We find remains of irrigation projects in desert areas because they've neglected the conservation that was necessary to keep the streams flowing to furnish the water for those ditches. And I think that conservation, to hand down an equal or greater opportunity to the next generation, is completely justified. Heaven knows we're handing them down enough debt that was incurred that had nothing to do with conservation, to be willing to give them a few roads and dams and water courses as we go along.

I have never been able to see the validity of an argument in favor of building dams all over Africa and Asia and Europe, and other places with American tax dollars, and then opposing building dams in the United States with American tax dollars. So I have voted against those and I have followed the Bible literally; decided to see that "charity begins at home," if we're going to spend money. For that I have no apology. I realize that that's looked upon as being a rather parochial, provincial outlook on affairs in many international circles but as a practical man who was raised in the country, it appeals to me, and I'm gonna follow it (chuckling) as long as the people of Georgia send me to the Senate of the United States.

Now it is a matter of record that this is not—these projects are not "pork barrel" projects; they all pay for themselves. We built the

Altoona Dam over here at a time when construction was much cheaper than it is today. We can—that dam cost thirty-two million dollars. I believe that was the first project in the entire comprehensive development of the Alabama-Coosa Waterways. Now that project has been in operation for fourteen years, but some two-thirds of the construction cost of this project has been realized through the sale of electrical power and in the measurable reduction in downstream flood damage. And that does not take into consideration the vast economic activity that has been generated around Altoona Lake. That all of you I'm sure have been there and know that that's a considerable business of itself.

Now Buford Dam on the Chattahoochee is another case in point. I didn't make any pledge about Buford but I had as much trouble or more with it than I did with Carters. I was told that if the river ever got as low again as in 1925 that Atlanta would be dead; they wouldn't have water enough there even to wash their children and the dishes, much less to carry on the great industries there. So I worked on that project awfully hard, and when we got that first million dollars, I heaved just about as great a sigh of relief as I did when the first million for Carters, for after you get 'em started, they go. And Congressman Davis and I will see to it that we complete this one and get the money from here on out. I want to thank him for his stalwart support for every project in Georgia. He's not narrow in his thinking. He looks after the people of the Seventh District; he's a diligent Congressman, but he's also a progressive Congressman who is willing to step over the district lines and assist those who live in other areas.

Now, you know something about Lake Lanier on the Buford Dam. Last year, almost eight million people visited Lake Lanier for sightseeing and to picnic, sail, fish, water ski, camp. In fact, Lake Lanier was the most popular last year than any that has been built as a result of federal river and water development. And there is every reason in my mind to believe that the economic return of Carters will match or exceed the experience at Altoona and Buford.

I have so often repeated one of my most profound convictions, and that is that water is the key to the future, that I hate to burden you with it here again. But our people shouldn't forget it, and they

Carters Dam

should teach it to their children, because there's no doubt on earth in my mind that the area that has the water in adequate quantities—clean water, unpolluted water—will be the—will dominate the future in this country.

We must assure the maximum utilization of our water resources; I do not propose to overlook any river in Georgia that has the potential to be developed. We must do the total job. Because with the rate of increase of population and its dynamic economy in which we are living today, a world that experiences revolutions in manners of living and habits of thinking and in the development of appliances and devices almost overnight, and not to speak of developing weapons that can—of tremendous danger—why we must not relax in our efforts to see that this great potential that is as valuable in maintaining the freedom of the people of the United States as some of the divisions in your Army and your missiles in your silos out in South Dakota and Montana.

I know that those of you here who have shown such an unselfish interest, have devoted so much time and energy without any monetary compensation to getting this project underway, will continue your interest in the development of our waterways.

And there's no question on earth that the bread that you cast on the waters will be returned tenfold when these projects are complete and under operations.

This is a happy day for me as it is for all of you. It's a high privilege to be here with you. Thank you (applause).

Georgia Press Association
9 July 1965

Senator Russell gave this speech at the awards banquet of the Georgia Press Association.[15] Because Russell had been ill, media representatives and citizens speculated whether he would seek re-election. On this occasion, however, a journalist reported that the Senator appeared fit. Russell informed reporters that it was premature to make a formal announcement concerning his plans.[16] In the address, given at Jekyll Island, Georgia, he called for a constructive partnership between the press and government. Russell assessed the economic gap between Georgia and the nation, the disparity in income among Georgians, and the challenge wrought by an increase in population.

* * * * * * * * * *

It is a privilege to be here tonight with my friends of the Georgia Press Association.

As one who has spent most of his life in public office, I feel I have obtained a liberal education on the ways of the press—if by process of osmosis. Most of my knowledge has been pleasantly gained, though sometimes it has been a bit painful. All of it has been valuable.

Over the years I have come to know many fine and gifted writers and editors. But I do not believe I have known a journalist who could match the sharp wit and trenchant pen of the late William B. Townsend of the *Dahlonega Nugget*.

Chancellor S. V. Sanford [University of Georgia] credits Bill Townsend with writing the most artful news story in the history of journalism. This item, in its entirety, said—quote—"Tom Jones' mother-in-law is visiting him anyhow"—unquote.

---

[15]Text of speech from Speech File, Speech and Media Series, Richard B. Russell Collection, RRLPRS.
[16]*Brunswick News*, July 3 and 10, 1965

There are some members of your profession, and mine, who hold that there must be an inevitable conflict between newspapermen and public officials. I do not share this view, although I have noticed that some editors seem to hold some office holders in rather low esteem—and vice versa.

But this is to be expected in the give-and-take of our robust political system. Personally, I think it is a good system. I have survived its tests in the past, and I am ready to face any that may lie ahead.

Thomas Jefferson considered freedom of the press to be one of the five great rights of the American people. He said: "If it were up to me to decide whether we should have a government without newspapers or newspapers without a government, I should not hesitate to choose the latter."[17]

The vital role of a vigorous and unfettered press in the American democratic system has not diminished since Jefferson's time. Indeed, it becomes increasingly crucial as government at every level continues to expand and to grow farther and farther away from the people.

As editors, it is your responsibility not only to inform our people, but to expose and root out the corrupters in government who betray the people's trust. You also have a duty to protect the rights and liberty of the American people from those who rob us of our sacred heritage as free men.

More than seventy-five years ago, Henry W. Grady [of the *Atlanta Constitution*] wrote a series of articles for a New York paper about the struggle of the Southern people to build a new life on the ruins and ashes of a conquered land. In one of these he said: "The desperate days are over. And now the world will witness a change in the South little less than magical. The ground has been prepared—the seed put in—the tiny shoots tended past the danger point."[18]

---

[17] *Writings*, Vol. vi, p. 55, in *Home Book of Quotations*, Burton Stevenson, ed., 10th edition (New York: Dodd, Mead and Co., 1967), 1602.

[18] Grady wrote these articles for *New York Herald*, 1880-1881; see Raymond B. Nixon, *Henry W. Grady: Spokesman for the New South* (New York: Alfred A. Knopf, 1943), 155-182.

Today, those seeds have come to full flower. Grady's dream of a vibrant, proud New South has in our time become a reality.

No more exciting evidence of this can be found anywhere than in our own state. Indeed, Georgia's growth and progress in the relatively brief period since World War II has been little short of phenomenal. We have gone far toward ending our economic dependence on King Cotton and toward achieving a sound balance between industry and agriculture.

Since 1947, we have seen the creation of more than a third of a million jobs for Georgians through new and expanded industrial development. Our pace of industrial growth is ahead of that of the South as a region, and several times that of the nation as a whole.

A key factor behind our progress has been the inspired leadership of Georgia editors from Grady's day forward. The press—the weekly papers particularly—are due major credit for the vastly improved state of Georgia's agriculture and industry.

As gratifying as our progress has been, we must not be lulled into a false sense of complacency. We cannot stand still. We must continue to drive forward.

The task for the future is three-fold: First we must close the income gap between Georgia and the rest of the nation.

We have made laudable progress in the past decade toward upgrading the economic lot of our people and in giving them more promising opportunities. In 1947, the average Georgian had an income two-thirds that of the national average. We have now raised this to better than three-fourths the national average.

This is good, but not good enough. Georgia still ranks forty-first among the states in per capita income. We are ahead of such Southern neighbors as Kentucky, Tennessee, and even North Carolina. But we continue to lag behind Virginia and Florida and most of the states of other sections.

We must not relax until we equal—and then better—the average for the country.

Second, we must endeavor to see that every section of Georgia shares to the maximum extent possible in our growth and prosperity.

No one takes greater pride than I in the spectacular growth of Georgia's major urban centers, particularly in Atlanta. If ever an economic miracle were taking place before our eyes, it is occurring today in the changing skyline, the dramatic expansion of commerce and industry, and the exploding population of metropolitan Atlanta.

This progress is shared generally by our other principal cities, but not—unfortunately—by all of the smaller cities, towns, and rural areas.

No section of our state must be neglected in the march of economic progress. The rural areas and the small towns of Georgia historically have contributed richly to the development, strength, and moral fiber of Georgia. They must not be denied full opportunity to participate in the dynamic growth now taking place within our borders.

I want to see Atlanta and the other metropolitan areas of Georgia continue their spiralling growth. I shall do all that I can to see that it does continue. But I also want to see us develop ways and means for assuring that all other sections will be equal partners in our progress.

Third, we must prepare and plan now for the vast increases that will take place in our population in the years immediately ahead.

I am sure that most of you are familiar with the recent population projects of the University of Georgia which forecast a population of almost six million people by 1975. Our economy must produce many thousands of new jobs within a relatively short time in order to keep pace with the anticipated growth.

This means our economy must do double duty: it must generate new jobs for our expanding population at the same time that we are striving to boost the general economic level of all our people.

Georgia clearly faces some difficult problems if we are to meet the challenges of the future and guarantee our continued economic progress. I have every confidence we will master those challenges if we will but make wise and prudent use of the great wealth of human and physical resources with which we are blessed.

In this regard, I am pleased that several Georgia communities have entered the competition as the site for the huge atom smasher to be built by the United States Atomic Energy Commission. This is further evidence that we are determined to make our mark in the new scientific age.

The proposed atomic accelerator would be a first rate economic and scientific prize for Georgia. It will be a permanent nuclear laboratory with a staff of two or three thousand engineers and scientists. It will cost almost three hundred million dollars to build and several million dollars a year to operate.

We have made an outstanding showing for this facility, but I would be less than candid if I did not say that our chances of landing it are slim indeed. Almost one hundred and fifty communities from throughout the nation are entered in the competition, and many of them are considerably ahead of us in existing nuclear science activities.

Despite the odds, I and the other members of the Georgia delegation are doing all that we possibly can to try to bring this facility to Georgia. If we succeed, we will have made a tremendous breakthrough in a scientific and industrial area that holds immense potential. If we lose, we at least will have carried the word of what Georgia has to offer for this type of activity to some influential quarters of government, science and private industry. Either way, I am confident our efforts will yield dividends in the future.

We have made some headway in bringing Federal research activities to Georgia. I am particularly proud of the half-dozen research laboratories that I have managed to locate at Athens and elsewhere in the state in the past five years. The plant investment alone of the research facilities at the University [of Georgia] approaches twenty-million dollars.

But this is but a fraction of what the Federal Government spends each year on research and development activities at the nation's universities. Up to now, neither Georgia nor the South has shared proportionately or fairly in the distribution of these funds. . . .

President [O.C.] Aderhold of the University of Georgia has pointed out that fifty-nine percent of all government-sponsored university research money goes to twenty-five institutions. Only three of these schools are located in Southern and border states, and none are in the Southeast. Yet the Southern region contains a third of the nation's entire college-age population.

It seems to me the Federal Government, which is supposed to be against such things, is engaged in flagrant discrimination against the South in the apportionment of these research funds. It is high time it ceased. Georgia and the other Southern states are entitled to share equitably in the intellectual, scientific, and economic benefits that flow from our own tax dollars that go to support Government research.

I, for one, refuse to concede that all the brains and intelligence are concentrated in a few enlightened pockets of the country such as New England, Chicago, Southern California, or even Texas.

During my time in the Senate, I have never hesitated to use every proper and legitimate means at my command to influence the location of desirable Federal activities in Georgia. These efforts have borne some fruit, particularly in the defense area over which I have some special responsibilities as chairman of the Armed Services Committee and of the Defense Appropriations Subcommittee.

I can report tonight that at the close of 1965 fiscal year some one hundred thousand servicemen and thirty-three thousand civilian employees were located at the fifteen major military facilities in Georgia. These establishments had a combined military and civilian payroll during the year of more than six-hundred million dollars. Still another two-hundred million dollars was spent for the operation and maintenance of these posts.

This does not include an additional half-billion dollars that was added to our economy in the fiscal year through military prime contracts awarded to private business firms in Georgia. All this adds up to a one-billion-three-hundred million dollar annual shot in the arm to our state's economy.

Former Congressman Carl Vinson and I on occasion have been criticized for Georgia's substantial participation in the country's essential military and defense activities. I can assure you that this is the kind of criticism I do not mind in the least. I welcome it.

So long as I remain a member of the Senate, I shall continue to advance Georgia's interest in such matters with all my vigor and ability—and with apology to no one. I shall do so confident in the knowledge that Georgia has as many advantages to offer for these activities as any other state in the Union—and considerably more than most.

The members of this audience are well aware that I do not support all of the economic and social measures that are advanced under the banner of the Great Society [of President Lyndon Johnson], just as I did not support all those proposed by previous administrations.

I cannot in good conscience vote to spend the taxpayer's money on any program that I deem to be unnecessary, unsound or of doubtful constitutionality. Yet it is sometimes intimated that because of my opposition to some pet program the people of Georgia might be denied the benefits from it.

This may make an interesting conversation piece in certain circles, but it is punitive doctrine that I would not advise any Federal bureaucrat to try to put in force. Regardless of whether I vote against a given program, if it becomes law over my opposition I shall endeavor to see that our people participate fully in its benefits.

The people of Georgia pay Federal taxes on an equal footing with those of every other state. They have an inherent right to share in the benefits of every Federal program on the same equal footing. . . .

III.

Speeches on Military Preparedness

[Atlanta – Armistice Day – Nov. 11, 1953 –]

Glad to be here –

American Legion –

Composed of those who have fought Country's battles. Its members are citizens who have pledged their all as the measure of their patriotic devotion. Common tie

Unity of men whose loyalty has been tested – Bond cemented by Common purpose – resolve – Sacrifice

Bond Strengthened by united determination to serve Country in peace as they served in war –

Proud of Legion Membership

Handwritten notes, speech on Armistice Day, Atlanta, Georgia, 11 November 1953.

Armistice Day
11 November 1928

Mr. Russell prepared this address for delivery at the Gordon Military Academy (now Gordon College) in Barnesville, Georgia.[1] He celebrated the devotion to duty of young American soldiers, and pledged that their heroism during World War I would not be forgotten. Drawing upon a premise that guided his entire career in government, he insisted that soldiers sent to battle must be supported with "every resource of our country." Russell also assessed the United States' constructive motivation for involvement in World War I. He contrasted the nation's poor preparation for battle with the soldiers' "unequalled . . . fighting power," and praised the "high ideals" of the American Legion and Auxiliary.

* * * * * * * * *

The occasion we are met to commemorate is one that is recognized around the world. It marks the end of the greatest and most destructive war the world has ever seen. Just over ten years ago the red tide of battle flowed with such fury that some thought the Armageddon was at hand. Then came the memorable Armistice of November 11th, 1918. The news was received all over the world with the greatest joy and our centers of population showed a spirit of carnival. In their reaction to the horrible dread that hovered over almost every home the first Armistice Day was spent in universal rejoicing.

With the passing of the years Armistice Day has assumed a more solemn meaning. We approach it with silent prayer for those heroes who made the day of peace possible but did not survive to see or enjoy the fruits of their sacrifices. We reconsecrate ourselves to the service of our common country with the firm resolve to do our part to make its future worthy of the sacrifices of the past. We should lend our

---

[1] Text of speech from Speech File, Speech and Media Series, Richard B. Russell Collection, RRLPRS.

energies to promote the day of universal peace among all of the nations of the world. To those who returned to their homes broken in body or mind—who left the bloom of their youth on the battle fields of France—to them we renew our pledge that their heroism has not been forgotten, and seek to alleviate the pain of the wounds of honor received in their country's service. And we should commit ourselves, unequivocally and steadfastly, to the principle that if war must come again—that if it is impossible to avoid its horrors—then every resource of our country—men, material, wealth, industry, agriculture, commerce, all of talent and capacity and energy of every description, shall be drafted to make the supreme and united and unselfish fight for the national triumph. It is not enough to draft the young manhood of this nation without as exacting a draft on all we possess. And when we enact this principle into law and national policy, we will have less of war, if we do not abolish it altogether.

I deem it unnecessary to attempt here to trace in detail all of the causes of the great war or the events leading up to our participation. Suffice it to say, that for the first time in history the world saw the greatest country on earth summon her sons to the colors without a single sordid or selfish or ulterior purpose. None of the impulses which have always steeled the hearts of men for battle motivated us as we grasped the sword. We did not fight for lands or cities or for a "place in the sun." Ours was the greatest empire on earth, a vast domain stretching from ocean to ocean, with populous cities, fertile fields, great plains that stretch in measureless sublimity, and mountains that keep company with clouds and stars.

We did not go to war for national glory. The history of our courage needed no embellishment at the hands of this generation. From the time a group of weak and struggling colonies, nurtured on warfare with French and Indians had thrown off the yoke of England, we had never known defeat. From Saratoga and Yorktown to Santiago and Manilla, we had proven our bravery.

We did not strike for freedom for ourselves. We had the greatest democracy in the world. For a century and a half our land had been an asylum for the oppressed. Our proudest boast was that all of our citizens were free and equal.

Armistice Day

We did not strike to enslave others. By the arbitrament of the sword it had been determined that none but freemen could be within our borders.

Not for wealth, for through the peaceful medium of commerce, our vaults contained all of the gold and silver in the world.

But in an age devoted to crass materialism and rapacious selfishness, with the world enveloped in darkness, these United States presented to a war-dazed mankind the glorious spectacle of a self determining people taking up arms for an ideal as high and noble as that which moved Sir Galahad in his quest for the Holy Grail.

The mind and energies of a great people were directed to the lofty ideal of insuring every people the right to determine for themselves the form of government they should have.

This was a miracle which was spiritual in its aspect. No sooner was it performed than we worked another which was not spiritual, but material. The declaration of war found us without arms or army. From a state of pitiful unpreparedness in an armed and warring world, almost overnight our country was transformed into an armed camp. With a weak nucleus in our regular army and men who had received some military training in schools in the country, we set about the task of making a fighting machine out of a mass of untrained citizens. I know that the people of this community are thrilled with pride when they reflect on the important part played by the sons of old Gordon [Military Academy] in this great endeavor, both in training and on the battle fields of France. And in the land of spirits in the Great Beyond I know that there was rejoicing on the part of those patriots who wisely planned here an institution which could contribute so freely of the talent of preparedness to our country. Not only in the training camps but on the bloody fields of France was this institution in the forefront. Among those laid to sleep beneath the skies of France, 3000 miles from home, were two members of my class, Tom Read Beasley and Paul B. Minter, both killed in action, facing their country's foes.

As we did not possess a large standing army, our enemies comforted themselves with a false sense of security, and allowed us a minimum of four years to really be a factor in the War. We were sending men by the thousands within a few months—citizen soldiers, called from farm and office, counting-house and shop. While our allies rejoiced to see the manpower of America pouring into France, they too were doubtful of their value as soldiers with the limited training they had received.

I will not recite the story of the part played by the American soldier in bringing the war to a speedy end. Most of my hearers remember the history of the war perhaps better than I. The American Expeditionary forces had come to France with one idea in mind—to crush the German Armies who had fought the powers of the world to a standstill for four long years, and were at that moment knocking at the gates of Paris. From the first time they went into action at Chateau Thierry, through Belleau Woods and in the Argonne, until the Hindenburg line was shattered, friend and foe alike marvelled at the unequalled, natural, inherent fighting power of the American Doughboy. The stories of their daring exploits read as pages from the tales of Knights of old, translated to modern setting. The doubters of the Allied High Command gladly turned a large part of the war over to Uncle Sam. The leading exponents of Kulter saw the handwriting on the wall and the Kaiser prepared to remove his domicile to Holland. To my mind the most unusual feature of the whole war was the German complaint that the Americans did not fight according to the rules, customs, and usages which had by tacit understanding grown up for the conduct of the war. The Doughboy had but one rule: To strike the enemy wherever and whenever he saw him and always move forward whatever the odds or obstacles. By the late fall of 1918, the power of autocracy was crushed and through the courage and high purpose of American Soldiery, with the unstinted support and sacrifice of the entire nation, whether in uniform or not. On November 12th, ten years ago, God's sun rose once more on the world at peace.

The map of the globe has been changed by the war. The terms of peace provide for fulfillment over a number of years, and the staggering cost of the struggle must be borne by generations yet unborn. Despite the unselfish sacrifice of America, the world still gropes for a real peace based upon mutual understanding and good will. The dominant hope of mankind is the outlaw of war. How far we are from this much sought goal no man can say. We believe long strides have been made in this direction. But certainly the state of world affairs is such that we cannot afford to be deceived by dangerous, if well-meaning pacifists who advocate absolute disarmament. The temper of the world is well illustrated by the bitterness manifested by some of our late allies when we respectfully requested some settled plan of payment of the money loaned them in 1917 and 1918. To the bitter correspondent who wrote that the abbreviation "U.S." stood for "Uncle Shylock," we could well rejoin that the "U.S." stood for "Unquestioned Saviors" in 1918.

Whatever may be the true verdict of history on the varied phases of the Great War, one thing is assured. The part played by America will be stamped with unselfishness and crowned with rare courage. We have proven our sincerity by our works. While France was recovering Alsace-Lorraine, Italy dismembering Austria, and England reaching for colonies in every quarter of the globe, we only asked for the establishment of an era of good will on earth among all mankind. If the great day of permanent peace ever arrives the way will have been paved by American Sacrifice.

Any remarks on an occasion of this kind without reference to the American Legion and the Legion Auxiliary would be incomplete. With the victory won, the American Armies turned their minds and faces towards home. But a hundred thousand of the bravest of the brave had made the supreme sacrifice and were taking their last, long sleep in foreign soil, among strange if friendly people. Thousands of their comrades were so sorely maimed by the cruel wounds of war that theirs was a living death. They had fought and suffered side by side, the problem of an agreeable and just rehabilitation of these who had gone to war faced them. In every breast was the hope that younger brothers and sons should be spared the suffering of unpreparedness and discrimination. These men and women know what patriotism meant. Theirs had been tested by fires.

So there naturally sprang into existence this great peace time organization, as surely patriotic in time of peace as it had shown itself in time of war. This was the American Legion.

To my mind the preamble of the Constitution of American Legion is a document which in greatness is second only to the preamble of the Constitution of the United States. In every line of it can be found a text:

> For God and Country, we associate ourselves together for the following purposes: To uphold and defend the Constitution of the United States of America; to maintain law and order, to foster and perpetuate a one hundred percent Americanism; to preserve the memories and incidents of our association in the Great War; to inculcate a sense of individual obligation to the community, state, and nation; to combat the autocracy of both the classes and the masses; to make right the master of might; to promote peace and good will on earth; to safeguard and transmit to posterity the principles of justice, freedom, and democracy; to consecrate and sanctify our comradeship by our devotion to mutual helpfulness.[2]

Before our entry into the war, there was a sharp division among our people as to which side should prevail. On every hand there had grown up an army of so-called pros and -isms—Pro-Germans—Pro-Allies, and pacifists. We know now that there is no room in this country for any pros except pro-Americanism. Since the war there has been noticed abroad in the land a strange and insidious cult of anti-patriotism. We are confronted with the reprehensible spectacle of men who have taken bountifully of the blessings of our free government, teaching a doctrine that places the individual higher than the government that protects him, and with an imperious egotism, says that a sense of national pride breeds war and that a man is proud of his country when he has nothing else to be proud of.

It is the duty of every good citizen to combat this sentiment. The American Legion and Auxiliary, with its high ideals of National

---

[2]Seelye Jones Richard, *A History of the American Legion* (Indianapolis: Bobbs-Merrill Co., 1946) 363.

progress and well being needs the support and influence of all who cherish the history of this land in their efforts to instill real Americanism and love of this country and its institutions in the hearts and minds of all.

This dangerous sentiment to which I refer is particularly manifested by those misguided pacifists who advocate a policy of absolute National disarmament. We have never been a Militaristic people. The very nature of our government and the composition of our people insures that we never will. We know there will never be a war of aggression waged by these United States. But history teaches us in unmistakable lessons of blood and sorrow that the millennium is not at hand. A land as rich and favored as ours would be more helpless than a lamb in a pack of wolves if we were without means of adequate self defense.

The American Legion therefore advocates national preparedness. Not through any system of compulsory military training such as prevailed in Europe in 1914, and still obtains in certain lands. But through a national policy which insures that if it again becomes necessary for our citizens to become soldiers to defend their homes and loved ones, it shall be with a minimum of suffering and without discrimination between our citizens. I have already referred briefly to the Universal Draft. The American Legion has always advocated the governmental use of every resource of our country in time of national stress. It never wants to see again the sorry spectacle of dollar-a-day men facing machine guns, brigade fire, and hand grenades at the front, while dollar-a-year men wax fat on war time profiteering at home. No true American can rejoice at prosperity acquired through the suffering of their fellows and the gouging of our common government when it is helpless to protect itself.

If war must come again, which God forbid, American Soldiers must not return home to see a marble mansion on a hilltop for every soldier who lost his life upon the field of battle in his nation's service.

Those of the American Legion who were spared by Providence to return to their homes sound in body and mind, have not forgotten those unfortunate comrades who live in death, through wounds in France. It has labored for the Buddies who were broken on the cruel wheel of war. The gentle women of our Auxiliary use every God-given feminine art of softness to make their lot as easy as possible. One of the brightest pages of our national history is the loyal devotion of the Legion Auxiliary to our disabled soldiers and sailors. The Crimean war brought forth one Florence Nightingale. In America her name is Legion. Our people have done all that is possible to let these sufferers know that their sacrifices are not forgotten. A grateful government has also done much to provide for them every assistance that modern ingenuity can devise. They are remembered particularly on this day by poppy Sales and little gifts of remembrance.

We will make of this a day of remembrance and, as the gentle hand of woman has always sought to heal the wounds of war, we have left to women keeping green the memory and the graves of those who died for native land.

In almost every town of the land there is some little mother who cannot forget. Those of us who were fortunate enough to be spared unscathed, and those who profit by the sacrifices of those who fell, should never forget. So long as the pride of a country is in the achievements of its men and women its future is assured.

In America's Battle Abbey—at Arlington—we have erected a national shrine in which is entombed the remains of an unidentified soldier who fell in action in France. In pomp and martial ceremony—attended by a throng of people including the President and high officials, this unknown soldier was laid to rest in the shadow of our National Capitol. Symbolical of the spirit of America's appreciation, there is always a sentry on guard who marks with measured tread his watch, signifying that while we hold exercises but once a year in their memory, that America can never forget for an instant the limit of his sacrifices.

So long as there is one true American patriot alive, he will stand guard over this national shrine. It is the exemplification of the ideals, devotion, courage, and sacrifices of these who fell. The measure of our tribute marks the future hopes and aspirations of this Republic.

The mother of every unknown can nourish the secret belief that the one who received so lavishly of his nation's gratitude is her son.

Armistice Day

There beneath the warm Virginia sun, lulled with the breezes which come from the Potomac, sleeps in the kingliest tomb of all, an American soldier. Surrounded by the graves of Generals of High Command he takes the highest rank, because his sacrifice symbolizes the spirit of American patriotism. And each year on this day we meet in solemn tribute to assure those who died, that if the soldier is unknown, the cause for which he fought is everlasting, and that succeeding generations, until the end of time, shall keep the faith.

The emotions of the heart are so much stronger and more varied than the power of expression that I cannot express my sentiments here today. I thank you for your greeting. And I can only say that I am deeply sensitive of the honor you have shown me by asking me to talk to you on this occasion. I appreciate this opportunity to come back home. The warmth of my welcome exceeds that extended the prodigal son of the scriptures. As a student at Gordon for three years it was my privilege to live in Barnesville, to know the people of this community, to profit by their culture and learning, and enjoy the warm hospitality of their homes.

I am proud to be able to say that I am a graduate of Gordon. Dr. [Douglas Larkin] Watson [President] will vouch for the sincerity of this statement if he has not forgotten a scared and struggling Senior of the class of 1915, who more through grace and pity than through knowledge, finally attained a passing mark in calculus. Old Gordon has that indefinable atmosphere that we call, for the lack of a perfect description, school spirit. That something, which, having fastened itself to the heartstrings of youth, never leaves during this life, but always preserves and keeps bright the precious memories and recollections, as an ever vivid picture of the friends we loved and the days we spent within and around her classic halls.

A life not blessed with pleasant recollections of youth is poor indeed. Some of the most precious pages of my memory revolve around the scenes of my school days here. This town and its people have a corner apart in my heart. The greeting given me today adds another pleasant chapter to the book of my life, with the scene laid in Barnesville.

Defense Savings Program
10 November 1941

Senator Russell gave this speech in the Walter Little Room of the Hotel Dempsey in Macon, sharing the platform with State Defense Administrator Marion Allen.[3] The Senator was introduced by local attorney, Charles Bloch. By 1939, Germany had invaded Poland and Czechoslovakia, and President Franklin D. Roosevelt had requested of Congress funds to strengthen the nation's military. On September 6, Roosevelt announced that a German submarine attacked an American destroyer, and instructed the Navy to "shoot on sight." Just three days before this speech, the United States Senate voted to modify the Neutrality Act of 1935. The vote was fifty yeas, thirty-seven nays, and nine abstentions, climaxing a vigorous two-week debate. Russell did not debate this resolution on the Senate floor, but did vote to arm American flag ships.[4]

In this address, given less than one month before Japan attacked Pearl Harbor, Russell assured that the Nation would supply its "young men with the finest of the awesome material of modern warfare." While hoping that the United States could avoid direct participation in the fighting, he asked citizens to invest in the nation's defense savings program.[5]

* * * * * * * * * *

In these perilous times in which we now live, any meeting in the name of national defense is of great significance. This is all the more true when patriotic citizens gather to make their plans to provide for the treasury the necessary sinews of war to prepare our country for

---

[3]Text of speech from Speech File, Speech and Media Series, Richard B. Russell Collection, RRLPRS.
[4]*Congressional Record: Proceedings and Debates of the 77th Congress*, November 7, 1941, First Session, Vol. 87, Part 8, 8680.
[5]*Macon Telegraph*, November 11, 1941.

Defense Savings Program 213

protection against the great storms now raging over three quarters of the globe.

Just a little over two years ago we were living in a time of comparative peace. It is true that we had seen aggression by the totalitarian states against helpless nations in Africa and the brutal attacks of the Japs upon China, but here in a free America we did not apprehend any menace to our peace and security. We were slowly and painfully making our way out of a great depression, and were devoting all of our resources to the effort of making democracy work in this country.

Suddenly the mad genius [Adolf Hitler] whose shadow now falls across the entire world started upon his program of death and destruction in Europe, with eventual world domination as his goal. In two short years we have seen the [German] swastika sweep across all of western Europe and the steppes of Russia and into north Africa, and fly from the mastheads of pirate ships seeking to dominate the seven seas.

The evil genius of nazism has proclaimed to the world that the world is too small for the conflicting philosophies of government of democracy and totalitarianism to live on this sphere in peace. He announces that one or the other must fall. The German legions' marching song boasts, "Today we are masters of Europe; tomorrow we will conquer the world." Here in America, as prudent men, we have observed that they do not say "Except the United States." We have therefore launched upon the most stupendous program in the history of the nation to build invulnerable defenses for this country, to arm our young men with the finest of the awesome material of modern warfare, and to supply arms to those who resist aggression anywhere in the world.

Our country is not yet an active belligerent. We hope and pray that we may avoid sending our young manhood into the maelstrom of war; but in calm common sense we may as well face the issue. The test is on. As freemen we have accepted the challenge to determine whether the people's government can survive and preserve the people's liberties in a contest with a totalitarian state where human rights are despised, individual liberties unknown, and every man, women, and child is a cog in a ruthless machine dominated and directed by one master.

What do we propose to defend in this great national effort which will soon require such a great sacrifice from us all? It is the American way of life. We propose to defend liberties that we did not appreciate until they were threatened.

We prepare to defend that priceless heritage handed down by our forebears, under which our Republic in a comparatively short time has become the greatest, freest, and the happiest land that the world has ever known. With all of its weaknesses, democracy is the best form of government yet devised by human minds.

In 150 years we have made more progress than the world had seen in any previous thousand years of history.

Every citizen of this country, every man, woman, and child, wherever they may live, whatever they do, shares in the responsibility of doing his part to meet the present challenge of Hitlerism to the way of life of a free people. We have called our young men to the colors. A million and a half young men, the flower of American manhood, are today in training camps. They have been called from civilian life to be trained in the art of war, in order that they may defend America. Tonight, on the storm-tossed waters of the north Atlantic, American boys are standing at battle station on American warships, seeking the undersea pirates and the vultures of the air who would thwart our promise to deliver supplies to those actively engaged on the battle front against the forces of aggression.

This is a war of machines. No amount of human valor can prevail over a tank unless you are supplied with an equally efficient tank. Raw courage alone cannot prevail in the face of super dive bombers and tons of high explosives hurled from huge cannon. The front line in modern-day war extends from the fighting front to the assembly line. The man in uniform, while in imminent danger, is no more important than the man in overalls in the machine shop. We have an obligation to the man in uniform to supply him with all of the machinery of war that he needs.

At stupendous cost we are building the greatest Navy that the world has ever seen to give us overpowering forces in both the Atlantic

Defense Savings Program 215

and Pacific to see that no invader shall bring war to our shores. We have embarked upon a program to build acres of tanks and fleets of airplanes that will darken the skies. This is to keep our commitments under the Monroe Doctrine to protect the Western Hemisphere. This is to keep faith with the men in uniform, that they may not be at a disadvantage if sent to the field of battle.

Such a program cannot succeed unless the American people believe in it and are willing to cheerfully sacrifice for its success. Our way of life permits no slave driver to drive us to a task with the option of a concentration camp or a firing squad. In this democracy we depend upon the spur of conscience and the force of public opinion. This great program undoubtedly requires real sacrifices of a temporary nature in order that we may enjoy our rights and liberties in perpetuity. It will require money in such vast amounts as to stagger the human imagination to pay for fleets and tanks and guns and planes.

The representatives of the people have voted for the heaviest taxes our people have ever known. When these taxes are paid, and paid cheerfully, the taxpayer is making his contribution to the defense of America just as surely as the man in uniform.

This meeting here tonight is to encourage loans by every citizen to their government to provide means for the common defense. (Compliment Marion Allen and all connected with him on success of program in Georgia.)

There is an opportunity for patriotic service in lending to your government. Certainly Government bonds and stamps are the best security known to the world today. If they are not a good investment, then it is impossible to find one on the face of the earth, because all of the United States stands pledged to their payment.

A great responsibility rests upon both industry and labor to provide the tools of war before it is too late. The overwhelming majority of industrialists and of those who work in industry are patriotically and unselfishly laboring to supply arms for our forces and to send overseas. There are some exceptions. The weakest place in the armor of America is in the selfish greed of a minority of industry to exact profits out of the defense program. The great mass of the American people demand that in this emergency our Government deal firmly with both groups. Time is too precious to permit any man or set of men to endanger the security of America by delaying for one moment the production of the all important weapons of defense.

The pledge has frequently been made to the American people that no one would get rich out of this defense program. That pledge has not yet been fully kept. The President [Franklin D. Roosevelt] and the Congress owe it to the boys in the camps and the fathers and mothers of those boys to see that no unwarranted profits are made in this extremity. As a friend of the President and a supporter of his Administration, I have regretted to see the Government of the United States temporize with labor leaders who have put their own selfish aims ahead of the national welfare, and who have called strikes that threaten the success of the defense program. We cannot afford to have strikes as usual any more than we can have business as usual in this country if we hope to survive against the forces of evil which threaten us. It is unfair to the men in camps to dilly-dally and delay in getting them the proper arms. It is unfair to the overwhelming majority of American labor, who are patriotically working to the limit of their ability to arm America, to have a few domineering leaders bring into disrepute the cause of all of those who toil by arousing public opinion.

The Navy's Challenge for Service
August 1942

The Japanese attacked the United States' fleet and military installations at Pearl Harbor, Hawaii, 7 December 1941. The U.S. experienced other setbacks in the Philippines, Malaya, Burma, Indonesia, and the Pacific Islands. A United States' fleet was destroyed in the Java Sea and, mid-1942, the Japanese advanced in New Guinea and the Aleutian Islands, creating a great demand for more American ships and sailors.

To help fill this need, on 18 July 1942, Rear Admiral Randall Jacobs asked Senator Russell to record a speech to be used to recruit young persons into the Navy.[6] Jacobs prepared an "outline of material" that the Senator could consider using. Jacobs planned to send Russell's recorded statement "to any and all radio stations" and newspapers in Georgia.[7] In the message Russell emphasized how the Navy would provide young Georgians opportunities to both defend their country and to learn a job skill. The speech was transcribed in Washington, D.C.

* * * * * * * * * *

My friends:

The important part which the Navy, the Marines, and the Coast Guard are playing in this war, is common knowledge. The battle lines are far flung—over the oceans and isolated islands of the world. Troop convoys, arms shipments and supplies must be sent to our own forces and those of our allies. Enemy submarines are infesting the waters off our shores. Enemy battle fleets must be stopped while still far away, to prevent invasion of our shores.

---

[6]Text of speech from Speech File, Speech and Media Series, Richard B. Russell Collection, RRLPRS.

[7]Letters from Jacobs to Russell, in Speech File, Speech and Media Series, Richard B. Russell Collection, RRLPRS.

Because of the tremendous job which it has to do, the Navy is being expanded rapidly. New ships and new planes are being commissioned every day. And with every ship that slides down the ways—every naval plane that rolls off the production lines—new opportunities are opened to red-blooded patriotic men who want to serve their nation in its time of peril.

I was particularly happy to respond to the Navy Department's request to speak to you about the Navy and to tell you about the Navy's Challenge for service. A number of my relatives have served in the Navy—one of my brothers is now serving as an enlisted man—and we are all proud of the fine record which Georgia men already have achieved in the Navy in this war.

Several of our young men already have been decorated for bravery in action in the far Pacific, and enlistments in the Navy have been very high indeed in Georgia. The state of Georgia was ready to go even before Pearl Harbor—and when war broke out, enlistment stations all over the state were crowded with volunteers.

With the fine historic background which Georgians have for patriotism and bravery, it was no surprise for us to read the names of our Georgia boys on the rolls of honor that started coming as soon as war broke out. Let me read you the names of some of our Georgia men who have been decorated for their courage in the great battles that are going on out there in the Pacific.

Commander William L. Anderson of Sylvania and Millen, who was presented by Admiral Nimitz with the Navy Cross.

Lieutenant Commander James H. Brett of Cedartown and Statesboro, the Navy Cross.

Lieutenant Commander Lucius H. Chappel of Columbus, the Navy Cross.

Lieutenant Commander Robert E. Dixon of Richland, the Navy Cross.

Lieutenant Carl F. Faires of Atlanta, the Navy Cross.

Ensign Curtis Hamilton, a native of Monroe, the Distinguished Flying Cross.

Lieutenant Commander William Outerbridge of Tifton, the Navy Cross.

The Navy's Challenge for Service

William W. Parker, Seaman First Class of Bannethburn, the Navy Cross.

Lieutenant Commander Ashton B. Smith, the Navy Cross.

Jackson C. Pharris, a gunner, the Navy Cross.

This is only a partial list of Georgia's heroes. More are coming in all the time. You will note that the list includes officers and enlisted men alike. They are the kind of men of whom Georgia has always been proud—the kind of men who will be your shipmates if you join the Navy, the kind of men the Navy needs in ever-increasing numbers. Because this fighting Navy of ours is going to grow and grow—and it is going to fight and fight—until the last Jap warship, the last German sub has been blasted to the bottom of the sea.

So far America has been largely on the defensive. But as these new ships we are building—and these new men that are now joining up to go into action—the situation is going to change.

But let us not fool ourselves, the war is going to be long and hard. We are not yet over the hump. Our enemies are strong, and we were not prepared. We have lost much valuable ground that will have to be regained. And the Navy needs your help in regaining that ground.

Those boys fighting away off yonder in the far Pacific—or strange tropic islands—in the air and under the sea—they are fighting your fight—the fight for the preservation of your home and your liberties—the fight to save your mothers and fathers—your sisters and sweethearts—from the murder and pillage that have been the fate of the overrun nations of Europe. Those boys fighting out there are keeping America from invasion by the Jap hordes. They need your help—the help of every able-bodied patriotic man who can get into the scrap.

Let me read what the Secretary of the Navy recently had to say on the subject. I quote:

> Never in all history has the call for defenders of freedom been so urgent as at this moment. Brave men are needed—stout-hearted men—men who would rather fight to stay free than live to be slaves. . . .

That is what the Secretary of the Navy said about the Navy's need for men.

And in return for your services, the Navy can do much for you. Because of the opportunities which it offers for self-improvement, the Navy always has appealed to young men—in fact, the average age of enlisted men in the Navy today is only 19½ years. For the Navy is a great training—as broad as life itself.

The Navy today is a tremendous technical organization offering you work of every description. There are forty-nine different classes of jobs waiting for patriotic American men who select the Navy as their branch of our armed services. You can take your pick—radioman, machinist, carpenter, bos'un, aviation pilot, cook, baker, metalsmith, fireman, painter, and dozens of others. Whatever your job in civilian life, you are almost sure to find its counterpart in America's fighting Navy.

The Navy wants skilled fighting men. If you have had special training or are particularly experienced at your trade you have an opportunity to enter the Navy or the Naval Reserve with a Petty Officer's rating—which will give the higher pay, allowances, and responsibilities to which you are entitled.

But even if you don't possess any special qualifications, that does not disqualify you. The Navy affords you an opportunity to go to a trade school where you can get training worth fifteen hundred dollars in order to qualify you in the work for which you show an aptitude. If you're handy with tools—or if you like radio, photography, welding or any of nearly fifty other skilled occupations, here's your chance to get the finest training, and to use the best equipment the world has to offer. Costly metal lathes—marvelous telescopic cameras—vast power and tool plants—they're all part of the enormous workshop you can call your own.

And you'll be drawing pay while you learn. When you enlist as an Apprentice Seaman you're paid fifty dollars a month. After approximately two months, almost all Apprentice Seamen are automatically promoted, with a proportionate raise in pay. Then you move ahead just as fast as your own skill permits. The Navy wants you to get ahead, and the Navy will do everything possible to smooth the road for

The Navy's Challenge for Service

you. Over approximately fifty percent of the enlisted men in the Navy today are Petty Officers. And remember—every promotion means an increase in pay and allowances.

The United States Navy is building the world's greatest Naval Air-Arm. If you're interested in flying, this is your chance. And there are scores of jobs open to you besides actual piloting. You may qualify as an aviation machinist, metalsmith, photographer, gunner, observer, parachute rigger, bomber, and many other jobs. And remember this—every Bluejacket who receives flight orders, whether as a pilot or in any other capacity—automatically receives a fifty percent increase in pay. The experience you get in Naval aviation will fit you for a good job in civil aviation after the war. No matter what your training in the Navy, it will fit you for a better job after the war is over, and the enemies of freedom have been defeated once and for all. Some of the most important executives in American industry owe their success to the early training and experience they received as enlisted men in the United States Navy.

As an enlisted man in the Navy, you'll have a great chance to win your wings as an Officer Pilot. You'll be given the world's finest, fastest planes to fly—the Navy planes that are spearhead of America's attack. The requirements are simple—a high school graduate, physically fit, and between the ages of eighteen and twenty-seven. If you qualify you will become a Naval Aviation Cadet with pay of seventy-five dollars a month. You'll learn blind flying, gunnery, bombing, and navigation. And when you graduate you'll receive your Navy wings of gold and your commission as a Naval Officer.

The Navy considers its enlisted men the finest fighting men in the world, and has done everything in its power to care for their comfort and health. You receive the best medical and dental service absolutely free. Your food, board, transportation and clothing are all provided for. Even your dependents are taken care of by the government to ease you of financial strain.

You can enlist today in either the Regular Navy or the Naval Reserve. Enlistment in the Regular Navy is for six years. Enlistment in the Naval Reserve is for two, three, or four years—with the provision that you are free to return to civilian life as soon as possible after the war. Pay and promotions are the same in both branches. Any patriotic, red-blooded American man between the ages of seventeen and fifty can apply.

The United States Navy is the world's greatest training and conditioning school. This is your opportunity to take advantage of it. You can serve your country as an American fighting man—and give yourself a headstart in life at the same time.

Georgia has always been proud of her record for volunteers—and she can continue to be so, for the enlistments in percentage places Georgia very high among the forty-eight states. I am informed by the Navy Department that in the single month of May, 602 Georgians joined the Navy, and the number has been increasing steadily. If you want to join the Georgia heroes already at sea—and those in training school preparing to join them—there are recruiting stations at Macon, Albany, Athens, Atlanta, Augusta, Columbus, Rome, Savannah, and Valdosta. The officers at any of these stations will be glad to give you full details and take your application.

Report on Visit to War Theaters
28 October 1943

On 7 December 1941, the Japanese attacked the United States' fleet and military installations at Pearl Harbor, Hawaii. The nation experienced other serious losses in the Philippines, Malaya, Burma, and Indonesia. In 1943 the Allies began reversing their losses, and Senator Harry S. Truman charged Senators Ralph O. Brewster (Maine), Albert B. Chandler (Kentucky), and Richard B. Russell to visit, study, and report the status of the War Theaters. Russell chaired this investigating committee. They departed on 15 July 1943.

In reporting his *personal* findings to the U.S. Senate on October 28, Russell noted that this public account would "largely be a repetition" of statements made in Executive Session to the Senate on 7 October.[8] The Senator indicated that, in making the 37,000 mile trip, the committee did not "advise or interfere with Allied Military" personnel, but only secured "information" about "the provisions being made for the health and well-being of our troops." He looked for the "general atmosphere prevailing in each of the theaters." Russell described the state of transportation, hospital facilities, naval operations, engineers, and petroleum. He praised the "courage and resourcefulness" of soldiers in "combat."

* * * * * * * * * *

Leaving Washington on July 25, we flew to Presque Isle, Maine, and from there to a large air base in Newfoundland. From this field in Newfoundland [indicating on map] we proceeded to another large base in Labrador used by planes flying across the Atlantic for delivery to England. From this field in Labrador [indicating] we flew across the awesome ice cap, and peaks and glaciers of Greenland, following the Great Circle route to a field in Iceland [indicating]. From Iceland

---

[8]Text of speech from *Congressional Record Proceedings and Debates of the 78th Congress*, October 28, 1943, First Session, Vol. 89, Part 7, 8859-8866.

we went to the United Kingdom, where we spent a number of days, practically half the time with our Eighth Air Force. From a gigantic airport in southwest England we took off at midnight one night for Marrakech, in north Africa [indicating].

We spent more than a week in the north African theater of operations, and visited all the important cities along the Mediterranean, as well as Casablanca on the Atlantic, and all the troop concentrations that are scattered along the entire rim of north Africa, as well as the scene of the fighting there last spring. Leaving Cairo, we traveled across Arabia to Basra and Abadan (indicating) on the Persian Gulf. There, in a climate so hot that the actual temperature recorded by thermometer defies belief, our men are assembling and delivering to the Russians vast quantities of war material under lend-lease.

From this theater we proceeded to Karachi, in India (indicating), and thence across India by New Delhi and Assam Province and over the Burma Hump into China, visiting Kunming and Chungking. Coming back out of China we proceeded to Calcutta, and from Calcutta across the Bay of Bengal to Ceylon. From Ceylon we crossed the Indian Ocean to Carnarvon on the west coast of Australia. We were told that ours was the first land plane ever to make this flight across the Indian Ocean. We visited Port Darwin and Townsville, from which place we flew across the Coral Sea to General MacArthur's headquarters in New Guinea. Returning to Australia we landed at Brisbane, from which city, after a visit to Sydney and Melbourne, we took off for New Caledonia. We came home across the Pacific, stopping at Fiji Islands, Samoa, Christmas Island, and Hawaii on our way to Los Angeles, whence we took the last long jump across the entire United States to Washington.

This represents the route taken by the four-motored Liberator transport in which we left Washington. The party did not stay together throughout the entire trip, but went to different places within each area visited in other planes. The large plane in which we left Washington flew nearly 37,000 miles, and members of the committee traveled several thousand miles in other planes when visiting points where a four-motored plane could not land. About one-eighth of the total time of the trip was consumed in travel through the air. Most of the remaining seven-eighths was spent in an earnest effort to gather information.

Upon my appointment as chairman of the committee I announced that we were in no sense a committee on the conduct of the war, and that I did not consider it within our province to undertake to advise or interfere with Allied military and naval leaders in their direction of the strategy of the war. I did feel that the committee could perform a very useful function for the Senate by securing first-hand information from the various theaters of operations as to the provisions being made for the health and well-being of our troops, as well as finding out what the men were thinking and talking about, the condition of their morale, the suitability of the tools of war being produced at such great effort and expense, and the general effectiveness with which the war is being prosecuted. I also believed that the things heard and observed by such a Senate committee would be helpful in dealing with the questions arising from our relations with the other Allied powers, and in preparing for the many trying and complex issues whose solution must have final approval by the Senate after the war is over.

No one would claim that any person could become conversant with all phases of our far-flung activities in a trip of little more than two months' duration. All that one could hope to do was to get a fair idea of the general atmosphere prevailing in each of the theaters visited. This we endeavored to do by personal contact and observation. We slept in palaces and in pup tents. We ate with those who are directing the destinies of nations, and with enlisted men at their mess. We conferred with high officials of every government visited, as well as with the commanding officers in every theater of operations. We had explanations of strategy, tactics, and objectives, illustrated by maps and in some cases by moving pictures. We talked to wounded men in hospitals who had just been brought in from the front, as well as with men of all ranks belonging to every branch of the service.

We spent days with the Fifth Army as they were undergoing the final phases of intensive training in amphibious operations preparatory to the invasion of Italy, as well as with Commando units and

Marines training for jungle fighting in the South Pacific. We saw bomber and fighter squadrons briefed for attack take off in their planes, both from England and in the Pacific theater. We visited men in their barracks, and chatted with them as they relaxed in Red Cross canteens. We attended the moving-picture and the U.S.O. [United States Service Organization] shows, to which the men in the more remote places look forward so avidly.

The men who are actually fighting this war are thinking about post-war problems, as well as things at home and the conduct of the war. I wish that every Member of the Senate could have been with me to share my discomfort during a two-hour grilling by several hundred Servicemen in a Red Cross canteen in New Delhi, which they have named "Duration Den." It would have required not only all the powers of prophecy of the entire Senate, but full and frank replies from the heads of all the Allied powers to answer some of the questions propounded. Any idea that the men are only thinking about the end of the war and getting home would be disabused by a visit to any overseas station.

What I have seen and heard does not make me an expert on all things pertaining to the war, but I have a much clearer picture than I could possibly have gained by zealous attendance on committee hearings for twelve months. Not only is this war the greatest undertaking the American people have ever embarked upon, but even after having visited all the theaters of operations it is difficult to grasp the magnitude of the job to which the power and might of the United States and our allies have been harnessed all around the globe. It was a great experience to see first-hand the difficulties and obstacles which are requiring such a tremendous expenditure of human energy and material resources, and which demand ingenuity, heroism, and a spirit of sacrifice on the part of millions of our boys and girls.

The over-all problem of transportation involved in this war is so great as to stagger the imagination. It taxes to the limit the resources of our Nation and the human endurance of our people engaged in it. The most striking single difficulty is that involved in the effort to supply our forces in China and our Chinese allies. After having been brought thousands of miles by steamship into the harbor of Calcutta, every pound of supplies going to General [Claire L.] Chennault's gallant air forces in China must now be loaded or unloaded nine different times, as well as being flown over the towering peaks of the Burma "hump" before they can be utilized against the enemy.

The job of maintenance and repair in this mechanized war is an onerous one. Veritable factories must follow each army. American engineers and mechanics have built great machine shops at various places across the vast reaches of north Africa, on the scorching rim of the Persian Gulf, in Australia, and on the islands of the South Pacific, where planes, tanks, trucks, and ships are either assembled or repaired. I never ceased to marvel at their efficiency. We saw production lines at those remote stations receive airplane engines that seemed to be completely wrecked. A few hours later they emerged wrapped in cellophane, and as precisely tooled and efficient as a new engine coming from a plant in the United States.

One benefit we will derive from the enormous expenditures of this awful war lies in the training of large numbers of the finest craftsmen and mechanics in the world. Both the Army and the Navy have accomplished wonders in this respect. Boys who twelve months ago were either unemployed or doing work requiring no skill are today repairing the most delicate instruments, such as radar and radio equipment, telephone exchanges, submarine periscopes, and are working with the countless finely balanced machines which are necessary in the operation of airplanes, submarines, and other complicated mechanisms of war.

Every American may well be proud of the manner in which our armed forces have met the problem of maintenance and supply. Our difficulties have been so far solved that our troops are now unquestionably the best fed, best equipped, and best provided armed forces the world has ever seen. In some of the remote areas the ration is not as tasty and varied as one would like, but all of our men have plenty of nourishing food and clothes adapted to the climate in which they serve and fight.

The completeness of the hospital facilities both in the field and at permanent stations, and the speed with which the sick and wounded receive treatment are almost unbelievable. I do not think we failed to visit a hospital at a single place we stopped, and I talked with doctors, nurses, and patients. Men are recovering from wounds in a few weeks in this war which would have proved fatal heretofore, and the use of the sulfa drug, blood plasma, and new methods of treatment received by the sick and wounded in our armed forces is incomparably superior to the average treatment received by the civilian population at home.

All Senators have talked to eyewitnesses who have vividly portrayed some of the difficulties and obstacles with which our fighting men must contend in the course of operations, as well as the indomitable courage and resourcefulness of our boys who are engaged in actual combat. I shall not repeat them. All of us heard sagas of individual heroism and accomplishment which make the stories of the Knights of the Round Table pale in comparison. It was hard to believe that the quiet and modest chap you met in a hospital cheerfully bearing three or four gaping wounds was a hero who had either killed eleven Japs singlehandedly or had flown through the hell of fire which greeted the men who struck the Ploesti oil refineries. I shall never forget the emotions I experienced as I sat with fifty fighter pilots of the Eighth Air Force in England and heard a handsome blond squadron leader about twenty-five years old instruct his men on a mission across the Channel. He sounded as casual as if he were discussing the proper play to run in a football game. Nor can I forget the fine-looking boy, a veteran of six months' jungle fighting at nineteen, who twelve hours before had received a bullet in his leg while fighting the Japs in the Solomons. It so happened that I knew his family quite well. He was more interested in talking about conditions in Georgia than in New Georgia. After telling me that he hoped to be back in action within three weeks, he wound up by expressing concern about the people back home, saying: "Look after the folks at home, Senator, and we will take care of these Japs out here."

The fighting in Europe is against a determined, well-equipped, and resourceful enemy. It does more or less follow the orthodox conception of war. The war in the Pacific is a battle to the death. Tales of incredible and shocking brutality by the Japanese in the treatment of our men, including the wounded, make it easy to understand why no quarter is now being asked or given. The Japs had the early advantage of training in jungle fighting. They are patient and cunning. A Japanese sniper will tie himself in a tree and remain there for three or four days. Another will spend several hours crawling as short a distance as a hundred yards for a shot at an American soldier or marine. They have a great trick of slipping behind our lines and feigning death along a path on which reinforcements must travel and throwing a grenade into a detachment of our men. They had mastered all the arts of camouflage in jungle fighting. The best illustration I can use to describe the jungle fighting in the islands of the South Pacific is to compare it with Indian warfare in early colonial days, with the jungle more fearsome and difficult to penetrate than any primeval forest.

Our men have had to learn jungle fighting the hard way, but they have finally mastered it, and today they are beating the Jap at his own game.

As a member of the Naval Affairs Committee I undertook to observe as many of the activities of our Navy in the areas visited as possible. I am frank to say that I believe the Navy is doing a disservice to the many American heroes by overstressing its policy of remaining the "silent service." Sailors handled every one of the landing barges which took the troops and Marines ashore in the South Pacific, as they did in north Africa, in Sicily, and in Italy. They kept the noses of their ships, which are easy targets for bomb and shell, against the sands of the beaches until the last soldier and the last piece of equipment was ashore. Ofttimes the guns of destroyers and cruisers blazed the path for our infantry and tanks. Due to the constant vigilance required to fend off attacks by airplanes and submarines, the men manning these ships often do not get more than two or three hours' sleep a day for as long as a week. In Sicily one of our light cruisers broke up a tank attack by a regiment of the Hermann Goering Division just before it was apparently about to result in disaster to one of our divisions which had not had time to set up its heavy defense equipment. In my judgment the American people are entitled to know more about what the Navy has been doing in order that they may properly appreciate the sacrifices of the men who go down to the sea in ships.

It is inspiring to observe that in both the Army and the Navy morale seems to be higher where the hazard is greatest. This is particularly true of the men who man our "pigboats," or submarines. I had an opportunity to talk to the officers and men of many of our underwater craft who are carrying the war to the very shores of Japan. I asked a lad who was a member of the crew of a submarine in drydock at Pearl Harbor, where a huge dent caused by a depth charge was being ironed out, whether he would prefer service on a surface ship. His reply was, "Hell, no. It's safer down there than up above when those airplanes come in with their torpedoes and bombs."

Due to the great importance of China to the Allied cause, I regretted that our visit there was not long enough to enable us to have time to go more fully into the details of the situation there. We did, however, have ample opportunity to confer with Generals [Joseph W.] Stilwell and Chennault and to visit with the generalissimo and the leading figures of his government at Chungking.

Some of the conditions noted in China were most disturbing. Such industries as the country possessed were largely in the area occupied by the Japanese. The country has been in an exhausting war for a number of years, and they have suffered great losses. Chinese troops are poorly equipped, and in their present state of affairs are confined to defensive and guerrilla action. To apply the word "army" to the forces of China is not to use that word in the sense usually understood when referring to the armed forces of other leading Allied Powers. Their form of government lacks many of the elements of a democracy, as the term is generally accepted in our country. This generalissimo, Chiang Kai-shek, is a great patriot. In him rests China's last best hope of salvation as a free and unified democratic state. If any one man in China can accomplish this, he will do it. He is confronted with great difficulties, the details of which I shall relate.

Notwithstanding all his handicaps, the generalissimo refuses even to discuss peace overtures with the Japs, and the fact that China is still in the war as our ally requires the attention of 15 or more Japanese divisions.

In my opinion, General Chennault is one of the most brilliant soldiers this war has produced. With an incredibly small number of effective airplanes, he is contributing greatly to keeping China a factor in the war. Certainly no man has ever done more with so little. Considering the limitations upon him, General Stilwell is also rendering a great service to his country and the Allied cause.

It is requiring a superhuman effort to furnish General Chennault's air forces, but the maintenance of air bases in China is of such importance that we should attack the problem of supplying him with redoubled vigor.

On account of her proximity to Japan and her knowledge of the Japanese people, China has the most effective intelligence service on Japanese activities of any of the Allied Powers.

We received information from the most reliable sources in China to the effect that we were still continuing to underestimate the strength of Japan, particularly in the field of production. We were advised that instead of the 500 planes generally estimated here, the Japs were making more than a thousand planes a month, and were producing twice as much shipping as they were before Pearl Harbor. This may be the answer to the amazement of our commanding officers in the South Pacific as to where the Japs get the planes to replace the large numbers that are shot down so rapidly there.

In addition to the ocean shipping, the Japanese are manufacturing large numbers of lightweight shallow-draft wooden ships powered by Diesel engines. They are using them for interisland transportation, and in some cases over considerable distances. Much timber is being taken from occupied China for the purpose of constructing these ships, and we were also told that they had even used some of the trees from the Emperor's sacred forest in Japan for this construction. I asked some of our submarine commanders about this, and they confirmed the reports that we had received in China. These ships constitute quite a problem to our submarines. Ofttimes submarine commanders do not feel justified in expanding a long way from home priceless torpedoes in sinking such small craft. They surface, and sink them with gunfire. Practically all of these wooden ships are armed, and we have undoubtedly sustained some losses of submarines in these actions.

One unit of the Chinese Army is fully trained and equipped. Our transport planes which are flying equipment in to General Chennault returned with cargoes of Chinese soldiers. Many thousands of these men who could not be armed and equipped in China have been flown out to a point were equipment could be provided, and are now fully armed, completely furnished with motorized transport, and have been thoroughly trained in all of the latest methods of warfare. Our officers are confident that they are first-class fighting men and will give a good account of themselves when they come to grips with the enemy.

The first questions asked by every enlisted man and junior officer who has been overseas any considerable length of time is, "When are we going to get some leave to go home?" All of the veterans realize the value of the experience they have acquired in actual combat, and practically none of them expect to be released from service until the job is done, but there is an overwhelming feeling on the part of those who have been overseas for many long months that arrangements should be made to give them a respite from their trials and dangers, and a chance to see their families.

Every member of the committee is agreed that the War Department should immediately adopt some policy of returning troops home for a leave or rest after certain services have been performed. This has worked well in the case of the crews of our airplanes, who are allowed a fixed period of rest after a certain number of sorties, which varies in different theaters of operations. I believe it would be a great incentive to the men and would still further reinforce the fine morale that is now displayed if all of them had definite prospect of a visit home after the performance of a certain task or period of service for which they are assigned. For obvious reasons this is a difficult matter on which to legislate, but the committee has made strong recommendations to the War Department and the Navy Department that a fair policy of leaves be promulgated.

The one bright spot in many of the isolated places where our men are serving has been the American Red Cross and the U.S.O. troupes. There is no way to compute what these touches of home life have meant to boys who are working and fighting under almost impossible conditions. The girls in the Red Cross canteens have been worth their weight in gold, and the resourcefulness they have displayed in all conceivable circumstances has been amazing. We met several of the U.S.O. troupes. Some of them were tired and worn, but they were still carrying on, and I am sure that none of them have ever played to more appreciative audiences. A report to the headquarters of our forces in the Middle East on the trials of a group of these entertainers whose stage was the burning sands of the deserts enabled us to have a better appreciation of what these stage people are doing. The report read:

> Attitude of troupe so far is very good. Tonight will play Basra and depart for Khorramshaar tomorrow. Accordion now useless as heat melted wax.

Men who live close to death think on the spiritual side of life. We attended church services at several places, and were much impressed by the manner in which the chaplains are carrying out their multifold duties. We likewise visited several cemeteries where rest those heroes who have made the supreme sacrifice. Even in the haste and confusion of war our honored dead have not been neglected. Those who have loved ones or friends who have fallen in battle would be comforted if they could see the well-kept cemeteries where they sleep, and the solicitude of the chaplains in charge to have every grave properly marked amidst surroundings of appropriate dignity.

Any account of our observations without a word of praise to the Navy Seabees and the Army Engineers would be incomplete as well as unjust to some of the heroes of this war. From the frozen lava beds of Iceland to the blistering sands of the deserts, these men work as high as twenty hours some days constructing facilities that are essential to modern war. When the history of this war is written, their unselfish sacrifices and tireless labor should adorn one of its brightest pages. To date they have received far too little credit.

I was very much concerned to note that for some reason many of the most recent of our allies and our late enemies have great expectations as to what they are to receive from the United States in the way of relief and rehabilitation. It is very unfortunate that their expectations are so high. The widespread idea that we are preparing to look after all of the needs of the world and to restore the destruction wrought by this war has caused me seriously to question the wisdom of delegating to a civilian agency the responsibility of handling relief and rehabilitation abroad. The establishment of a large civilian agency with widespread activities is likely either to generate unnecessary bitterness by failing to fulfill hopes that are excessive or else prove to be a more expensive undertaking than the American people should be compelled to finance. I believe it would be much better for all concerned if the people of north Africa and Italy, particularly, were frankly given to understand now that, while willing to assist to a reasonable extent, we do not consider it the responsibility of the United States to rebuild destroyed cities or embark upon any longtime program of relief. . . .

I hope that I do not sound callous when I say that in my opinion this relief should be on a temporary basis, and so far as adults are concerned should be confined to the very minimum, a sufficiency for a short period to maintain life, but kept so small that it will not stifle a desire to supplement the ration received from us through other efforts. We should be very careful not to publicize or embark upon a policy which will either lead to greater misunderstanding or result in stupendous charges against the Treasury that our people should not be called upon to meet.

Wherever we went we were most courteously received by the officials of the British Empire. I was much impressed by their frankness in discussing not only the conduct of the war but post-war problems. The people of England have made great sacrifices in this war and have displayed a fortitude, in the face of constant danger, which we might well emulate. Many of their cities have been heavily bombed. The food in England was poorer than in any other place we visited. All clothing is strictly rationed. Civilians have practically no gasoline and are converting their cars and trucks to charcoal burners.

The British people have hospitably received the American soldiers who are stationed in their midst. From a military standpoint, they have displayed every quality that one could ask in an ally. The British Tommy is a first-class soldier. Wherever I had an opportunity to visit with our Navy, both enlisted men and officers spoke in glowing terms of the skill and seamanship and the courage of the British tar. The Royal Navy is still living up to its finest traditions. The heroic exploits of the Royal Air Force already belong to the legends of this war. As fighting men they are good partners to have in a scrap.

We had some opportunity to observe the operation of the British Government not only at home but throughout the Empire. I came home with a healthy respect bordering on envy for the efficiency of the British in administration, and in the handling of their relations with other nations, and in their own vast dominion. The British have a definite foreign policy with respect to every corner of the globe. Every civil servant and every officer of any rank is apparently fully acquainted with Empire policy as it applies either militarily, diplomatically, or commercially. Every action of the responsible officials of government is designed to promote that policy.

If our Nation has a definite policy which extends longer than six months after the conclusion of the war in any of the far-flung lands in which American troops are fighting and American dollars are being spent, I was unable to find anyone among our officers abroad who could define it.

We cannot afford to rely upon even so splendid an ally as the United Kingdom to protect all our interests, or there will be inevitable conflict and confusion after the war. Our civil agencies abroad are numerous, but too often they are either working at cross purposes or, worse to relate, in some cases have no apparent purpose. Our post-war interests are being neglected, and we stand to get very little or no return from our immense expenditures.

In places our representation abroad was apparently weak. Too many of our representatives still appear to rely upon ancient protocol and the easy ways and flowery terms which have been in vogue in the past. This is a day of realism, as might be expected when great peoples are fighting for their very lives. Realists are directing this war in the field as well as in places of power, not only in enemy-lands but among our allies. We would do well to assume a more realistic attitude. In my opinion all of our civilian agencies operating outside the United States should be coordinated in the hands of some two-fisted

American who has an understanding of American interests in all international matters. The old type of kid-glove diplomacy, including high-flown but vague phraseology, does not have any place in today's international dealings. . . .

We should keep closer check on the expensive tools of war that we are dealing out on such a gigantic scale under lend-lease arrangements. In the Mediterranean area and the Middle East our British allies have stressed the fact that they have given large quantities of war supplies to Turkey as very effective propaganda to gain the good will of the 250,000,000 Mohammedans of the world. Much of this military equipment transferred by England to Turkey is American-made and American-financed equipment, and was transferred to England under lend-lease. Every sensible person realizes that we will not be paid in full for all of the material of war which we have advanced to our allies under lend-lease. No one really expects it. In my judgment, it is a very poor policy to permit lend-lease equipment, paid for by the people of the United States, to be used to buy good will even for our closest friend when good will is such an important commodity. If it is good business for England to get credit with Turkey and the friends of Turkey for helping that nation in time of danger, it would seem to me to be worth something to the United States.

In like manner some of the equipment which is included in the British transfers to Russia is American-made or American-bought. American food handled on a lend-lease basis has likewise been used by the British Food Commission to feed refugees and other hungry peoples of the earth, and I doubt that the recipient is always aware of the fact that the United States was the true benefactor.

I would be the last to do or say anything which would cause any breach between our country and our British allies. I believe that the future peace of the world largely depends upon a complete understanding between us. However, matters of this kind can surely be adjusted without disturbing good relations. No people are perfect, including our own; and I feel that there will be a better understanding and more mutual respect between us and less possibility of feeling which might prevent or postpone a complete accord after the war if such matters are worked out as we go along.

One source of irritation to our men who are serving in that large portion of the world which is under the aegis of that great news agency, Reuter's, is the paucity of news as to the American war effort. After having traveled for practically a month in that area I can understand how they feel. On some days it would have been difficult from reading the papers to know that the United States was participating in the war at all. National pride, of course, colors our own news, and we are not slow to boast about the accomplishments of our armed forces.

However, it seems to me that, on the whole, our press has been much fairer with our allies in reporting the war than they have been with us. I could give many illustrations, but this excerpt from a leading paper in Australia illustrates what I am talking about. The article was written on the day that Italy surrendered. Despite the kindness with which our troops have been received in Australia, it is disturbing to an American soldier there to read:

> There is great joy in Britain that Italy's downfall should so largely be a British Empire affair. Empire forces were responsible for ninety percent of the battles from the first battle in East Africa right to the final landing on the Italian mainland.

All in all, the morale of our troops in India appeared to be lower than in any other theater. India is in many respects a very depressing place for troops to be stationed. This great country of 350,000,000 souls is a land of contrasts, of great wealth of the few and indescribable poverty and filth of the many. A great famine is sweeping some of the provinces, causing unspeakable suffering and many deaths from starvation. . . .

The days that I spent in India, however, did confirm me in the belief that it would require unremitting investigation over many years to even faintly understand the so-called Indian problem, and that those who have never been there, but have a five-minute solution, are extremely foolhardy. . . .

This war of mechanized transport, involving millions of vehicles from huge ocean liners to the innumerable jeeps which have become so indispensable, is consuming petroleum products in staggering amounts. Up to now we have been depleting our petroleum stocks at a ruinous rate, supplying not only our own forces but those of our allies. It is high time to utilize the petroleum deposits of other parts of the world. Otherwise, the end of the war will find our own deposits practically exhausted.

The President's statement this week that plans are being made to accomplish this is highly gratifying. There may have been sound reasons heretofore for not more widely employing the huge deposits of the Persian Gulf. These reasons were based upon difficulties of transportation. With the opening of the Mediterranean and the great increase in construction of shipping, there is no longer any valid reason for not giving our oil deposits a rest, and tapping those of other areas.

At one time we were shipping high octane gasoline to Russia, which has great petroleum reserves, but lacked refineries. Refineries have now been supplied Russia. We should no longer be compelled to draw on our dwindling petroleum reserves for use in most of the foreign theaters of operation.

All of us are concerned about American rights in air bases and air facilities which have been constructed at our expense all over the world. There should be no delay in having some definite understanding and agreement as to the post-war rights of our commercial aviation. Certainly we occupy a better position to negotiate such understandings now than we will after the war is over. We cannot expect to have sovereignty over all bases that we have constructed for military purposes, but we should be able to assure to American enterprise an equal chance with others in these bases we have paid for, and the right to operate in all parts of the world.

Air power is the decisive factor in this war. With the great developments being made daily in aviation, the peace of the world and the outcome of any future wars will depend directly upon air power. Planes must have bases from which to operate. We should begin now to plan for the post-war period, both to assure the future defense of the United States and to assist in maintaining world peace on a basis of justice and equality.

Many of our close offshore bases are built on lands under foreign flags. I have never been satisfied with the 99-year lease given the United States in the destroyer deal negotiated by this country before we entered the war. This is not any 99-year country! Where would we be today if [Thomas] Jefferson had handled the Louisiana Purchase on any such basis, or if our rights in Florida, or if even the Alaska Purchase, had been subjected to any such limitation? If we can be trusted for 99 years to occupy and develop defenses on the lands belonging to our allies, but essential to our defense, there is no reason why future generations, who will still be paying for this war, should be denied the protection these bases afford.

Time can bring remarkable changes. War will move much faster in the future than it has even in this day of blitz. With the tide of lend-lease running high from our shores, future generations of Americans should not be subjected to the danger of having these bases, built and maintained by Americans, used against them 100 years from now. It should be possible to work out some arrangements which will give us permanently such protections as these bases may afford.

There are many other important spots on the globe which have been fortified and developed with American money and sweat, which will become increasingly important to the defense of the United States with the rapid improvement of air and sea transportation. The smaller the world becomes, the closer are these bases to our shores.

I invite the attention of the Senate to the importance of some arrangement with the Government of Iceland in the post-war period which will permit us to use the very expensive facilities we have constructed on that island. A glance at the map will show that heavy bombers and submarines based on Iceland can close all of the shipping lanes of the north Atlantic. In any future war, control of Iceland means control of the north Atlantic Ocean. . . .

In the Pacific our boys are already fighting and dying over and around the islands that were mandated to Japan after the last World War. Much more precious blood will be shed before the Japs are finally rooted out. Certainly as a result of the sacrifices of these men, and to prevent the further killing of the boys of the second or third generation moving back into these islands in some future war, we should have some definite policy with respect to the future status of these islands that will assure the defense of the United States, as well as contribute to the peace of the world. We have rights in these islands that are being purchased today with the blood of American boys.

I spent several days on the island of New Caledonia, one of the westernmost of the Pacific islands. This is a French possession. In order to assure an open sea route to Australia and the bases of operations against the Japs in the islands of the Pacific, we have spent many million dollars fortifying this island. It has a fine, natural, landlocked harbor. We have built wharves and docks, seaplane bases, airfields, and roads, barracks, and hospitals, and placed heavy defense artillery to beat off the strongest Japanese attack. We have in operation at our bases there some of the finest repair and machine shops that I saw anywhere in the world. In brief, New Caledonia has been transformed by American dollars and American sweat and sacrifice into an all but impregnable fortress. So long as it is in friendly hands and we have any considerable naval and air power, no enemy from the west can with safety attack either North or South American without first reducing it.

In the past we have heard a great deal about the fortification of Guam. I do not know what future plans or program for the fortification of Guam the American Congress will be compelled to pass upon; but I believe that if we could obtain rights in New Caledonia and utilize the fortifications and facilities already existing, it would save much of the expense of fortifying Guam. It seems to me that negotiations should be entered into at the earliest possible date looking to the acquisition, by fair and just arrangements, either of title to all of New Caledonia or perpetual rights in and to the bases and facilities we have constructed. I know that there are those who will hurl the charge of imperialism at such suggestions and claim that they are in derogation to the terms of the Atlantic Charter. I do not think that there is anything imperialistic about it. Call it what you will, it is a realistic step to prevent another generation of Americans, who will undoubtedly still be paying for the present war, from being compelled to pay again in blood and treasure in taking these islands back from the same enemy who may obtain them if we follow the policy of take and abandon after this war is over.

American boys will soon be dying to free the soil of France from a foreign invader. We are now equipping many French divisions in north Africa with American arms in order that they may join in the fight for the liberation of France. We are supplying the French people in north Africa with petroleum, clothing, and many other articles through lend-lease. When the mother-land of France is freed from the German invader we will undoubtedly spend huge sums for relief and rehabilitation in France. It is not too much to ask that for the sake of the future defense of American we be given some rights in an island which means nothing to the defense of France but may be vital to our own defense.

Nothing that I saw in the course of my travels would justify any confidence that the war is nearly over. Indeed, I believe that overoptimism is one of the enemies which the American people must constantly fight, day and night. The German Army, though extended to the limit, is still a most formidable military organization. Their first-line troops are still the equal of any in skill and fanatical bravery. . . .

Any hope for an early defeat of Germany must depend upon the collapse of the Army due to shortage of fighting equipment, or to a break-down of civilian morale and revolution within. They are taking a terrific pounding by day and by night from our gallant airmen and the R.A.F. [Royal Air Force]. We will soon be in a position to increase substantially the bombing of Germany from bases in Italy as well as from England, and the number of German factories destroyed and families driven from their homes will greatly increase.

But all of this is not done without losses to us. The Germans have turned from the production of bombers to fighter planes in the effort to stop the destruction of their homeland from the air. They are devising new methods such as the rocket guns and small parachute bombs dropped from the air in the effort to destroy our air forces. While our military authorities say the price we are paying is not excessive in comparison with the destruction our air forces are causing, we must frankly face the fact that the increasing tempo of bombing likewise brings about increasingly severe losses of our own in men and equipment.

In the Pacific we have only whipped the Japanese in the outposts of their ill-gotten empire. The bulk of their Army and the major units of their Navy have not yet been brought into action. We have a long, hard, bloody job before us, and I fear that the sacrifices, shocks, and losses we must yet endure are much greater than the average American citizen anticipates. . . .

Mr. President, what I have said is the record, as complete as I can make it, of my remarks in the executive session of the Senate on October 7. It has not been altered materially in either form or substance. I tried to be factual, and to speak as objectively as possible. . . .

Every patriotic American expects our country to do its full part in this war, but I do not believe that doing our part requires us so to keep our light under a bushel that, where permitted to think, we are expected to speak in whispers of the contribution of our own country to the cause of Allied victory.

I therefore am not greatly disturbed by that portion of the American press or officialdom which sees ghosts every time any person in American public life has the temerity to suggest that it is proper for our allies to appreciate the extent of our efforts and sacrifices in this war as we appreciate their efforts and sacrifices. We have come to a pretty pass if a citizen of the United States cannot support with wholehearted devotion the cause of his own country without subjecting himself to the charge that he is anti-British or anti-Russian. . . .

I yield to no one in the fervor of my desire for the closest unity between the Allied Nations to achieve the victory over our common enemies. I am as anxious as any man for the United States to cooperate with Russia, England, China, and the other Allied Powers in maintaining peace in the years to follow that victory. I believe that any lasting world peace must have as its keystone a complete understanding between the United States and the British Empire. But, Mr.

President, this cooperation and understanding cannot be had except upon a basis of equality and frank and fair dealings.

Frank discussion will always dissipate the clouds of suspicion. It will promote a better understanding between all the Allied Nations in the trying days ahead of us after the victory is won. It will pave the way for the necessary sense of appreciation of sacrifices in a common cause which begets good will between peoples. On such good will and understanding any permanent peace for this stricken world must depend.

University of Georgia Alumni
13 June 1946

The United States and its allies celebrated victory in Europe on 7 May 1945, and over Japan on 14 August 1945. The newly-created United Nations convened its first session in London on 10 January 1946. It was in this setting that Senator Russell gave the address below to graduates of the University of Georgia.[9] During this postwar reunion, seventeen former classes of the University paraded to the Chapel on campus where Marion Smith, Class of 1903 and Chair of the Board of Regents of Georgia, introduced Russell.

After praising the nation's mobilization for World War II, the Senator insisted that its strong military defense be maintained. Desiring a "permanent peace," he opposed isolationism, warning that nations must learn to live together or "die together in an atomic war."

In defining the proper province of labor in society, Russell warned against "monopolies in any form." The following year, the United States Congress passed the Taft-Hartley Bill, legislation Russell said guarded the rights of American workers while requiring persons under contract to meet their legal responsibilities.

* * * * * * * * * *

I am deeply grateful for the compliment paid me by the invitation to speak to you today. It has been my invariable experience that to accept an invitation to speak while the Congress is in session is a sure way to bring up for disposition legislative matters of transcendent importance. Today is no exception to the rule. I had great difficulty in getting a pair in the Senate on the important measure now under consideration.

However, I have not been privileged to meet with the Alumni Society since the year 1928, and I made up my mind to come back

---

[9]Text of speech from Speech File, Speech and Media Series, Richard B. Russell Collection, RRLPRS.

to the campus for this meeting today without worrying about legislative matters. After all, the Senate and the Government of the United States got along without me pretty well for about 150 years, and I am sure that it will endure for many centuries after I have departed the halls of Congress. This is the first meeting of the Alumni Society since the end of World War II. Our university has gone through six of our country's wars—the War of 1812, the War with Mexico, the War between the States, the Spanish-American War, World War I, and the greatest of all wars—World War II.

This institution has grown and expanded with our State and nation, and more of the sons and daughters of old Georgia participated in World War II than in any of the other conflicts. More of them gave their lives in their country's service. As we meet here today, it is but fitting that we should pay tribute to those from this institution who played well their part in every theater of war and on each of the Seven Seas where armed forces of our country were deployed against our aggressors. The sentiment in every heart is "tears for those who made the supreme sacrifice and will not return—cheers and all honor to those who were spared and came back to us."

We may take great pride not only in the heroic service of our fellow alumni, but in the wholehearted devotion with which this institution was dedicated to the war effort. Its staff and all of its facilities were unstintingly placed at the disposal of the War and Navy Departments, and the official records at Washington disclose the notable contribution made by our Alma Mater. Dr. S. V. Sanford [President, University of Georgia]—peace to his ashes—spent many long hours in Washington and undoubtedly hastened his passing by his efforts to utilize to the fullest degree everything that this institution had to offer in the mobilization and training of the vast citizen Army and Navy which won the war.

It is likewise gratifying to know, now that the war is ended, that the greater part of the student body, which overtaxes the capacity of this school, is composed of veterans who are now undertaking to make up for the time spent in their country's service. All of these things add to the glory of the institution that we love and affectionately hail as Alma Mater.

Americans are not a militaristic people, and we have never maintained considerable military forces in time of peace. As before, the outbreak of war found us unprepared. I shall not deal with the miraculous achievement of a free people in organizing the finest army and navy in the world and forging the weapons of war, not only for ourselves but for our allies. Suffice it to say that our civilian armies, composed of men who had been taunted as too soft and too spoiled to fight, proved themselves the superiors of the professional soldiers of the Axis powers. The foul attack at Pearl Harbor unified our people as one, and enabled us to again crush our enemies in battle.

VJ [Victory over Japan] Day brought World War II to an end. We are now engaged in the great struggle to build the machinery for a permanent peace.

The most costly and oft-repeated mistake of mankind is the erroneous idea that victory in war brings peace. Since the earliest days of recorded history, men have gone forth to die in battle in the mistaken belief that by overcoming an enemy on the field of battle he could assure peace in his time and spare his children the horrors of war. Until now mankind has never learned the oft-told lesson of history that peace cannot be assured merely by winning a war.

The men of my generation won a war in 1918, and thought that thereby we had brought about permanent peace. Again history showed that permanent peace cannot be assured by crushing the aggressor of the hour. Within a quarter of a century three times as many young Americans as were called in 1917-18 were compelled to leave their homes to save our common country and our cherished institutions.

Victory brings a cessation of hostilities. It may destroy some dictator and his scheme of world domination which threatens mankind everywhere. Victory in battle may put down the forces of aggression for the time being, but it has never secured the establishment of permanent peace. The yearning for peace in the hearts and minds of the people of the earth are always infinitely greater just after the sacrifices of war. The human tendency to forget in periods of armistice [what] we have experienced between wars has heretofore lulled people into a false sense of security. It has caused them to refrain from making the sacrifices necessary to assure a permanent peace.

Those who gave their all, and all those who sacrificed in any degree in the greatest of all world conflicts from which we have just emerged, suffered that their loved ones and their fellow countrymen might enjoy the blessings of peace. They had before them the ideal of the right of all men everywhere to enjoy the blessings of freedom, to stand upright without fear, to live and to work and to strive to succeed, and to hold such views on religion and government as they might choose in a blessed atmosphere of permanent peace.

Despite the yearning for peace in the hearts of the common men everywhere, we are confronted with the bald fact that the obstacles and the difficulties in the way of a complete world understanding to bring about peace and freedom are greater than they were even in 1918. It is little wonder that the faint-hearted are discouraged. However, the danger which menaces civilization is so great that we must resolve to contribute as patriotically and as unselfishly to the peace offensive as did the men who stormed the beaches of Normandy and Iwo Jima. There must be some way, somehow, to bring into reality that day of permanent peace for which people everywhere in the world are praying and hoping. We must not become discouraged or deterred from our sacred purpose. We must realize each and every day that our duty to labor for peace was not relieved by the surrender in the red school house at Reims or on the decks of the battleship *Missouri*.

As civilization has progressed through the years, each generation has evolved weapons of increasing destruction. World War II was not only the bloodiest and most destructive war that the world has yet seen, but it ushered in the atomic age. The sacrifices of those who fell should have been a sufficient challenge to the world to create a system of settling disputes without war. It had not done so in the past. Even the great destruction of this war might not have sufficed to bring about world sanity if the bomb which fell on Hiroshima had not posed so dire a threat to world survival.

As a member of the Special Committee on Atomic Energy, I sat through several weeks of hearings on matters related to this lethal weapon. As I listened to the scientists describe the bombs of Nagasaki and Hiroshima as being near the bow-and-arrow stage as compared with the possibilities of future bombs, I could not escape the feeling that I was living in another world. If men resort to war again in the age of the development of planes and rockets and atomic bombs, the war will be over in a matter of hours, and the casualty list will be so great that the few survivors will probably never compile it. The human family is faced with the grim necessity of learning how to live together in peace or of preparing to die together in an atomic war.

Isolationism is all but dead in this country. It is our duty to see that it is not revived. The clearly established foreign policy of the United States is to meet all of the other nations of the earth more than halfway in reaching agreements for a just peace and for the settlement of future disagreements which may arise without resort to war.

We are not an imperialistic people, and in the very nature of our institutions we will never be an aggressor against other nations. Our representatives have gone into every conference of nations with clean hands and no cards up their sleeves. We not only contributed to all of our allies during the war, but are today making enormous loans and expending large sums of money in the effort to prevent world suffering and to restore the ravages of war.

We have acceded to every reasonable demand of our great Russian ally for security. Some of the concessions that we have made hardly seem justified, but in our effort to allay all suspicion and to give evidence of our good faith we made them. Despite all our concessions the victors have not been able to agree upon a peace treaty with Germany, Italy, and Japan, and the wheels of the United Nations have been stalled by the use of the veto power in every matter involving Russia.

It is difficult in our fair land of freedom to understand why there should be any great trouble in men of sound sense and good will getting together and building an enduring structure of peace. During the war we clothed all of the allied nations with the cloak of democracy, and made the issue a war between democracy and dictatorship. In war phraseology, the dictatorship of the communists in Russia and the dictatorship of Chiang Kai-shek in China were lumped together as democracies. Our admiration for the fighting prowess of the Russians and the capacity for resistance displayed by the Chinese was great. We fostered the myth that these dictatorships were all democracies under the skin with us and the British.

If we are to make a frank approach to the problems before us, we must now admit that the wartime honeymoon of these dictatorships with American and British democracy was a marriage of convenience. We will never successfully deal with the problem of world peace if we do not pull our heads out of the sand and face conditions as they really exist.

The efforts of the representatives of our government to build an enduring structure of world peace are in the very nature of things difficult enough. Their strivings to maintain the supremacy of man in the context with Statism and to work out a fair peace are certainly not made any easier by the self-styled super-liberals in this country who defend and plausibly explain every demand of the Russians, whether in the Balkans, in Korea, or in North Africa, while parroting *Pravda* and Moscow Radio with the patent falsehood that our government is imperialistic in its designs.

I have no quarrel with communism in Russia if that be the form of government the Russians desire. I do have an unspeakable contempt for the fellow travelers in this country who seek to poison the minds of the unthinking by their subtle attacks on the men of good will in positions of responsibility in our government whose only aim is an enduring peace. These fellow travelers have adopted the primary propaganda principle of all those who have hated democracy in recent history that if you will get up a big enough falsehood and reiterate it loudly and often enough the masses of the people will eventually accept it as truth.

There is no difference of opinion expressed in Russia over the views of the communist government on any international question. There are many sound reasons for this apparent unanimity of opinion. In this country, freedom of speech is being sorely abused. One group is openly communistic, and in a recent meeting in Madison Square Garden urged their sympathizers and fellow travelers to encourage strikes in every section of the United States, to seek to prevent amicable adjustment of any labor dispute, and to try in every possible way to disrupt our economy in the critical reconversion period. To their credit, be it said that this group boldly wears the badge of communism and openly advocates measures to destroy our form of government. They are not as dangerous as the group that denies the communistic label, and who subtly work under cover.

There has been seen in the halls of Congress the amazing spectacle of representatives elected by the American people denouncing our country as being imperialistic while finding excuses for Russian policies. Within the past few weeks employees of the Federal Government met in Atlantic City and organized a union. They proceeded to pass resolutions denouncing the United States and Great Britain for not immediately removing troops from various war sections. One delegate offered a motion to include a denunciation of Russia for the same reason. He was howled down and the original resolution was adopted.

This same union adopted a constitution which in effect asserts the right to strike against the Federal Government. Without exception every President of the United States has stated that there is no such thing as a right to strike against the Government. This is true for the very simple reason that a government which can be strike-bound is not a government at all.

There is such a thing as abuse of freedom of speech, and the spectacle of Government employees evincing their allegiance to a foreign nation while on the payroll of the United States comes in that category. I believe that there are enough loyal American citizens to fill every position in our Government, and that the time is at hand when this issue must be determined once and for all.

Those of our citizens who have the onerous duty of devising and defending our foreign policy are of course properly subject to criticism in a free State, but they should be spared attacks in the back by employees of their Government on such wild and unfounded charges while carrying on their negotiations.

The Russian press and radio seek to capitalize on these attacks. The teeming millions who live within the "iron curtain" have no other source of news, and they of course assume that these attacks upon

American foreign policy represent a large measure of public opinion in the United States, and that instead of pursuing a policy of altruism we are engaging in a grab game and imposing upon the rights of the weak.

Every loyal American citizen, while reserving the right of constructive criticism, will support the efforts of our Government to bring about a United Nations organization upon which both the weak nations and the strong may rely for equal justice.

Unfortunate though it may be, power is still the dominant factor in world politics. The voice of our representatives who are engaged in critical international negotiations will soon be muted if we pursue a policy of demobilization and disarmament which renders us impotent as a military power. Neither can we discharge our obligations to the United Nations without maintaining a strong military establishment.

Military service in time of peace is not attractive to the average American. However, thousands have died to win the victory. It is unthinkable that any considerable number of our young men should be unwilling to do their part after the dangers of battle are past to contribute to making secure the peace. Permanent peace is the most priceless gift which could be bestowed upon the world, and it cannot be achieved without some sacrifice.

It is all too evident now that permanent peace cannot be secured by mere platitudes nor written formula. The United Nations must be given the strength and virility which will enable it to function in the cause of peace. This will be hard and tedious work. We must exhaust every possibility to come to an understanding with Russia. Without it we cannot be assured of peace. There is no danger of a war in five years, or probably ten, but unless all of the peoples of the earth accept in good faith the structure of international accord which we are seeking to build through United Nations, we will plant the seeds of another war which will bear awesome fruit in the next generation.

Our relations with our allies as we seek agreement must be maintained with the dignity befitting our position as a great nation. We must strive for tolerance and understanding of the viewpoint of others. This does not mean appeasement and surrender, for we have learned through sad experience that this will not work. Conditions do not justify military alliances with any one or two nations. Such a step would be sure to confirm the ill-founded suspicions which now divide us. We must depend upon the consuming desire for peace which is universally a part of human sentiments and instincts in all countries, and by seeking to appeal to that sentiment, and dealing with patience and firmness and with infinite labor, we will not fail.

The most important contribution which can be made by the average man is to present the same unity of purpose in the fight for peace which made us invincible in time of war. Unity of purpose and an unselfish desire for peace on the part of all the free peoples of the earth will eventually make itself felt even through the so-called "iron curtain." Such a spirit of solidarity, stemming from the hearts of all free men, will eventually prevail over an apparent solidarity imposed upon the many through fear of the ruthless power of a few men.

We are far from that unity today. Unrest and confusion always follow in the wake of war. It is not surprising that there is so much confusion in our country today, now that we have found momentary release from the common danger which cemented us together during the war.

If we are to properly support the efforts of our country to bring sanity and agreement to the international front, we must eliminate the internal strife which plagues us today. Production was the key to victory in the war. Reconversion and production are today the key to victory in the fight for permanent peace. We must forego the fight for personal and selfish vantage to forge the weapons for peace.

Our representatives at international conferences hear the confusion of voices and the din of strife at home, with men offering old panaceas which have failed and new definitions which fit their purposes. In recent weeks there has been much discussion of a proper definition of modern liberalism, and as to what constitutes a political liberal. This debate has brought forth some strange concepts. There are those in public life who take the position that to be a true liberal one must advocate revealing all of the secrets of atomic energy to all the world before having any agreement through the United Nations denying the use of atomic energy for destructive purposes or any provision for inspection to see that no nation seeks to take advantage of others by preparing for atomic warfare. In this group are usually found those who take the position that every demand made by Russia in international affairs is always right, and that the United States is an imperialistic power for opposing Russian policies anywhere in the world.

Such people usually undertake to prove their liberalism in domestic affairs by proclaiming that they have never voted for any bill which organized labor opposed or against any bill which organized labor advocated. I do not accept this definition of liberalism. I refuse to let people belonging to that school of thought define liberalism for me. By their standards I would be a reactionary.

The American people demand liberal policies on the part of their Government. Such policies are necessary to make us strong at home and respected abroad. However, in our quest for international understanding, the great masses of our people expect reciprocity from the other nations of the earth, and demand that they be protected from any threat of aggression from any source until the United Nations is generally accepted and clothed with the authority and power to assure world peace.

To make our nation strong at home, the true liberal believes in the greatest measure of individual freedom for each man within his own sphere, so long as he does not impinge on the rights of another individual or threaten the welfare of the whole. A true liberal believes in equal rights to all. That means equality before the law and equality of opportunity for all of our people. It does not mean that you can equalize the wealth of the country by dividing it up at stated intervals. God created men with different aims in life. He did not create them as exact equals in talents, in ability, or in degree of ambition.

Government administered by men can and should work for equality of opportunity and for those measures of security which do not require the surrender of freedom. But it can never completely equalize the lives of all of the people of the state without total regimentation and the destruction of all individual liberties.

Under my conception of liberalism, the state cannot tolerate monopoly in any form. This is true because monopoly is the natural enemy of individual freedom and the free state. A democracy cannot tolerate a political monopoly whereby a few men impose their will upon the many. We have long waged war with economic monopoly, the great combines in finance which have denied individuals an opportunity to improve their lots in life and threatened control of the free government of the majority.

Within the past few months our government, and indeed the very lives of our people, have been threatened by strikes against the government. This is a form of monopoly. It has focused the attention of the people upon the importance of fair and just legislation which will place upon organized labor a responsibility toward the public interest in some manner commensurate with its present position of power. This legislation should not and must not deny the right of labor to strike in ordinary circumstances, or the right to organize into unions of their own choice, or to collective bargaining. It should in no way hinder or discourage the age-old aspiration of the toiler to a higher standard of living and the better things of life. But on the fundamental principle that no single group of men can assume a power which threatens the government formed to protect the public interest and to protect the welfare of all the people, labor must recognize that the public interest and the welfare of all is paramount to the rights of any group.

An arrogant labor leader can be as dangerous to the life and health of the American people as an arrogant captain of finance. Both must recognize that they possess no right which is not subordinate to the Government which protects them.

I am sustained by the profound conviction that the sound common sense of the majority of the American people will make the proper verdict on the many perplexing questions which confront us. I believe that we will work our way out of this welter of confusion to a higher ground than that which we have known. We will not seek to attain unity by crushing one group for the benefit of another, but by holding firm not only to the form but the spirit of democracy.

I have an abiding faith that the men and women who have passed through these classic halls and who constitute the membership of the Alumni Society will be found in the forefront of the fight against tyranny in any form, either at home or abroad. We will not succeed in securing universal acceptance of the principles of the United Nations organization merely by damning communism or totalitarianism in any form. We can only achieve that end by making democracy work in these United States as a lesson to the world. We will not make democracy work in these United States merely by damning either capital or labor or any other segment. We can only make democracy work by practicing it in our daily lives and taking the time and the trouble to measure up to the responsibilities of citizenship in this great republic.

American Legion Convention
15 October 1951

On 25 June 1950, less than four years after the end of World War II, troops in North Korea invaded South Korea. To prevent what he perceived to be the Soviet Union's domination of Asia, President Harry S. Truman sent United States military personnel to help defend South Korea. Senator Russell gave this address to more than 5,000 delegates to the thirty-third Annual American Legion Convention in Miami, Florida.[10] The President of that national organization was Erle Cocke, Jr., a Georgian and friend of Russell. In this speech, the senator praised the American Legion for their loyal duty to country; he described how their "comrades" once again were called to a "trial of death"—this time in Korea. The Senator depicted the fight as one between "freedom and slavery." Lamenting that the United States had not remained adequately prepared to defend its interest in the world, he asked citizens to sacrifice to defeat the "blanket of tyranny."

* * * * * * * * * *

Mr. Commander, my Comrades of the American Legion, Ladies of the Auxiliary, Ladies and Gentlemen:
It is a high privilege to address this gathering.
It is likewise a source of profound *personal* pleasure to have this opportunity to pay a public tribute to Commander Erle Cocke.
As a fellow *Georgian*, I was naturally gratified by his election as National Commander of the American Legion. As a fellow *American*, my gratification swelled into pride—great pride—at the magnificent manner in which he has conducted himself during his administration.
His sterling patriotism—his energy—his ability—have carried the voice of the Legion—the voice of Americanism—throughout our

---

[10]Text of speech from Speech File, Speech and Media Series, Richard B. Russell Collection, RRLPRS.

American Legion Convention

land. He has exemplified nobly the high ideals of one of the great organizations of our nation. The Legion is proud and the nation is proud of his record of service.

In an organization dedicated to loyal and devoted service of country it is natural that such men must arise to the top. The Commanders of the Legion have traditionally been men whose lives are marked by public service—"service to the community; service to the nation." They have well reflected the spirit that has held the Legion together during the span of its existence.

The American Legion is composed of men who did not shed their desire to serve their country when they doffed their uniforms. They have one common bond—wartime duty in the Armed Forces of the United States. Together with the members of the Auxiliary, they have one common goal—the preservation of this nation and its institutions.

Ladies and Gentlemen, I salute you. You represent an organization trying to advance no special interest except the interest of patriotism. Your objectives are above sectionalism; above self-seeking "pressure" groups; above the internal hatreds that threaten our country.

In these perilous days, you are a bulwark of strength—a beacon of Americanism seeking to guide these United States through the reefs and shoals of internal subversion and external aggression.

It is for this reason that I speak to you tonight of the critical problems that confront our nation.

In past years, these conventions have been held in an atmosphere of joy and merriment. Old friendships have been renewed amidst nostalgic reminiscences of Paris, London, Hawaii, Melbourne and the other places that held a fleeting respite from the horrors of war.

This year, there will still be the joy—the merriment—the reminiscences. Gloom and dark melancholy have never been characteristics of the American people. Nor should it be otherwise.

But underlying the celebrations, the revivals of old friendships, the gaiety—will be the grim realization that in another land Americans are gathered for a far different purpose.

These young Americans—many of them your comrades in arms of a previous war—are assembling at this hour for a trial of death. As we discuss the problems of a nation's survival, they are confronted with the grim problem of individual survival. As we pledge our loyalty in words and declarations, they are pledging their loyalty in blood and agony.

It is many a mile from here to Korea but nothing we do—nothing we say—can take us very far from those men. We are bound to them by the strongest tie that can cement mankind—the gratitude of a free people towards those who have sacrificed to preserve our free institutions.

In the darkest hours of this nation's travail of birth, Tom Paine wrote the ringing declaration, "These are the times that try men's souls." With the independence that followed *that* victory at Yorktown, Paine declared: "The times that try men's souls are over."

Unfortunately, there have been few generations of Americans who have escaped this trial. The men who are crouching in foxholes tonight—who count an hour of sleep as a vacation and a can of C-ration as a banquet—are now going through trial by fire.

Although we are far from the battlelines—separated by an ocean and a continent from the horrors of blood and slaughter—we too are on trial. We at home must make the decisions that will determine whether those who have fought and died in Korea—those who have served in other times of danger—have fought and died in vain.

The problem before us can be stated simply. The differences between freedom and slavery—between God and Godlessness—are crystal clear. We are confronted with a powerful but degrading force which seeks to enslave all mankind. This sinister menace has already succeeded in subjecting vast areas of the earth to its totalitarian rule and is reaching out ever further in its plot to subvert human liberties.

It is the greatest worldwide conspiracy against the basic dignity and freedom of man known to human history.

Only the United States possesses the strength—the power—the resources, to stand firm before the threat of global subversion. Only our strength can inspire other free nations—some of whom sleep at

American Legion Convention

the very feet of the bear—all tired by wars and threats of wars—to make the effort necessary for their own survival.

In such a situation—we as Americans have only one choice. We cannot fail to rise to the ringing challenge that comes down to us from the sacrifices of the myriads who have fought for freedom in the past.

We, as American citizens, must steel ourselves to make the sacrifices which are necessary to defeat the forces of darkness and evil.

We, as American citizens, must be ready to pledge our all to guarantee the survival of our civilization and its institutions.

We cannot—we must not—ignore the centuries that man has struggled towards freedom and dignity and permit the earth to be enveloped in darkness.

A year ago there was real cause to question our ability to meet the danger. Patriotic men asked themselves: "Even if we make the sacrifices—is there time?" It was a fateful question. It can be said that it was a time when our nation was weak—weak not in spirit, but in armies, ships, planes and the weapons of war.

We had failed to heed the lessons of our own history. Ignoring the warnings of the American Legion and other patriotic and farseeing groups in our country, we had dissipated our military might. Our strength was a little more than a shadow of the magnificent fighting machine we started dismantling in 1945. We had again *suffered* the delusion that peace was to be found on the bargain counter. We were to learn again that there is no such thing as cheap national security.

The outbreak of Communist aggression in Korea in June of 1950 sharply underlined our mistakes. We awakened overnight to the realities of this decade—a decade in which only America—and a then woefully unprepared America—stood between the free world and slavery. We are paying a price for that mistake—paying it in waste—in suffering and in blood

History will undoubtedly record that only two things provided us with the time to correct our costly errors. They were our ability to deliver a stockpile of atomic bombs anywhere in the world and the fighting hearts of the gallant little group of American soldiers and marines we were able to land on the peninsula of Korea.

Upon those relatively slender threads hung the fate of all mankind.

In the year and more since the outbreak of fighting in Korea, we have come far. We have almost tripled our Army and more than doubled our Navy and Air Force.

We have not completely solved our problem of a trained citizen reserve adequate for any emergency. We have made a long stride forward. With the stout help of the American Legion, we have built the framework for a system of Universal Military Training. In January we must complete the job. Universal Military Training and an effective reserve force of citizen soldiers is the keystone in the arch of our future defense. To attempt any other method of military preparedness over long years of tensions will be disastrous to the national economy.

We have maintained our atomic superiority and propose to increase it.

We have taken the ships of World War II from mothballs and placed them in modern fighting trim.

We have approved greater forces for General [Dwight D.] Eisenhower in Europe and aided and inspired our allies to strengthen their armies.

We have appropriated the staggering sum of 137 billion dollars for our defense, including the production of atomic weapons.

Although we have gone far, we still have far to go. Our stockpile of strategic materials is far from satisfactory. Many of our weapons—including practically all of the "fantastic" new armaments we have heard so much about lately—are still in the pilot stage or on the drawing board.

Nevertheless, it is my considered opinion that the United States today is in a position to guarantee its own survival. I do not mean that we have reached a stage of total security. Such does not exist. But I do mean that once again we can take our destiny into our own hands.

That is a blessed state. In this world of fears and conflict there are few nations that can claim to be the masters of their own fate. We are able to stand unafraid and squarely face the threat of militant world communism, even though it be armed to the teeth.

This is a precious gift that we must not *treat* lightly—must not *lose* through indifference—must not *dissipate* through cowardice or irresolution. The United States holds the most *priceless* of all freedoms—freedom of choice. If we throw it away, the blanket of tyranny will smother the fires of liberty. They will not burn again for centuries.

The American people have been deeply troubled by the course of our fight against the menace of communism. There is no doubt that the course we have pursued and are pursuing in Korea has served its purpose. There is no doubt that the sacrifices of our fighting men have brought us precious time to rearm. And—finally—this action, following on the heels of Greece and the Berlin airlift, gave earnest to the whole world that we would match our words with deeds.

The American people are patient and long persevering in their quest for peace. But that patience is not without limit. We will not indefinitely play as bloody a game as Korea under rules that limit the use of *all* our strength.

We hate war, but once involved, from Bunker Hill to Okinawa, we have fought to win.

For almost four months, there has been *talk* of the meetings seeking an agreement to end the Korean conflict. In good faith we *have* met our adversary with complete willingness to terminate the fighting on any honorable terms.

Whatever be his real purpose, the enemy has until now shown more of a disposition to manufacture propaganda than to end the war.

The American people are tired of deceit, of subterfuge, of trickery and of knavery. The American people are tired of *words* of peace and *deeds* of treachery. The American people are tired of double-talk negotiations which can be indefinitely prolonged to permit the enemy to resolve internal difficulties or to build up his strength.

If it becomes manifest that talk is merely a cloak for treachery, the American people will demand the application of other methods and new measures to bring the Korean struggle to a conclusion.

In a larger sense, the life and death struggle between the slave world and the free cannot be terminated at Kaesong. The aggression in Korea is but an incident in the communist blueprint for world conquest. At practically every point on the rimland of communism there are powder kegs—powder kegs whose fuses reach back to Moscow. Up to this moment the master plotters in the Kremlin have set off two of them—Korea and Indo-China. At a stroke they can touch off Iran or Yugoslavia or elsewhere. These master plotters think to sit safely in the Kremlin while they exhaust us with fighting their unthinking slaves. They would protect the citadels of communism while callously sacrificing the hovels of its puppets.

The enemy seeks to place us in the position of firemen dashing madly about the city in frantic efforts to quench innumerable fires started by a nimble arsonist. Let the scheming arsonist beware. The free world well knows the lair of its chief enemy. It is not deceived. We will not be bled to a slow death through the manipulation of satellites and slaves. If he continues this course, one of the fires will get out of hand and consume the home of the arsonist. When he overreaches himself the principal arsonist will be brought to book.

Let not the aggressor misinterpret our desire for peace as weakness. Let him not mistake our patience as irresoluteness. Let not the aggressor err in thinking our desire to rebuild the shattered world is due to cowardice or lack of faith in ourselves.

Our paramount goal is world peace—peace in which mankind everywhere can prosper and grow strong. We do not want war—even though we are strong and free—we do not want to impose our will upon any other people. But we are a proud breed. When attacked, we are a *fighting* breed, a people who carried our flag from Berlin to Tokyo—who have never seen that banner trail in defeat.

Faced with a foe who recognizes no argument except strength, war is not inevitable. We may find through strength the way to peace. If we can marshal overwhelming might, the enemy will not risk total destruction. But if we become careless or irresolute, or tire in our efforts, war—total war—is certain to come.

We are far from that ideal state of preparedness which would appeal to the prudent. We have far to go in building our Army, our Navy and our Air Force against the day of further aggression. We have many problems to conquer, including that of traitors in our midst who prefer an alien flag—an alien ideology—to our own.

We must be ready if the day of final reckoning is to come—as it will come with certainty if the aggressor continues in his aggression. But if that day is to come, we will meet it as befits our heritage.

The tyrants in the Kremlin have it within their hands to pursue a course which will plunge the world into war. Confident in our strength, we know that it will be a war that they could never win and which would bring them to ultimate destruction.

Let us not weary in pursing the path to adequate preparedness. It is the only hope of peace—it is the only road to security—the only means of preserving our institutions.

Ladies and Gentlemen, these are times of peril—of trial, tribulation and sacrifice. As free men we must freely elect to follow the course of salvation and victory. I know the spirit of the Legion. I know that you will not fail. I know that America will not fail in the supreme hour of decision.

Douglas Chamber of Commerce
8 December 1959

Senator Russell gave this speech to a large crowd at a Douglas, Georgia, Chamber of Commerce dinner.[11] Because of the continuing Cold War with the Soviet Union, he advised maintaining a strong military capability. Responding to the Soviet Union's successful launching of a satellite, Sputnik I, the Senator stressed the importance of developing "futuristic weapons."[12] At the same time, Russell observed that "tensions" between the United States and "Russia" were easing. With considerable candor, he explained the "juvenile jealousy" among branches of the military, the problem of getting "objective advice" when choosing "weapon systems," and the degree of education required to operate modern instruments of war. The text was marked, "excerpts for Douglas speech."

* * * * * * * * * *

Almost from the end of World War II, our nation and the Free World have lived under the threatening clouds of a cold war brought about by the aggressive designs of international communism.

Our people believed that after V-J [Victory over Japan] Day, we would enter a bright and promising new era of world peace and international understanding. Accordingly, we began dismantling the great war machine that had smashed the Axis powers in the most devastating war in history.

But the dream of a genuine and lasting peace was illusionary. It became apparent almost immediately that our wartime Russian allies had no intention of disarming and of becoming a peaceful member of the family of nations.

---

[11]Text of speech from Speech File, Speech and Media Series, Richard B. Russell Collection, RRLPRS.
[12]*Douglas Enterprise*, December 10, 1959.

On the contrary, [Joseph] Stalin [of the Soviet Union] merely took up where Hitler had left off. Though his methods were somewhat different, his goal was the same—the domination and enslavement of free men the world over.

The grave danger posed by international communism was not lost on the American people. They met the challenge.

As they have always done in times of clearly seen national danger, the American people willingly made the sacrifices necessary to support a military establishment adequate for our national security and survival against the communist threat.

Today, and continuously since Korea, there has been a broad public understanding of the crucial importance of maintaining the numerical strength of the Armed Forces and of equipping them with the advanced weapons of modern warfare.

Such a defense effort, of course, is extremely costly. It is hardly necessary to state that the defense budget alone amounts to roughly half of all Federal expenditures. This does not include foreign aid or the cost of the atomic energy program.

In the long run, however, it is less expensive to maintain a fairly constant defense effort, as we are now doing, even though the cost is measured in many billions of dollars.

It would be far more costly to follow the unrealistic famine or feast program of reducing expenditures in times of momentary calm and embarking on crash spending programs when a crisis looms.

Within the past few months, we have seen a few hopeful signs that relations are improving between the United States and Russia and that world tensions are easing.

This cautious optimism has been inspired by the peaceful-sounding tones of Premier [Nikita] Khrushchev and stepped up diplomatic activity between the East and West.

Our own President [Dwight D. Eisenhower] is now engaged in an unprecedented international tour in an attempt to convince the peoples of the world of the peaceful intent of the American nation. All our hopes and prayers go with the President in his arduous undertaking.

But we must not permit ourselves to bask in the false sun of complacency.

Until Khrushchev proves his words of peace with deeds of peace it would be foolhardy to relax our military preparedness.

The dedicated communists speak in many tongues. But they respect only strength and power. It would be suicidal for this nation and our Western allies to undertake to deal with our avowed enemies on any basis other than strength and power.

The maintenance of an adequate defense force, therefore, remains the first order of business for the American people. Indeed, it is the first order for survival.

Since the national security demands continued high-level defense spending, a heavy responsibility rests on the Executive Branch of the Government and upon the Congress to make those expenditures count.

The American taxpayer, who must foot the bill for our defense program, does not expect to buy security at bargain-basement prices. But he has every right to expect—indeed, to demand—that his defense tax dollars are being spent as wisely and efficiently as possible.

I am one of those who has been highly critical of the petty rivalry and juvenile jealousy among the different branches of the Armed Forces. As Chairman of the Senate Armed Services Committee, I have undertaken as best I could to put an end to foolish competition and senseless duplication of effort by the services.

Some observers believe these problems are symptomatic of a faulty defense organization. They maintain that the only way to avoid dissension and rivalry is to abolish the separate services and combine all our defense components into a single department.

I do not believe the answer is as simple as that. Even if the Army, Navy, and Air Force were combined into one service, there would still be competition among parts of the organization discharging different functions under different names.

Under our present law, the power and authority of the Secretary of Defense over the separate Armed Forces is unquestionable.

Until the Secretary has fully utilized all the authority now at his command to compel a higher degree of inter-service cooperation and teamwork, I am unconvinced that the existing organization of the Defense Department should be uprooted.

Civilian control over the military is a long-honored and accepted principle of our government. It was, in fact, written into our Constitution by the Founding Fathers.

Our professional military leaders have shown no inclination to disagree with the propriety or wisdom of that principle. In fact, all the evidence indicates that they approve of it.

But our professional military leaders and the country as a whole have a right to expect competent civilian direction of the defense establishment.

One of the great handicaps to competent civilian direction of our military efforts has been the excessive turnover of civilian secretaries and assistant secretaries within the Defense Department.

Since the present Administration came to power less than seven years ago, there have been three different secretaries of defense. The most recent incumbent of that tremendously important office took over only last week to serve for a little more than a year. Changes in other civilian officials in the Pentagon have been too numerous to mention.

The Department of Defense has become so large and complex, and the decisions so critical, that persons of even a brilliant intellect cannot make informed judgments without on-the-job experience.

There are, unquestionably, many civilian leaders in the military establishment who are there to fulfill an unselfish duty to their country. They are men of high caliber and unassailable patriotism.

But, unfortunately, there have been other civilian officials who have served short periods in these jobs because the title is impressive or because the office affords a considerable amount of prestige. Many assistant secretaries and under secretaries have served for relatively brief periods—enough to get the distinction in their obituaries but not long enough to acquaint themselves with the duties of their office.

The direction of our defense effort is a grimly serious business. It requires dedication, experience, and ability far above and beyond the call of duty.

Unless responsible civilian officials are dedicated and give the government service after they have learned their jobs, their decision-making function passes by default to the professional military men. Whether or not anybody likes it, that is the inevitable result.

The staggering complexity of the military establishment and the development of highly technical new weapons imposes a great responsibility on members of Congress who must provide the funds for the defense program. The compression of time and distance by missiles, aircraft of supersonic speeds, and electronics requires decisions based as much on scientific competence as on traditional concepts of military doctrine.

It is becoming increasingly difficult to obtain objective advice when a decision must be made between competing claims for appropriations by advocates of different types of weapon systems. Most of the persons familiar with these advanced weapons are identified with a military department, or a contractor advocating one of these at the expense of another.

Not only are weapons themselves becoming more scientifically complex, but so are the skills that are needed to man the weapons of modern warfare.

Throughout most of our history, an eager young person with a high school education or less could be trained to become a thoroughly competent soldier, sailor or airman. But missiles and electronic equipment now being developed virtually require the services of holders of graduate science degrees to man them.

The Atlas inter-continental missile, for example, is so complex that it almost takes a team of college professors to fire it. And even they frequently fail to get the rocket off its launching pad into flight.

There seems to be little doubt that today we are lagging behind the Soviets in our missile and space program. This has terrifying implications for the safety and security of our nation.

To spur our lagging efforts, we sorely need what the scientists call a "quantum jump." In layman language, this simply means that we may have to skip some phases of the conventional step-by-step development on weapons systems. Instead, we should focus our efforts on developing futuristic weapons that will provide a striking breakthrough rather than devoting great amounts of time and money in perfecting weapons that are obsolete before they become operational.

Let me give you an illustration of what I mean.

For some time, a controversy has been raging over defense against manned bombers. This is, to be sure, an area that cannot be neglected. We must have a margin of safety in providing a defense against the possibility of such a bomber attack.

But I fear that too much of our effort has been based on the assumption that an attack from conventional aircraft is the principal danger that we face. Reliable indications are that the primary threat is from missiles—not bombers.

Yet, in the last session, Congress was called upon to decide between two competing systems of missile defense against manned bombers, both of them enormously expensive. We very probably will have to come to grips with the same question next year.

None of the great problems involved in providing for the defense of our common country are easy. And nobody has all the answers.

The task of providing that defense vitally concerns all of us, and part of the responsibility for it devolves upon each of us.

By working together in a spirit of determination and sacrifice, we will continue to maintain a defense establishment that is second to none—one that will guard our country, preserve our freedom, and protect our future.

Dalton High School
13 December 1962

In 1958, the Soviet Union successfully launched a satellite, Sputnik I. This achievement caused leaders in the United States to accelerate plans to explore space. It also provoked the nation to reevaluate the means by which students were being taught math and science. In April 1961, under the John F. Kennedy Administration, in Bay of Pigs Invasion, more than 1,400 exiled Cubans were defeated attempting to invade Cuba to overthrow Fidel Castro. In 1962 the Soviet Union began placing intermediate range ballistic missiles in Cuba. In response, Kennedy instituted a quarantine upon all offensive military equipment shipped to Cuba. In the end Premier Nikita Khrushchev ordered his Soviet ships not to attempt to break through the blockage.

During this tense Cold War atmosphere, Senator Russell gave the speech below to students and faculty at Dalton High School.[13] He emphasized the importance in the contemporary world of mastering the "field of science and production." Praising teachers as "heroes of" the "cold war," Russell noted the new "opportunities" in space, and the "dangers" on earth that awaited students. The Senator warned against allowing the federal government to usurp powers allocated by the Constitution to the states. Russell called for a national "fabric of spiritual values." Fred Burdick, President of the Senior Hi-Y Club, introduced Russell to the audience. Following the address, principal Charles Bowen presented the Senator with a bedspread as a reminder of the importance of the chenille industry in Dalton.[14]

Principal [Charles] Bowen, Superintendent Hale, Mr. Putnam, distinguished members of the Faculty and Student Body of Dalton High School, honored guests and my fellow Georgians.

---

[13]Text of speech from Speech File, Speech and Media Series, Richard B. Russell Collection, RRLPRS.
[14]*Dalton Citizen News*, December 14, 1962.

Dalton High School

It has been all too long since I have had the pleasure of a visit with you here in Dalton and Whitfield County. I therefore welcome most sincerely the privilege of being with you today. Most especially is it gratifying to have the opportunity of meeting with you at Dalton High School, one of the finest and proudest in the entire State, and one which has, over the years, helped produce some of Georgia's leading citizens in business and industry, agriculture, government, and the sciences.

I am glad to be here with you today and have the opportunity of meeting a new generation of Dalton High students, who will soon take their place beside their predecessors in positions of leadership throughout every strata of our society.

But a few decades ago, the good life that we take for granted now did not exist for many and in fact, the world, it seems, was for the few and the very few.

Education was not known by many and a few grades of elementary school—and for most, only a few lessons in reading and writing by the fireside at home—was the extent of the educational training held by a vast majority of people in our state and nation.

Any man who held a high school diploma was looked upon as very well educated indeed and that was, of course, before many of our Georgia high schools were anywhere nearly as well equipped with learned faculty and modern teaching facilities as they are today.

This state and nation of ours, and for that matter, the entire world is changed almost beyond recognition from my grandfather's day and his father before him.

In the old days, the man who had the broadest shoulders and could wield the meanest weapon could succeed in life. But now, with education, even the less physically strong can make great advances in life and can contribute much to society.

In our fierce struggle with world Communism, it is imperative that this nation make every effort to combat the horizons of ignorance at home while winning minds abroad. We must advance in education, particularly in the fields of science and production. And, of course, we must retain our traditional allegiance to the humanities and the social sciences.

It is reported that Russia is out-distancing the United States in the number of advance-degree graduates they turn out. But it is my firm belief that, in quality, American education is vastly superior to that of any Communist nation and will ever remain so, for we are free men. We question all things with open minds and are perfectly at liberty to draw any conclusions that we may desire and so state them publicly for all to hear and learn.

In this country, we say "an informed people is a free people." The opposite is true in Communist lands. Textbooks in schools are slanted to support policies of government. Education is devoted to training young people to support the Communist Party and to training technicians toward that end.

So far we have managed to keep our schools from being entirely controlled by the Government. Of course, Russian schools are strictly regulated by the Government—with the curriculum and teaching methodology prescribed by a Ministry of Education.

We are fortunate in America in that, in spite of low salaries and sacrifices in terms of greater material advancement, we have always had in this country dedicated and selfless faculties in every division of our school systems, and we are moving ahead in the training of new teachers of even greater quality.

Teachers—elementary teachers, high school teachers, college teachers—all are of greater importance than at any time before. They are indeed heroes of this cold war and will be in the front lines of our ultimate victory.

Teachers are contributing as much to the defense of the nation as are the soldiers keeping an hourly vigil at the Guantanamo Base in Cuba, in Berlin, in Laos, and the other critical trouble spots over the world. It is the service of American teachers that will ensure our future, for only the educated are free.

Our students and our faculties know what Lord Brougham meant when he said: "Education makes people easy to lead, but difficult to drive; easy to govern but impossible to enslave."

You who are now the students of today have before you the greatest challenge of life in the history of the world. Yours is a world filled with unusual new opportunities, yet one fraught with dangers and pitfalls never dreamed of by earlier generations.

It used to be that there was a considerable span of years between one great advance in almost any area to an improvement or a modification or another advance in that area. Nowadays, it seems that just as soon as one new device in our daily lives is perfected and made available, another comes out just as quickly to render the previous edition obsolete. We are in the space age, or what historians will probably call the "early atmospheric" age. Our State of Georgia, I believe, is going to be a major participant in this new era of our existence and will benefit significantly in many ways—including in an economic way in this adventuresome and exciting day which is just beginning. Georgia is situated geographically to command a sizeable portion of our expanding and growing space program, and I think our participation in this area is going to increase.

Outer space is our newest frontier, and I often wonder what will follow from there. This nation and the world are on the brink of the most fantastic scientific revolution in history. In weather forecasting, in communications, in education, in new materials and techniques for industry, in medicine, and in many other fields, we are going to benefit directly from the space research program now under way.

For health and human betterment, consider, for instance, the miniature instruments, "sensors" I believe they are called, attached to our astronauts to give their physical responses in space flight. This device measures heart beats, brain waves, blood pressure, breathing rates, etc. In civilian life, these instruments, which could be called "electronic nurses," are already being applied to hospital patients so that they can be watched by remote control. The moment a patient's condition changes, it is instantly recorded and a warning flashed. These sensors are components of what we might call an automated hospital of the future.

I read this spring of an electronically rigged helmet that was used during spring football practice at Northwestern University to obtain data about the degree and kind of a headshock received by football players. This apparatus, located in the crown of the helmet, resembles that used by our space experts in telemetering critical data back to earth from the astronauts. The research at Northwestern is to determine minimum standards of performance for football headgear.

Doctors now foresee a battery-powered television system, small enough to be swallowed, transmitting an "on the spot" pictorial report from a patient's stomach.

The car you drive will reflect the progress of space science. Among the "things to come" are miniaturized electronic controls for automobiles, capable of maintaining highway speed, slowing the car to avoid obstacles and stopping it in dangerous situations. The power plants of tomorrow's automobiles may be no bigger than a coffee can—burning new fuels with much greater efficiency.

These are just a few of the "things of tomorrow" that are with us today or will be in the near future.

As government grows larger and infiltrates almost every segment of our existence, you will have to have a greater knowledge of that government. It will be incumbent upon you to maintain an awareness of what has made our national government in these United States strong throughout the great span of years of our history, yet flexible enough to cope with the problems of new years and of new ideas.

Our government was built upon the sound principle of a system of checks and balances which divided the powers of the Federal authority into three separate and distinct branches—the legislative, the executive, and the judicial.

In recent years, unfortunately, there seems to have developed in Washington a race between each branch of our government to see who can usurp from the other powers never given and never intended. All of us have observed the lessening of those powers of government expressly reserved for the States in the 10th Amendment of the Constitution as much of the influence and authorities of the several states have been absorbed into one huge, monolithic Federal Government.

The Executive Branch is now claiming widespread authority by the "stroke of a pen" on an Executive Order. This authority was never granted by the Constitution.

The Supreme Court has entered into the field of legislation and has sought to write the law of the land instead of deciding what the law is, or interpreting it, by means of legal precedent which was the accepted role of the Court until some ten or fifteen years ago.

This trend in our nation, if allowed to continue unchecked, will ultimately bring down this great government that we have constructed and lead to the complete destruction of our fine American civilization—the greatest known to man and the envy of the world today.

I urge you to read your history. To study the lives and philosophies of our early American statesmen. Learn about Thomas Jefferson and his magnificent contributions to our society. Read of [Alexander] Hamilton and [Andrew] Jackson, of our early patriots [Nathan] Hale and [Patrick] Henry, who placed country and principle above petty prejudice and partisan politics.

Ours is not a world at peace, and there has hardly been a moment of international tranquility in the last decade. I see little hope for such in the immediate future. No one wants more than I to avoid the consequences of war and especially a nuclear holocaust, but I am convinced that our best chance of survival and of avoiding war is to insure that this nation maintains a powerful military establishment capable of deterring any enemy military attack.

There are great dangers that confront us. These powerful new weapons that man has created are more than able to bring about our own destruction and the destruction of all that we have known and loved in this nation and indeed in this world.

As a member of the Joint Committee on Atomic Energy since it was created and as Chairman of the Senate Armed Services Committee, I have sometimes emerged from a lengthy session when the potential of these great weapons that we possess is outlined and described and found myself shuddering and wondering if I am not in the midst of a hideous nightmare. No one would be more willing than I to destroy every atomic weapon on earth if a realistic program of disarmament could be adopted. However, I am completely opposed to adopting any wooly-minded plan which in any way would depend upon the word and good faith of the Communist leaders. For, if we did so, we would risk our own suicide and would insure our ultimate destruction.

I, of course, would much prefer to expend our energies and the billions upon billions of dollars spent for national defense for peaceful pursuits and the building of a better America. But I am not willing to spend our energies and money for building a better country for Russia to take over and enjoy after they have enslaved the builders.

Our national defense structure, our military strength, whatever the cost, whatever the price we may have to pay, are our only insurance policy against war and world catastrophe.

As a nation and as a people, we will have progress, but it is necessary to weave into that progress a firm fabric of spiritual values, our greatest American heritage. We must maintain a spiritual atmosphere in our country if we are to challenge Communism. Communism is an idea, and we must combat it in that form as well as on a battlefield if we are ultimately to achieve victory, as surely we will. Our American dream embodies a set of ancient spiritual values, a moral code, which must remain forever with us.

America's greatest hope is in her young people. The legacy of this nation will soon be in your hands. And it will be your greatest task to insure that the moral code, the spiritual values of America are ever with you as you go about your lives as citizens of this great land of ours. With this thought in mind, I am fully confident that America will persevere as she has always persevered, and the great hope of Christmas, of peace, joy, happiness, and love, shall become the reality that we all so prayerfully and earnestly seek.

Gordon Military School
26 May 1963

Senator Russell gave this speech at the dedication of the new Alumni Memorial Auditorium at Gordon Military School (now Gordon College), in Barnesville, Georgia.[15] Attending the dedication services was Hugh Gordon of Athens, Georgia, grandson of General John B. Gordon, Confederate General for whom the institution was named. Russell was introduced by Robert J. Marshburn of Homer, Georgia. A full dress military parade by the Gordon Cadet Corps followed the dedication.[16]

After reviewing world conflict observed since his graduation from Gordon Military Academy in 1915, Russell praised the prosperity, character, and "cultural advancement of our country." To continue this progress, he argued, the military must remain strong and the cost of government should be curtailed. Rather than base foreign policy upon aid to other countries, the United States should promote "enlightened self-interest."

* * * * * * * * * *

General Daniel, Colonel Light, my old friend, Bob Marshburn, distinguished members of the Faculty, students of Gordon Military College and my fellow Georgians.

I have been in public life now for some forty years and one of the real pleasures that accompanies such a career is the opportunity to meet with my friends over the State, at meetings of many varied descriptions. I suppose I have made literally thousands of speeches and have attended an infinite variety of occasions, not only in Georgia, but across the length and breadth of our great land. But I can honestly say that I have never enjoyed myself quite so much as upon

---

[15]Text of speech from Speech File, Speech and Media Series, Richard B. Russell Collection, RRLPRS.
[16]*Georgia News Gazette*, May 30, 1963.

this occasion, where you have honored me today by your cordial invitation to come home again to Barnesville, Lamar County, and Gordon and dedicate this impressive new structure.

I know that this is truly a homecoming for me, for here on this stage sit some of the best friends that any man on earth could possibly have, the members of my Class of 1915 here at Gordon.

It's been a good many years now since we left Gordon to begin our journey along the road of life. The old school has changed so much and I am proud to know that it is growing by leaps and bounds.

This new building is ample evidence of the physical growth of our school. It is a monument to planning and foresight on the part of the Administration, together with the Board of Trustees, so ably headed by my friend, D. B. Cannafax.

Gordon, now in its 111th year of service and inspired by the gallant and illustrious General John B. Gordon [of the Confederacy], is among the oldest schools in the South and is the pioneer of its kind in the State. It has been a pathfinder or trailblazer for education in Georgia and its long-continued traditions of intellectual achievement and activities designed to develop a student socially, physically and spiritually, warrant our Alma Mater's proud boast of being the finest preparatory school of its kind in the South.

The world has turned over many times since that spring of 1915, when my friends here and I left this hallowed ground to forge for ourselves in a strange world that we thought, even then, to be complex and difficult.

But, even in that year, the peace on earth that still eludes us was shattered, and World War I raged upon the continent of Europe. Except for little more than a decade after the conclusion of World War I, peace, real peace, has never been a permanent or an accomplished fact in our society.

Before 1915, the forces of Communism, which are upon us today with the might of a deadly tornado, were spawned by a German vagrant named Karl Marx in his filthy tenement room across the sea, and in only three years after our graduation here, in 1918, this awful tyranny burst upon a stunned world in the form of the Red Revolution in Russia.

Since 1915, we have witnessed the greatest economic depression ever known, which saw millions of people unemployed in our nation and hunger, starvation and want rampant in our land and abroad. We had little time to rejoice in a recovery for in the wake of this awful period there came the rise of Nazi tyranny in Germany, combined with the Fascists of Italy and joined by the militarists of Japan.

Again in our lifetime came a war which spared few nations and one that made its mark in the annals of history as bringing about the most terrible and wide-spread destruction of lives and property yet known to man.

Today a cold war, as real and as deadly as any other conflict that we have seen and one which offers no promise of an end in the immediate future, has caused drastic changes in the lives of all of us and again, in 1950, we were forced to take up arms to prevent the naked aggression of Communism in Korea.

So, the era of adult life that those of us entered in 1915, has not been a tranquil one and we have never known the security of international peace that this nation has sought in spite of the conflicts and the dangers and the perils which we as a people have been subject. But in spite of all the difficulties that we have encountered over the past forty and fifty years, our nation, our people, have continued to prosper, grow and succeed.

The American people in this latter half of the 20th Century are enjoying an era of unprecedented prosperity and have built a civilization which is the envy of all mankind, unmatched by any nation or any people throughout the eons of history.

Under our blessed free enterprise system and a government of limited Constitutional authority, our nation has not only endured but has grown stronger in the face of perils which would long ago have destroyed a nation not as fundamentally sound. The people of the United States have a greater purchasing power, have more, buy more, possess more and use more food, clothing, housing and everything else than all the people of Europe, Asia and Africa combined. These are obvious and very practical achievements of the American people under the system in which we live.

American industry, the team work of capital, management and labor, produces in such abundance for American markets as to make our nation the financial banker of the whole world. American agriculture has provided the abundance to enable our country to be the breadbasket for the entire world. We do not know famine and food shortages in the United States; our problem in this area is one of over-production and vast surpluses of foodstuffs.

In no nation on earth does the working man, both in industry and on the farm, enjoy a life that is comparable to that known in our country. This fact alone explodes the basic premise of the theory of Communism, which pits class against class, workers against management. In the United States, hours and days of labor have been regulated. Working people ride to work in their own automobiles instead of walking or riding bicycles as in other countries. Here clothing is purchased with one-third the hours of labor that are required in the most favored countries of the eastern world. Our homes are larger and filled with labor-saving devices even yet unknown in foreign lands. Also, we have achieved the widest distribution of good living standards among more of our people than elsewhere. Farmers own their own farms and we have legislation that enables them to enjoy a fair return for their labor.

Perhaps an even greater product of American freedom is the cultural advancement of our country, fraternal lodges, service and luncheon clubs, recreational clubs and charitable organizations abound in every city, town and hamlet. All are developing new heights of public service. Religious worship, of every faith, is welcomed within our country and is a potent influence for lasting good.

We are rapidly approaching the day when almost every qualified American young man and woman, whether financially able or not, may receive a college education and this progress has in great part been made available by the generous development of scholarship foundations on the part of American private interests and liberal credit programs by our state-supported institutions.

But as impressive as our material wealth may be and the large strides that we have made, we cannot as a nation and as a people be compelled throughout all time to maintain the burden of supporting not only ourselves, but three-fifths of the entire population of the world.

The Communists are wise enough to know that the American system of government can be broken down in possibly two ways. One is by military aggression, for which we must be eternally vigilant and always prepared—the cost is great, but it is an insurance policy which we are compelled to bear if we are to survive. The other is by bankrupting the American people and forcing a breakdown of our economy by excessive taxes over a long period of time.

Part of the ritual of every Session of Congress is to vote additional millions and billions into the foreign aid program, that all-time monster of world wide bureaucracy. A few years ago an Indian newspaper man said that the American foreign aid program, private as well as governmental, verges on the lavish. He said, and I quote, "The Americans do far more good than is good for themselves." We have spent a total of some 33 billion dollars in foreign economic aid since the Marshall plan ended in 1953. This figure is for grants alone and does not include the additional billions in loans, military aid or technical assistance.

The resulting evils and great dangers to our nation and our economy which these continuing increases and unlimited expansions of the foreign aid program have created, are now coming back to haunt us, the sum of which will be felt not only for the remaining years of this generation, but for the years of generations of Americans yet unborn.

As the thermometer of foreign aid expenditures goes up and up into vast incredible proportions, the economy of this country becomes dependent on these annual increases, which have for so long been a part of that economy. The economies of recipient countries become dependent upon it and the chances of curtailing these expenditures becomes harder and harder each year.

In some countries the economies were not so geared to receive the great influx of every conceivable form of aid and, for example, in the case of Korea, we saw a once-proud government grow fat and grow corrupt and the economy ruined because of the lush American dollars being poured into that country with little supervision and no accounting asked.

For the same reason in July, 1962, we had to suspend our foreign aid program in Haiti because of wide spread corruption and open and flagrant stealing upon the part of a handful of high government officials. We had spent 94 million dollars there, yet the people of that pathetic little country continue in poverty and they are 90 percent illiterate.

Our foreign policy has been built upon the principle of foreign aid. In the last Session of Congress, when the House of Representatives saw fit to install cuts in the amount requested by the Administration, the President became alarmed and literally begged the House Committee not to slash the program. The Secretary of State and a horde of aids invaded Capitol Hill and said that without foreign aid the American foreign policy as it is now constructed would fall to pieces.

In my opinion, we have already wasted many billions of dollars, but it is not too late to reconsider the course we have pursued to date and to initiate a foreign policy based upon initiative, thought, creativeness and above all, enlightened self-interest.

We hear so much these days about newly emerging nations, about these countries who are gaining independence and are breaking away from the old colonial powers. In almost every case in the last five to ten years, of those new countries raising its flag of independence, one of the motives of that new independence is to cash in on the American pot of gold that awaits every new country only for the asking in every corner of the globe.

The simple facts are these, my friends. Our country will soon be unable to support itself if it continues to carry the load for every other nation under the canopy of heaven, including Communist countries whose avowed purpose is to bury us. Our economy cannot stand the strain. Our people cannot be asked forever to undertake such a load, the greatest that any people of any nation in all of history have been asked to bear.

Our own population is rapidly growing and we must now plan for the future when money may be less plentiful, but people to feed, house, clothe and educate will be more plentiful. In the last twenty years, our population grew from 134 million to 186 million, an increase of 38 percent. In 1980, it is expected that our American population will be some 260 million, an increase over today's figure of 40 percent.

Despite efforts for the past seventeen years on the part of this nation to help the war devastated areas and now the so-called new countries, it seems the biggest dividend we have received in the sum total of this most important aspect of our foreign policy is in the form of ill-will, hatred and bitterness and willingness on the part of those receiving American aid to embrace Communism as a philosophy and a way of life.

The arguments which are made each year in favor of these foreign aid appropriations and of the increases which are requested might well have been played from a phonograph record of the arguments in connection with the first program which was ever submitted to the Congress.

We were told then that this program was necessary in order to mobilize allies who would fight by our side. There was painted the same gloomy picture of the sickness and suffering. If I had the slightest opinion that increasing foreign aid appropriations would enable us to avoid war, there would be no ceiling to which I would not go in the appropriation of these funds and that is the same feeling that I have for defense appropriations, if, in fact, foreign aid monies would really contribute to the prevention of war and preservation of world peace.

There is nothing in the history of the entire foreign aid program that would justify such a conclusion. We are told each year that, if our government does not provide the funds each time it is asked, then automatically and almost immediately the asking nation will turn to the Communists and will march into their camp with banners loudly proclaiming.

I believe it is a well-known fact that the Russian program of foreign aid has never so much as half-way equaled ours and that they have never loaned, much less given, a single ruble where there were not strings mightily attached for a long time to come. My friends, I will never vote to legislate at any time on the basis of what the Russians have said or done. Indeed, I find ludicrous the constant harangue of those who would have us eliminate everything in our system of economy and government, indeed our very social traditions of hundreds of years standing, which they say might afford a basis of propaganda to the Communist world.

It is doubtful whether the Communists need any basis for propaganda, for in that field they are expert, if not supreme. Moreover, if we are to eliminate every social, economic and political principle to which we are devoted as the solid core of our great progress as a nation, we will ourselves become nothing more than Communists in the process.

I think we have gotten ourselves into a completely untenable position by attempting to tailor our policies in order to escape the Russian propaganda machine. Does anyone for one minute ever think that the Communists will praise us for the good we have done and not capitalize upon every fault, real or imaginary, that they can produce?

Little laudation will be forthcoming from Communist sources and every lie, trick, use of deceit and falsehood that is known will be employed against us. My advice would be for those responsible for the conduct of our affairs to take off the fancy gloves and fight back with bare knuckles—we do not need lies and tricks to use against them. We can tell the truth on the Communists and they will think we are giving them hell.

When this nation changes its policies to move in any area, in any direction, because of Russian propaganda, then we are enmeshing ourselves in a net from which we cannot possibly extricate ourselves and which will eventually strangle us.

My friends, the President has said that these great demands in foreign aid funds, made on our taxpayers each year, are, in his words, vital to our national security. I say the immediate reduction of our national budget, which is swollen, increasing from year to year, is vital to our national security.

I would be more than willing to vote for a tax cut this year, if that cut would be accompanied by a genuine reduction in federal spending, both domestic and foreign. But we can never reduce our taxes and we

Gordon Military School 285

can never reduce our domestic spending without first reducing our foreign spending and placing a halt on this foreign aid monster, born of our generosity, but in the end so capable of cruelly and unmercifully devouring us and breaking our back as a great nation and a great people.

I know the American people now as in the past can be counted upon to make whatever sacrifices may be asked of them to insure our nation's security. Our budget for defense purposes alone, some 53.7 billion projected for 1964, is greater than the total aggregate budgets of France, England, Germany, Canada, Australia and Belgium combined, but even then that is a small price to pay for our very freedom and our cherished civilization.

Indeed, one of the United States' biggest foreign expenses is to maintain our armed forces abroad. We have military forces stationed now in some 109 countries and territories across the length and breadth of this planet. There can be no thought of economizing with the only shield of our freedom and that, my friends, rests altogether, totally and absolutely on the ability of this nation, not only to defend itself against Communist aggression, but upon its greater ability to obliterate the Russian nation, its leaders and its people, if war is forced upon us.

There is no doubt in my mind that, had not [Nikita] Khrushchev and his Kremlin cohorts been utterly convinced of our superior retaliatory and striking power, we would most likely have had war in Cuba when the President forced Mr. K[hrushchev] to back down, and we hope, rid that island fortress of the missiles and the bombers.

Our President's initial action there was wise and courageous and it was effective. But, I have been tremendously disappointed by his apparent weakening and backing away from our original demands of a complete evacuation of all Soviet forces and the guarantees of on-site inspection that we were promised.

We had the one great opportunity when it was discovered that aggressive weapons had been placed by the Red Bear [Soviet Union] but ninety miles from our shores, to go in and rid this hemisphere of the missiles, the Russians, Castro and Communism all in one packet.

A resolution warning the Russians on Cuba and defining for all the world to see what aggression there would consist of, had been passed by the Congress only a few months before. I drafted that resolution and I know what is in it. But the President, I am sorry to say, did not heed my advice to him, which I gave at the White House in a meeting before he made his historic October address.

Though we are faced with grave provocation and the Communist threat is real, our policy must always be flexible enough within its strength to be ever alert for the path toward peace that we all so earnestly and prayerfully seek. In dealing with the Communists, we must have no illusions. But, we can never afford to abandon the hope, an everlasting hope, that the men in the Kremlin will see the realities of the only alternative to a genuine peace—the horrors of nuclear holocaust, with the resulting death and destruction that is really beyond imagination, and that reason will finally prevail.

My friends, I have talked too long.

I am proud to be home again and have the high privilege of participating in this day of dedication of this newest evidence of the growth of our beloved Gordon Military College.

I wish I could offer you the answers and solutions for our problems, but there are no easy answers, no total solutions.

The road toward the good life is a difficult one—for the individual and for the leader entrusted with the responsibility of his country, But I have an abiding faith that you young Georgians, as have your forefathers for more than 230 years, will be in the front lines in the leadership of our State and Nation—working, striving, always toward the goal that our great nation shall forever maintain its high position in the world around us as the land of the free and the home of the brave.

Georgia Association of Broadcasters
13 June 1965

Senator Russell gave this address to the 30th Annual Convention of the Georgia Association of Broadcasters at Callaway Gardens, in Pine Mountain, Georgia.[17] The speech took place during the Annual Awards Banquet, where the Senator was presented a bronze plaque naming him Georgian of the Year. Governor Carl E. Sanders of Georgia made the presentation. The broadcasters praised the Senator for being a "leader, defender, promoter, and inspiration to the citizens of Georgia" for "almost forty years."[18]

Russell recalled the early role of radio in the lives of citizens and in his own political campaigns. Turning to foreign policy, he contrasted the decisive and effective way the United States troops were recently sent to the Dominican Republic to prevent a potential "Communist take-over" there, with the indecisive means by which the Vietnam war was being managed. He had "never" found any "advantage" to the United States being involved in Vietnam.

* * * * * * * * * *

In this nation of free men and free enterprise, there have been many spectacular successes among the diverse elements that comprise the American economy. Without question, one of the foremost success stories of our era has been the fabulous rise of the broadcast industry.

In little more than a single generation, broadcasting has developed from a struggling handful of pioneer and primitive radio stations to a giant complex of more than 5,000 radio and 600 television stations.

---

[17]Text of speech from Speech File, Speech and Media Series, Richard B. Russell Collection, RRLPRS.
[18]*Southern Advertising and Publishing*, July 1965, in Speech File and Media Series, Richard B. Russell Collection, RRLPRS.

There are few among us who have advanced beyond the cradle but have not yet reached the grave who do not spend a portion of every day listening to radio or watching television. The fare we hear and see ranges all the way from the Metropolitan Opera to horse opera; from outer space to Peyton Place. Yours is indeed a versatile medium.

I suppose some people would think it not very politic of me to admit that my own career in public life virtually spans the era of commercial broadcasting. Perhaps I should hasten to explain that my career began at an extremely early age.

One of my most vivid memories of the early days of radio in Georgia was the unforgettable style and voice in which Lambdin Kaye used to sign WSB off the air. You always knew the time had come to go to bed when you heard that inimitable voice proclaim: "This is the *Atlanta Journal*, Atlanta, Georgia. WSB, the voice of the South at the Biltmore. The *Journal* covers Dixie like the dew."

Not only do I recall the early days of radio but I even helped to make some early broadcasting history. I have been told that the first political broadcast to originate in Georgia was a program aired over WSB in 1930 by a group of friends who spoke in behalf of my campaign for governor.

Later in that same campaign, I made my own radio debut with a 30-minute talk over WSB. That program has double meaning for me because the time was paid for through nickel, dime, and quarter collections taken up by the school children of my home county. As I recall, the cost of those thirty minutes was about $75. After hearing of some of today's time rates, I know what they mean about "the good ole days of radio."

The impact of broadcasting on the daily lives of all of us—young and old, male and female—is so profound as almost to defy description.

Radio and television provide entertainment for our leisure hours and company for our lonely ones.

They provide up-to-the-minute weather data to help us plan our days and our work, and to warn us of impending dangers from floods, hurricanes, and tornadoes.

They keep the farmer abreast of the latest market trends so he can select the most profitable time to sell his livestock and crops. By the same token, businessmen frequently rely on radio and television for spot reports from Wall Street and other focal points of commercial activity. Broadcasting performs another essential economic function as a major advertising medium for retailers, merchants, and manufacturers.

I have noticed that broadcasters are always among the first to volunteer their services and their station's time to advance civic causes and community projects. The past efforts of this Association to combat the appalling slaughter on our highways is typical of your many public-spirited activities.

But the single most important mission of radio and television is helping to keep the American people well informed on the happenings in their communities, in the nation, and in the world.

This task is shared by all the news media—those of the printed word as well as those of the spoken word. It is a task that is becoming increasingly crucial in these ominous days when onrushing events such as those in Southeast Asia have such vital meaning to all of us.

You recognize—and are frequently told—that the broadcaster has a responsibility to the public. But I suggest that the public—and the public's representatives in government—also have a responsibility to the broadcaster. That responsibility is to see that radio and television stations are allowed to operate with a minimum of government regulation and restraint.

The system of broadcasting we enjoy in the United States is unique among all the nations of the world. Ours is the only system in which commercial television and radio stations are owned and operated almost totally by private industry. In every other country the broadcast media is owned and operated wholly or in part by the government.

The concept of government ownership and government operation of the broadcasting media is totally incompatible with the American system of free enterprise and individual liberty. We neither want nor need such a pernicious and potentially evil system in this land of freedom.

Over the last weekend, all America thrilled as Majors [James] McDivitt and [Edward] White achieved another historic milestone in man's relentless drive to expand his knowledge of science and his conquest of space. We marvelled at the incredible technology and machines that enabled the astronauts to live for four days in space, and to travel 1,600,000 miles in orbital flight at speeds above 17,000 miles an hour.

Someone has said that man has learned more about the physical nature of his world and universe in the decades beginning with World War II than during all previously recorded history of the human family.

This undoubtedly is true. Yet it is sometimes difficult to reconcile the giant steps of progress in the world of science and technology with the halting steps man has made in an even more critical area. For all his exploding knowledge of space, man has yet to learn how to live in peace with his fellows on the earth.

I do not like to strike a somber note on this happy and festive occasion. Yet I cannot in good conscience stand before a group of outstanding leaders, as is assembled here tonight, without expressing my growing concern over events now unfolding.

At this hour, upwards of 100,000 American soldiers, sailors, airmen, and Marines stand armed and battle-ready in two unhappy and explosive areas of the globe—in the Dominican Republic in our own Hemisphere and in Vietnam in the Far East.

In Vietnam, as the climbing casualty rolls grimly proclaim, American boys are doing considerably more than standing on alert. They are fighting—and some of them are dying—in a mean and dirty war that surely must be among the most frustrating conflicts in which American forces have ever participated.

There has been considerable improvement in the recent days and weeks in the highly dangerous situation that prevailed for a time in the Dominican Republic. We can take comfort in the fact that the threat to our security from that area has receded somewhat—though it has by no means disappeared.

The shooting and killing on that long-oppressed island was brought to a halt—and a Communist take-over probably averted—by the President's prompt action in sending in American forces. Had he failed to act when he did—and as he did—the story may have been tragically different. We might now be mourning the loss of American lives, and bemoaning the establishment of another Communist satellite under our very nose.

I have no sympathy for those editorialists and armchair generals who continue to disparage and criticize our intervention in the Dominican Republic. I am confident that the great majority of the American people approve and support the President's [Lyndon B. Johnson] timely and decisive action.

The humanitarian objectives behind that action was reason enough for sending in the Marines and soldiers. But the possibility of the establishment of another [Fidel] Castro [of Cuba] in the Caribbean was an even more compelling reason.

I believe the President's forthright action in the Dominican crisis has put the leaders of world Communism on notice that the United States will not stand idly by and see another of their puppets take control in this Hemisphere.

We have said in clear and unmistakable terms that the Monroe Doctrine means in 1965 what it meant in 1823—that we regard foreign interference in Latin America as a threat to our own peace and safety and that we do not intend to allow it. Above all, we have proclaimed to the world that we want no more Castros off our shores.

The United States' position in Southeast Asia is considerably more complicated than it is in our own Hemisphere. Our forces are in Vietnam at the request of a friendly government to help prevent a take-over by Communist rebels who are supported to a greater or lesser degree by Russia, China, and North Vietnam.

I can see why many Americans have difficulty understanding how our national interest is being served by the growing commitment of U.S. money, munitions, and men in Vietnam. I thought, and so stated at the time, that it was a mistake to get involved there in the first place; I have never been able to see any strategic, political or economic advantage to be gained by our involvement. Most of the military leaders whose knowledge and advice I most respect have warned repeatedly that it would be an incalculable mistake for the U.S. to engage in a full-scale land war on the Asian mainland.

The decision to go to the assistance of the anti-Communist government of Vietnam was made by President [Dwight D.] Eisenhower. The commitment he made was honored by President [John F.] Kennedy and even enlarged by President [Lyndon B.] Johnson.

Whether or not the initial decision was a mistake is now moot. The United States does have a commitment in South Vietnam. The flag is there. U.S. honor and prestige are there. And U.S. soldiers are there.

No man can foretell with certainty what the future course of events in Asia will bring. The monsoon season is beginning, and for the next several months conditions in the jungles and rice paddies will be tailor-made for the type of guerilla warfare in which the Viet Cong excel.

There are growing indications that the fighting may now be entering a new and perhaps decisive stage. Certainly the war is now entering its most dangerous stage—dangerous both from the likelihood of increased losses of American lives and from the possibility that Russia and China may intervene directly or under the guise of sending "volunteers" to fight along side the Viet Cong. The American people must be prepared to face up to either or both possibilities.

I hope and pray that I am wrong, but we seem to be drifting toward a situation in Vietnam that is in many ways similar to the Korean War. But in the case of Vietnam, we are at an even greater disadvantage than we were in Korea. This is due to a variety of reasons, including logistical problems, the instability of the [Vietnam] government, internal dissension, and the generally unfavorable terrain.

A heavy and onerous burden rests upon the shoulders of the President and upon his military and civilian advisers.

It is unthinkable that we would now abruptly withdraw our forces from South Vietnam, as some critics of our policy there apparently would have us do. This would mean the virtual surrender of all of

Southeast Asia to the Communists—including such stalwart friends as Thailand.

But it would have even graver ramifications. A precipitant U.S. withdrawal from Vietnam would undermine the faith of our allies in American resolve and purpose. It would weaken resistance to Communist aggression and subversion the world over. And it would shake the Free World coalition to its very foundations.

I am convinced that no one has yet come forward with the foolproof solution to the Vietnamese puzzle. The only thing that we know for certain is that there are no quick and easy answers.

In the absence of such a solution, I believe we have no choice but to support the course the President has charted—though recognizing, as we must, the gravity of the risks involved.

We can only hope that sooner or later the powers directing the Communist forces in Vietnam will be compelled to recognize the futility of their course of aggression, terror, and subversion. Perhaps we may yet persuade the Communists by our determination, strength, and force that the road they are traveling will lead ultimately to their own destruction.

Veterans of Foreign Wars Congressional Dinner 12 March 1968

Senator Russell gave this address to veterans, members of the United States Congress, and officials of the Executive branch of government at the Sheraton Park Hotel in Washington, D.C.[19] On this occasion, he was presented the Fifth Annual Veterans of Foreign Wars Congressional Award for service. President Lyndon B. Johnson made a surprise visit to the dinner, praising his "long time and good friend" as "a leader . . . of this country. If the nation is secure, and kept secure, all Americans will owe a great debt to" Senator Russell.[20]

Russell praised veterans who had sacrificed for the nation's security. Recalling his early opposition to the Vietnam war, the Senator advised finding an "honorable" means of allowing soldiers to "return home." Never again, he admonished, should Americans be sent to battle unless they would be supported by the "total wealth of our country." Should the war be continued, he advised, the necessary "air and sea power" should be deployed to end the "flow of weapons and equipment into North Vietnam."

* * * * * * * * * *

Commander-in-Chief [Joseph] Scerra; my distinguished colleagues of both Houses of the United States Congress; representatives of the Executive Branch; members of the Veterans of Foreign Wars; and guests.

It is indeed a high privilege to be with you this evening. I am especially honored to be the recipient of this coveted award. To have my name listed among the outstanding and distinguished Members

---

[19]Text of speech from Speech File, Speech and Media Series, Richard B. Russell Collection, RRLPRS.
[20]*Atlanta Journal*, March 13, 1968.

of Congress who have been selected by the VFW for this honor brings a feeling of deep humility.

The character and purposes of your organization give this award special meaning to me. And I accept it in the knowledge that you recognize—as I do—that the truly outstanding public servants of 1968 are the brave young men who have responded to their country's call to arms as you did in by-gone days.

These young Americans have laid their lives on the line and regretfully the English language has not provided us with adequate words to render to these men the tribute of which they are deserving.

Those of you who make-up this great organization have known first-hand the harsh realities of war.

Because of your own experiences in other times and other places, your understanding for the circumstances confronting the brave young men who fight under the American flag this very hour is deep and abiding.

Of all the important issues of our day, the grave and tragic situation in Vietnam is foremost in the minds of the American people and most assuredly, foremost in the thoughts of this audience tonight.

In 1954, when it was first proposed that we become involved militarily in Vietnam, I vigorously opposed the idea. The communists are probing all over the world and there are few places on earth where it would be more costly to support an United States military commitment than in Vietnam. In addition, it has always been my conviction that any military confrontation of communist aggression should be resolute and determined and involve the entire strength of our great land.

However, the time is now past to discuss the wisdom of our involvement in Vietnam. There is no place for hindsight under the present circumstances. We must deal with the situation as it exists at this moment.

Tonight we are confronted with a condition where over 500,000 of the finest of American manhood are in a distant corner of the world fighting under the American flag against Communist aggression.

We must now determine what must be done in order for these young men to return home under honorable circumstances in the shortest practical time at the lowest cost in U.S. and allied lives. I might add, parenthetically, that I, for one, cannot understand the oft expressed fear of the old-fashioned term, victory.

We have already paid the price of over nineteen thousand American lives, the value of which is incalculable, not to mention the cost in terms of National wealth, to convince the communists that we will observe our every commitment to aid those who are really willing to fight against communist aggression.

If we abandon that principle we would abandon in the jungles and the rice paddies of Vietnam, the heritage of greatness, freedom, and courage that has marked this country since its birth.

We have just experienced the bloodiest month in the course of this war during which we lost over 2,000 American lives. The Vietnam war has been depleting our national resources at the rate of almost $2½ billion per month and we have pitifully little to show for the price we have paid.

I have devoted most of my years in public service in trying to insure that we are militarily the most powerful nation in the world. I am happy to say in this presence that I have had no more steadfast ally in this effort than the Veterans of Foreign Wars.

I, therefore, feel confident that you feel as I do that there are clear alternatives to remaining indefinitely submerged in a strategy of self-imposed restrictions with the rising casualties and the unending need for additional troops which accompany this strategy.

As for me, my fellow Americans, I shall never knowingly support a policy of sending even a single American boy overseas to risk his life in combat unless the entire civilian population and total wealth of our country—all that we have and all that we are—is to bear a commensurate responsibility in affording him the fullest support and protection of which we are capable.

Under the basic policy on which our society rests, each American is, in his place and in his way, equally obligated to contribute to the defense of this nation. It is inconsistent with our history, traditions, and fundamental principles to commit American boys on far flung battlefields if we are to follow policies that deny him full support because we are afraid of increasing the dangers of those of us who stay at home.

It is a confession of moral weakness on the part of this country if we are afraid to take any steps that are necessary to diminish the fighting power of our enemies in Vietnam.

For three years, many of us, including many military leaders, have urged that we utilize our air and sea power to the fullest extent to prevent the flow of weapons and war material into the hands of our enemies to be used in the destruction of our youth.

If we are not willing to take this calculated risk, we should not still be increasing the half million men in Vietnam who are exposed to danger daily from weapons that might have been kept from the hands of our enemies.

We hear a great deal about limited wars. I would point out that there is no such thing as a limited war to men engaged in actual combat. While it is a sound policy to have limited objectives, we should not expose our men to unnecessary hazards to life and limb because [of a] limited war.

I shall continue to insist upon the employment of our air and sea power to stop the constantly increasing flow of weapons and equipment into North Vietnam. If we continue to fight this war according to the rules that are now dictated by our enemies, no end is foreseeable. It is, however, easy to foresee the constant loss of life and wealth and the sorrow visited upon many thousand more American homes.

Most of the steps that we have taken to bring this war to a conclusion have been about two years late. Time will no longer stand still for us, and we should move with dispatch to apply the military power available to us to convince Ho Chi Minh of the wisdom of desisting from his aggression and agreeing to a civilized solution.

Again, let me express to you my heartfelt appreciation for the honor you have bestowed upon me. I shall strive with every power of my being—to deserve it. Thank you—thank you from the bottom of my heart.

Admiral James Forrestal
Memorial Award
20 March 1969

Senator Russell gave this address at the Washington Hilton Hotel, Washington, D.C. He was joined at the head table by General William Westmoreland, Stanley Resor, Secretary of the Army, and Senators John Stennis and Margaret Chase Smith.[21] On this occasion, Russell was presented the National Security Industrial Association's highest honor, The James Forrestal Award for 1968. Although quite ill, when delivering the speech, the Senator stood "ramrod stiff," and "only near the end did he tire slightly, and even then there was no waver in his Georgia drawl."[22]

Senator Russell praised the National Security Industrial Association for its contribution to the nation's defense. He explained the necessity of a constructive partnership between "government and industry." Russell recognized the contributions made by industry during World Wars I and II. He warned, however, that "with power comes responsibility"; consequently, in the future, federal expenditures should be judiciously monitored by government. While noting the need for "urbanization programs, education, and job-training," and recognizing concerns for "poverty," Russell cautioned that the nation's military must remain strong to meet unexpected threats. In his 1941 speech to 4-H Clubs (reprinted in this anthology), Russell advocated maintaining a strong Navy so that "no enemy from across the seas can ever land on American soil." In this 1969 speech, the Senator explained how the world had changed: "The Atlantic and Pacific Oceans that so long served as protective moats around our homeland have . . . shrunk to puddles and the once friendly skies are now broad avenues of approach for massive missiles of destruction."

---

[21]Text of speech from Speech File, Speech and Media Series, Richard B. Russell Collection, RRLPRS.
[22]*Atlanta Journal*, March 21, 1969.

* * * * * * * * *

Distinguished guests, ladies and gentlemen; I knew Jim Forrestal. I knew him well. I respected his judgment, admired his devotion to duty, and was moved by the depth and intensity of his patriotism. It is, therefore, with a deep sense of humility and appreciation that I accept the memorial award that is tendered in his name. I shall always try to be worthy of this high honor.

While I might question your judgment in your choice of the recipient tonight, I have no such doubts as to the values of the purposes of your organization. You provide a vital link between government and industry in areas of national security. Only through close cooperation and coordination between those who make the tools of defense and those who use them can we be certain of timely development and production of the best military material.

James Forrestal was right in believing a close working relationship between government and industry is essential to the security of the nation, and upon that principle, he founded this organization.

We owe much to the inventiveness, the resourcefulness, the skill and—most of all—to the dogged determination of American industry. This is particularly true in times of crisis, when the chips are down.

I remember vividly that day in May, 1940, when President [Franklin D.] Roosevelt called for a production goal of 50,000 aircraft a year for our Army Air Corps and Naval aviation forces. Many knowledgeable people thought this was impossible and that the President was engaging in nothing more than propaganda or patriotic rhetoric. Yet, only two years later, in 1942, industry produced 47,675 aircraft and in the following year almost doubled that number. By the end of the war, we had turned out 273,757 airplanes—a truly fantastic record.

This example is but one of many near-miracles accomplished by industry when the need was greatest. It should give all Americans a feeling of reassurance to know that industry, if called on today or tomorrow, stands ready to perform other such marvels.

However, advanced technology has brought a radical change in the concept of military preparedness. From colonial times onward, it was no great feat for gunsmiths who produced the weapons used by the earliest settler to provide meat for his table and defend his home to produce likewise the standardized muskets or rifles for the organized armies.

Even during World War I, some industries could adapt civilian production to military requirements. And as late as World War II, automotive manufacturers managed to change their production lines to build tanks and jeeps rather than family cars.

Today, however, the sophistication of both military and civilian technology has brought about a diversification of the production base. Even the manufacture and marketing of consumer goods has become complicated, and the production of weapons of global reach, instant delivery, and incredible destructiveness is infinitely complex. Lead times of five or ten years are now required for many of our weapons.

Coupled with this there is a need for instant preparedness in today's uncertain world. The Atlantic and Pacific Oceans that so long served as protective moats around our homeland have—defensively at least, shrunk to puddles and the once friendly skies are now broad avenues of approach for massive missiles of destruction.

Moreover, the invasion of Czechoslovakia [in 1968] is ample proof that the doctrine that might makes right is still the canon law of Communism, whether it be the Russian brand or the Red Chinese version. Nor can we be lulled into any false sense of security because they may be momentarily diverted to other problems. It is imperative to maintain a defensive posture so strong as to make any aggressor deliberate long before he strikes the first blow.

The part that the industrial group plays in this military capability has increased tremendously during our lifetimes. But there are those in this country who look upon that growth as unhealthy. Some are earnest seekers of peace, who believe, however illogically, that by weakening our defenses we shall somehow encourage the better nature of aggressor nations.

There are some others who would redirect our national emphasis into other programs of national importance. But there are still others who are motivated by a fear of a gigantic industrial-military complex controlling our country. In regard to the latter, I find nothing inherently wrong in close coordination between defense and the industrial complex. In fact, it is essential if we are to maintain our defense at optimum levels of preparedness.

However, I would be less than frank if I did not express a word of caution. With power comes responsibility. It remains for industry to recognize that responsibility and act accordingly. To bulwark this, the government must continue to maintain close supervision and control over operations involving the military and defense oriented industry. Big industry should welcome this as their first and best line of defense against unfounded charges. I believe that your patriotism should ensure your cooperation.

Now let me speak for a moment about the growth of a disturbing element in our society which I view as a dangerous cancer if allowed to go unchecked.

It is the attitude of many Americans—particularly of many young Americans—toward the Vietnam War. When first participation was proposed, I opposed it as ill-advised. But we are in it. And American boys are out there dying in large numbers. They are out there fighting, figuratively, at least, with one hand tied behind their backs and a feather pillow in the other. Personally, I have been far from satisfied with the way the war has been fought but we have a duly chosen leader who is Commander in Chief and we have laws to govern our participation.

It is understandable that the youth of our country would prefer to carry on their civilian occupations, to study, to progress, to take part in the good life that goes on about us. But this does not justify the waves of desertions, the draft-card burning, the sit-in protests, and the hosts of other activities bordering on sedition.

I do not intend for this to be a flag-waving speech, but I for one, am proud of our flag. I am sure you get the same thrill as I do when I see it unfurled. But today it is being desecrated with offal and burned in defiant mockery.

Recently I watched a group of protesters parading with flags and banners. The banners read "Ho Chi Minh will win" and other such tripe. These people hold the land of their birth with scorn and derision. They constantly question and belie our aims, while they attribute to the enemies of our country the loftiest motives.

They donate blood to the Viet Cong. They are silent when the North Vietnamese brutally torture men, women, and children but are virulent when we defend ourselves. It is difficult for me to understand why Hanoi can be held a sanctuary while it is always open season in Saigon.

These people, if they are truly Americans, should reexamine their motives as well as their actions. Let them also reexamine the expressed motives and grisly actions of the followers of Communism. Let them ask themselves how much they have contributed to our country's welfare; how much they have worked to build this great land of ours.

Were they to go to these countries they support by their deeds—China, Russia, North Vietnam—or to their captives—Poland, Latvia, Lithuania, Hungary, Czechoslovakia, to mention only a few—I wonder if their reactions might not be different. In passing, let me say that I think our country can struggle along without them. Perhaps they would find out how fortunate they were to be born Americans. Perhaps they would then realize the stupidity of their protests—protests that would be harshly dealt with in almost any of the countries I have named. To condone, to excuse, to permit such actions is inimical to the best interests of all that civilization stands for.

We have other problems related to defense. One is the soaring costs of weapons, equipment, and other material. Defense costs have just about doubled in the past ten years. Total appropriations requested for Defense in fiscal year 1970 amount to a little over $80 billion.

The basic reasons for this mushrooming cost are not hard to find. We are fighting a war that costs at least $25 billion a year. We are also trying to curb inflation that has reduced our purchasing power so that today's dollar will buy only slightly more than what eighty cents would buy in 1958. And we are also finding our weaponry vastly more complex and thus more costly than in the recent past.

An M-1 rifle cost $31 to produce in 1946. An M-16 today costs $150. The *Forrestal* aircraft carrier cost $190 million to build in

Admiral James Forrestal Memorial Award

1951. The nuclear-powered *Nimitz* today has a price tag of $545 million. The F-84 fighter aircraft which was used during the Korean war was built for about $465 thousand. Today's F-111A has a current price of $6.8 million.

Other costs of government have increased similarity. In addition the government has taken on many new commitments. For just one of these, the war on poverty, the budget request for this coming year totals $27 billion.

As a result the average taxpayer keenly feels the pinch in his pocketbook. Because of its magnitude, much of his reaction centers on defense expenditures. An unpopular war is a prime target. Another is the overall cost of defense itself. I have noticed a ground swell of public opinion reflecting a growing unwillingness of people to pay the ever increasing cost of more and more sophisticated weaponry.

The only solution to all this, to me at least, is for some hard thinking on all levels, leading to solutions that will guide our future course.

There are those among us who, at the hoped-for conclusion of the war in Vietnam, would utilize the $25 billion windfall of "free assets" and pump it into urbanization programs, education, job-training, poverty, and other similar measures. Many people would urge the elimination of the 10% tax surcharge. Perhaps something can be done in each of these areas.

However, with my close connection with military preparedness, I am not unmindful of the increasing demands of our defense establishment. Partly as a result of our Vietnam operation, defense stocks of material and hardware have been drawn down markedly in the recent past. The replacement of these, the introduction of new weapons, and the modernization of those now in use will all call for expenditures of large sums if we are to maintain our defenses at home and honor our commitments abroad. There would be little gain to a course that would win a war against poverty in our backyards if we jeopardize the security of our very homes.

These are a few of our many problems. They are closely linked to your own livelihood and deserve your studied thought and response.

Only through the concerted cooperation of our best minds can we realize our collective aspirations.

Without optimism in the future, however, life would be a poor play indeed. Thus we owe it to ourselves and to succeeding generations to work fervently toward peace and understanding among nations.

History has a way of pulling some curious tricks out of the bag. Perhaps economic and social progress among all peoples will act as a great deterrent toward aggression. Mankind does not prefer to lose in a holocaust more than it can gain by a hollow victory. Perhaps enlightened leadership will lead to greater understanding, quell suspicion, and provide a lasting *detente* or even friendship among nations.

This is our dream, the longing of all democratic peoples. At present it is only a dream, but perhaps in the years ahead it may become a reality. It must if civilization is to survive and progress.

And so, to the members of the National Security Industrial Association, I wish you continued success in developing America's production potential. And again, I want to express my heartfelt thanks for the honor that you have bestowed upon me tonight.

IV.

Speeches on Civil Rights

[Cairo – Oct 29, 1953]

Thank Pitcher

Glad to be here – congratulations on great day – would have been a credit to large city –

Always glad to attend R.E.A. meetings. Brought about Revolution in American Agriculture.

My part in bill – in appropriations What it has done to farm home – Women – Children – Production – Added to total prosperity by purchase of appliances – Affected industry favorably – Labor

Greatest Single program to Happiness and prosperity.

Handwritten notes, speech at a meeting of the Rural Electric Association, Cairo, Georgia, 29 October 1953.

The Poll Tax
17 November 1942

During his campaign against Senator Russell for the United States Senate in 1936, Governor Eugene Talmadge sensed that he was losing the election, and introduced the topic of racial integration. Talmadge attempted to link Russell with President Franklin D. Roosevelt's New Deal programs that he said favored blacks. For example, Talmadge maintained that the New Deal taxed white Georgians to pay "huge pensions" to elderly African Americans, thereby decreasing the pool of minority workers.[1] Although re-elected to the Senate, from this campaign Russell learned how precarious was a southerner's elected office.

In this speech, during Senate debate, Russell opposed House Bill 1024, legislation introduced to abolish the Poll Tax.[2] He claimed that the Poll Tax was not used to deny African Americans the right to vote. Referring to blacks as "an uncivilized race," the Senator argued that state governments should make their own decisions.

* * * * * * * * * *

Mr. President, when I was interrupted by the parliamentary inquiry, I think I was discussing some of the history of the poll tax in my own State. I do this for the reason that the report of the majority of the committee on the bill sought to be brought up arrives at the conclusion, and states that this legislation is necessary because the several States devised the poll tax as a means of disfranchising the Negro in the eight Southern States.

I challenge that statement, Mr. President, and denounce it as being absolutely false and without foundation. Back in the days of colonial Georgia, when we were living under King George III, there

---

[1] *Atlanta Constitution*, August 29, 1936.
[2] Text of speech from *Congressional Record: Proceedings and Debates of the 77th Congress*, November 17, 1942, Second Session, Vol. 88, Part 7, 8897-8905.

was a poll tax of 4 shillings and 6 pence in the colony of Georgia, which any voter was compelled to pay before he could avail himself of the privilege of the franchise in voting for the members of the colonial legislative body.

It has been urged here that it is undemocratic and improper—yea, unconstitutional—to require a man to go forth into battle for a State which would levy a tax upon his right of exercising the franchise. That would be news to those from my State of Georgia who entered the Continental Army and gave their all in order that we might enjoy the independence and the rights and privileges which are ours as American citizens today. At that time some people from other sections of the country, from which sections today people are trying to force this bill down our throats, were still making a great business of selling us Negro slaves, and the poll tax was then in existence. Yet it is said here that it is necessary to pass this bill because the poll tax was devised as a means of disfranchising the Negro.

In the Revolutionary War the colony of Georgia made a record of which it might well be proud. The youngest of the Thirteen Original Colonies, it was the only one which had ever received any direct monetary grants from the British Crown. For that reason many of the people were kindly disposed toward the British Government, for unusual favors shown. Brother was arrayed against brother. Some of the most horrible tragedies of all our history, equaling that when Sherman passed through spreading his trail of devastation and woe, were incidents which occurred in the battles between the partisan bands of patriots and Tories in Georgia during the great struggle for independence. Nearly every house in the State was burned, most of the men were killed or wounded, and the women and children suffered indescribable horrors. The Tories and British brought in the Indians to complete the work of destruction.

But the revolutionary patriots never wavered, and despite the fact they had a poll tax they carried on through it all to victory and freedom for us all. . . .

Then, Mr. President, we come to that tragic fratricidal strife of the [eighteen] sixties, when brother was arrayed against brother in the greatest tragedy of all our American history. The poll tax was in effect

The Poll Tax

in Georgia during that war. After four years of heroic service upon the battlefields of Virginia and the West, the Georgia soldier accepted his defeat in good faith with his other southern comrades and returned to his home. My State suffered more from that bloody and awful struggle than almost any other State. It is not generally known, but in the Battle of Chickamauga, fought on Georgia soil, more men were actually killed in battle in 1 day than in any other battle of the Civil War.

The southern soldier came home, it is true, to find his home in ashes, and saw his wife and children coming up to greet him on a path which led from a house which had been occupied by servants when he marched away to war. But he had courage, Mr. President, even though he lived in a community which levied a poll tax. He faced the situation as a man, and, standing in the fire-blasted ashes of all he held dear, he faced the east and swore he would build there on the ashes of the old civilization an even greater and brighter civilization. He carried on under great handicaps. There in that tragic era of reconstruction his every movement was made under Federal bayonets. His civil courts and authorities were stricken down. He was disfranchised. He was not even permitted to vote if he paid the poll tax, because he was proscribed by reason of having fought for the rights of the States which he regarded as dearer than life itself. He found all the institutions of his Government overturned and military Governors operating the States.

In that day, Mr. President, that tragic day, the military Governor of my State called for the gathering of a constitutional convention to write a new State constitution, to give force and effect to the amendments to the National Constitution which had been adopted here in Washington. In the election of delegates to that constitutional convention the average white man in the South was not even permitted to vote, and the election was held in the shadow of Federal bayonets. That convention, Mr. President, was known in Georgia as the Negro-carpetbagger-scalawag convention. Perhaps Senators from other sections of the country are not familiar with those terms. A carpetbagger was someone from outside the South who came into the South at a time when the people were helpless, in search either of a home or of a political job with the new governments which were being instituted, or to prey upon those who could not defend themselves. The name is derived from the fact that the man brought all his possessions in a small valise, which was called a carpetbag. Many carpetbaggers left after a few years, and left with much more than they brought. Some of them, be it said to their eternal credit, stayed in good faith in the South. They saw the conditions there, and today the viewpoint of their children is the same as the viewpoint of the children of those who fought on the side of the Confederacy. Some of the best citizens of my State are those who moved into that State immediately after the War between the States.

Mr. President, a scalawag was one who was born and reared in the South. More often than not he had perhaps, through force, served in the southern armies. Generally, however, he was a shirker or a straggler when a battle for the South and southern rights and honor was at its hardest. He was one who, when he came home and saw his own prostrate and bleeding people ground into the earth, instead of casting his lot with them and seeking to bind up their wounds, abandoned them in their hour of distress and went over to the carpetbaggers and the Negroes, and fawning upon them for the purpose either of getting political preferment, or of securing plunder and booty from a helpless people, joined hands and went into the forefront of those who had come from abroad to persecute his own helpless people.

Mr. President, it is little wonder that in their hour of agony the Southern people regarded the scalawags who added to their distress as being more infamous than either Judas Iscariot or Benedict Arnold. Even the soldiers from the North who were stationed in the South held the scalawags in unspeakable contempt because they had abandoned their people in their hour of trial and groveled before the Negroes and carpetbaggers. They were without principle and without conscience.

That was the complexion of the constitutional convention which assembled in my State in 1868 to rewrite a State constitution. Negroes, carpetbaggers, and scalawags met to frame a constitution for the State of Georgia, but when they met they wrote into that constitution a poll-tax provision as a requirement for voting, and I imagine that they would be utterly dismayed today to know that in this late hour it is said that the States had no right to levy this poll tax, and that it was necessary for the Federal Government to project itself into the State with some sort of a super-carpetbag-scalawag proposition as this from Washington, to go down and tell the people of the State what kind of a constitution they are to have, and to undertake by a mere Federal statute to repeal in the constitution of a sovereign State a provision which has been in it a hundred years.

Mr. President, I do not stand here as any advocate of a poll tax. It may be outmoded. It may be that the time has passed when it is necessary for people in their poverty to levy a head tax for any purpose, but I want to say, Mr. President, that it is very difficult for some Senators from the wealthier States to understand how important every dollar is that we are able to get into our State treasuries to make our schools operate in some of the less fortunate States which have been so long exploited.

That 1868 convention in Georgia wrote into the constitution the provision that this tax should every year be set up as a special fund for education. It is assessed against white and black alike. It is applied to the education of white and black alike. Yet we hear it said that it is a device framed by the eight Southern States to disfranchise the Negroes. That is most absurd. It is utter poppycock. It is as utterly without foundation as any contention which has been made in this body since I have been a Member here.

The poll-tax provision should perhaps be repealed, but insofar as Georgia is concerned it should be repealed by the people of Georgia. The Federal Government, after accepting us into the Union when we ratified the Constitution in 1788, with the poll-tax provision in our constitution, and after having let it exist even through the trying days of the Reconstruction, has certainly no right to invade my State now and attempt to hold it up to public scorn, and say "Here are these Southern States; they are so backward that they are not capable of administering their own affairs. We have got to go down in there from Washington and rewrite the constitution for them, and tell them what they can and what they cannot have."

No; I am no advocate of the poll tax, Mr. President, but I am a bitter opponent of any effort by the Congress of the United States to strike down by statute the Constitution of the United States and my State constitution, particularly when the effort is motivated by some of the influences which I see here behind the bill. It is supported by every professional South hater in the United States. Oh, those backward, illiterate southerners, with the lowest per capita income in the United States, trying to get a little money to keep their schools open to educate their youth down there through this tax, are then held up to national scorn. The professional South haters join hands with the professional reformers to come down there and reform us on the ground that we are not capable of looking after our own interests.

Mr. President, the people from my section did their bit in the Spanish-American War. They fought—and some of them died—as bravely and as truly as did the people of any other section of this Republic. They came from a section which had a poll tax. In the First World War they came from a community which had a poll tax, and no question was raised that they should not fight because they came from States where a poll tax was imposed. It is only now, after 150 years, that statesmen have been developed who are able to perceive that the poll tax is so iniquitous that it is violative of the Federal Constitution, even though it was in effect at the time the Constitution was approved.

We thought we had perhaps a few statesmen back in the early days of this Republic. We have been taught at school—and it is still in some of the obsolete history books—that those who framed the Constitution of the United States were men of some little ability. When the Constitution was framed no prohibition against the poll tax was written. On the contrary, the right of the States to levy it was specifically protected in that great document. The poll tax was in existence when the Constitution was approved. We thought we had some statesmen back in the early 1800's. In the early days of the 1800's, in the dramatic moments which led to the War between the States, we thought that some of our statesmen were men of ability. In some quarters, Clay, Webster, and other great men have been recognized as men of some ability. But, oh no, Mr. President, the true Messiahs had not yet put in their appearance. The men who strode across the stage of history in that period were mere weaklings when it came to really perceiving what was unconstitutional. When we compare them with these present-day giants who look back to 1785, and read in the minds of the colonial legislature of Georgia, an objective to disfranchise the Negro through a poll tax, those men were nothing.

We fought through a World War in 1917 and 1918. There were men of some ability in the Congress at that time. The Senator from Kentucky [Mr. (Alben) Barkley] was a Member of Congress at that time. The war was fought and won without anybody making the amazing discovery that it was illegal and unconstitutional for a man to be called upon to fight for a State in which a poll tax was imposed. For 150 years, down to the year 1939, not even the most fanatic of the advocates of centralizing power in Washington ever imagined that the Federal Congress had the power, by statute, to wipe out the provisions of a State constitution which has such a long historical background. It remained for the great Senator from Kentucky and the Senator from Florida [Mr. (Claude) Pepper] to make the amazing discovery that all these years we have been living under a vicious, unconstitutional system which they would now remedy by a simple statute.

Mr. President, I know something about the forces behind this bill. I took the trouble to run through the hearings before the Senate Judiciary Committee. I would not deny to any person who ever lived the right to appear before a Senate committee and give voice to his views and opinions. However, Mr. President, I resent some of the things which have been said about my people and my State. A witness who appeared with the Senator from Florida in support of this bill, a witness who is temporarily sojourning in my State, made the statement before that committee, not once, but two or three times, that it was the practice in the State of Georgia for certain persons to buy up a large number of poll tax certificates, and for one person to take those certificates to the polls and cast a large number of votes with the certificates.

Mr. President, there was never any greater fabrication of any matter before any committee of Congress in the history of the Republic. The statement to which I refer is false and untrue. There is no such thing in my State as a poll-tax certificate as a license to vote. The poll tax is not paid at the time of voting. The voter is not required to submit any form of certificate or showing whatever when he presents himself to cast his ballot. The constitution of the State of Georgia requires that the poll tax shall be paid six months before the holding of the election. The registrars make up the lists of voters by going to the office of the tax collector and ascertaining who has paid his poll tax. There is no such thing in my State as a poll-tax certificate as a license which is brought in by a person when he presents himself to exercise the right of franchise.

No State in the Union has fairer, cleaner, or purer elections than has the State of Georgia, which I have the honor in part to represent here. I resent the imputations of the holier-than-thou Members of Congress who have the bill in charge that the measure is necessary to assure pure elections in the Southern States. The original House bill, the text of which is before Senators at the present time, states that because of pernicious political activities in the South it is necessary for the Federal Government to invade our State and undertake to clean up elections among our poor, ignorant, and backward people, who do not know how to handle themselves.

Of course, Mr. President, in a matter of this kind equity means nothing. The sponsors of the proposed law never heard of the rule that he who seeks equity must come into court with clean hands. Men of that ilk care nothing of equity and decency. The "holier-than-thou" Members of Congress who have been anointed by the machine of Boss Kelly in Chicago, that great humanitarian and pure political organization, urge the passage of this bill on the ground that it is necessary in order to clean up elections in the State of Georgia. Mr. President, there is more fraud and corruption in the Kelly machine or the Hague machine in five minutes than there has been in all the Georgia elections in the past 50 years combined.

I resent some of the forces which are behind this bill. I have no quarrel with communistic Russia as a fighting organization. The

The Poll Tax

Russians are powerful partners to have in a scrap. I have no objection to the people of Russia having the form of government that they desire. I am perfectly willing to go to the extreme limit in getting together all the tools, machinery, and material that we possibly can assemble, and go to great lengths in getting them to the battle front in Russia, to be used against our common enemy. However, Mr. President, I do not appreciate the fact that Mr. Earl Browder, the head of the Communist Party in the United States, is identified as one of the leaders in connection with the proposed legislation.

I am somewhat familiar with the program of the Communist Party in this country. Before there shall ever be a vote upon the pending bill in this body I propose to read on the floor of the Senate some of the documents of the Communist Party which have been scattered from one end of the South to the other. Speaking of disunity, if there ever was an effort to array one race against another, it has been made in the South by the Communist Party which is now sponsoring this bill.

The only thing which has done more than the Communist Party through the distribution of pamphlets to tear down good relations which men of good will in both races have painstakingly and earnestly created over a long period of years has been the proposal of measures such as that before the Senate at this time.

Mr. President, I have pamphlets which have been circulated by the Communist Party which demand that the States from the Potomac River to the Rio Grande, including Texas, shall be turned over wholly, solely, and exclusively to the colored people. The pamphlets state that the white people should be put out of those States bodily, and if they are not hurled out they should be liquidated, or made slaves of the blacks of those States, and that those States should be made into a great black communistic republic. For some time those leaflets have been scattered by the Communist Party in my State, and I shall exhibit them on the floor of the Senate before the debate is concluded. So when I see proposed legislation which bears the imprimature of Mr. Earl Browder and the Communist Party I scan it with unusual care.

I have seen pamphlets pertaining to the legislative program of that party. This bill is near the head of the list. The sponsors propose to follow it by other legislation which would wipe out all our registration and qualification laws and allow some little Federal official from some other State to preside at every polling precinct in the South during every election, not only congressional, but State and local as well. When I see them getting ready to make this the first step of such a program I resent it, and I shall do all that lies within my power to block that first step. Now, Mr. President, we have in Washington other organizations sponsoring the measure. We have Walter White, a Negro who runs the N.A.A.C.P. [National Association for the Advancement of Colored People], who is a great sponsor of this legislation. I understand that White used to be a constituent of mine. He has moved away now, and he has a good job as a Washington lobbyist. Of course, he has to have something to promote or the income will run out, and so he always has a bill. He has a right to urge his bill; but he is behind this legislation, and he appeared before the committee in conjunction with lobbyists from other colored organizations who are doing more to destroy wholesome racial relations in the South than men who have almost given their lives to build up good relations have been able to establish over a long period of years. It is a great tragedy, Mr. President, that we have men who in their haste to secure votes in some sections commit themselves to legislation like this without realizing the full implications of the legislation.

Mr. President, I shall not attempt to address myself to this subject at any length today. I do want to point out that as to those who are referring to the opposition which has been presented to the bill as being guilty of a filibuster, as engendering national disunity, the leadership has but to make a simple motion at five minutes past two to take up the bill to enable us to proceed to debate it upon its merits, to strip it of all the sham and pretense that have been thrown about it, to dispel all of the fogs of misrepresentation with which it has been shrouded, and to let the American people see what is really in the measure. It is merely a political punitive expedition into eight Southern States, and the forerunner of other efforts of the Federal Government to take charge of all of our election machinery. Vote for

The Poll Tax

it if you will; cram it down our protesting throats if you can; I predict that the day will come when you will regret having given all power to the Federal Government and left the States impotent. . . .

I desire to say now, Mr. President, that we who are defending ourselves here, we who are not only undertaking to protect our people but who are expressing our resentment at having them held up to scorn and attack with subtle abuse, have a right to avail ourselves of any privilege which is open to us. For my part I propose to avail myself of every right I have. Let the proponents make the most of it. Your warrants of arrest will not deter us in this fight. They will not stifle my protests or abate the contempt that I feel for some of the forces and motives back of this bill.

Mr. President, I notice that there is a tendency on the part of some Presiding Officers—and I certainly make no reference to the great Senator who is our present Presiding Officer—to take short cuts to deny Senators their rights under the rules, and to avoid seeking Senators who are standing upon their feet clamoring for recognition, look in another direction as if they are hoping and praying that some other Senator will seek recognition, and all the looking is away from those of us who oppose this infamous legislation, and it is all toward those who are seeking to cram it down our throats. In the consideration of the measure we are entitled, as Senators know, to a fair and square deal under the rules of this body. I, for one, shall insist and fight to the limit of my power and strength to see that no Member of this body is denied even one jot or tittle of any right that is his under the rules and precedents of this body merely because he opposes any such invasion of the States and infringements of the rights of the people of the States as is proposed in this legislation. This bill would lynch the Constitution of the United States and the constitution of the State of Georgia, but we shall endeavor to see that the rules of the Senate are not also raped and violated in the process.

Mr. President, there are probably some who are urging this legislation in good faith. They should perhaps be forgiven on account of their ignorance as to what they are doing; but they are doing more to cause race feeling and confusion in the South, they are doing more to delay the elimination of the poll tax in the Southern States, than is any person who might be in favor of retaining the poll tax. The poll tax is on its way out. It has already been voted out in North Carolina; there is no poll tax in the great State of Louisiana; there is no poll tax in the State of Florida, among the Southern States; and, Mr. President, I understand that the Democratic Party in Tennessee proposes to repeal the poll tax in that State this year. I happen to know that it was to be proposed in the Georgia Legislature this year to have the constitution so amended as to abolish the poll tax in the State of Georgia; and if a measure to that effect were submitted to the people of Georgia on a vote, as a voter in that State I should vote to repeal the poll tax as a State function.

That is one question, Mr. President. It is another to have to be compelled to stand on the floor of the Senate at intervals year after year and defend your people against legislation which is conceived with the idea of smearing the South and of putting the southern people in the light of being unable to attend to their own affairs. Let the poll tax be repealed, if it should be, at the proper place. We have not yet come to the state of affairs in Georgia where we need the advice of those who would occupy the position of the carpetbagger and the scalawag of the days of reconstruction to tell us how to handle our internal affairs. We have good government in our States. We have pure elections in our States. I say, further, Mr. President, that we are treating the Negro fairly in our States; and the Negro who is living with us there is not aided any when Walter White and these other Negro lobbyists get up legislation of this kind and bring it on the floor of the Senate.

Mr. President, I challenge all human history to show another instance where in the brief span of seventy-five years as much progress has been made by an uncivilized race as has been made by the southern Negro who was sold to us as a slave by our friends from the East but a short while ago in the life of a people. I challenge all history since the beginning of man to show any country or any people where two races as different as the white and the black races have been thrown together under such conditions as those by which the blacks and the whites have been thrown together in the South and where as

The Poll Tax

much progress has been made in the brief period of seventy-five years in establishing fair and just relations between those peoples.

Oh, there are injustices, there are abuses; but I say that despite the burden that we have been carrying in the South, those injustices and those abuses are not any worse, if as bad, than those imposed between two different strata of society in the States which have practically no Negroes today.

I am tired of having the South pilloried with this type of legislation. Any fair-minded man who will study the history of the last 75 years would commend the South on the great work that we have done. Under the leadership of our own people those who were ignorant slaves 75 years ago have made great strides forward. They have been provided with educational facilities largely at the expense of the whites. Many of them own their own homes or businesses, and some have accumulated wealth. No minority race under similar circumstances has ever enjoyed as large a measure of justice and freedom in such a brief period. We have worked hard and painstakingly down through the years to evolve a plan of having the Negro in our midst with the least possible friction, and we have made remarkable progress in adjusting the inevitable problems and conflicts which arise when two races live side by side.

We have made this progress in spite of all the reformers, publicity seekers, vote hunters, and South baiters and haters who harass us year after year by undertaking to tell us from Washington how to run our local affairs, and make a business of criticizing the South. If you expect by this or similar legislation to force social equality and the commingling of the races in the South, I can tell you now that you are doomed to failure. You do a great injury to the southern Negro by urging legislation of this kind, and even though you have the votes to enable you to pass the law, you will never be able to enforce any such system in the Southern States. The Negroes are building up a social system and a civilization of their own within the social system and civilization of the South, but it is separate and apart, and you cannot bring them together by law or edict. It is not to the interest of either the Negro or white race that this should be done.

If some of you zealous reformers would but direct your attention to worse abuses and injustices that are nearer home and leave us of the South, white and black, alone, as we work out this problem, it will be much better for all concerned.

So, Mr. President, speaking as one Member of the Senate, I consider the motion to project this matter into the Senate at this time the most inexcusable one of which I have ever known. It is not justified by any fact or condition that has been brought to the attention of any committee of the Congress. Not a single committee has had before it a witness to testify that any pernicious political activities are being carried on in the Southern States. Not a single witness has appeared to testify that there is any different condition existing today than there was in 1785 when the poll tax was first imposed in Georgia. On the contrary, the Southern States are wiping this tax out step by step. If this bill shall be passed, if it shall be crammed down our throats and the Southern States shall be invaded and their election machinery taken over, there will be torn down in the twinkling of an eye something that has been constructed very painstakingly and by the rule of trial and error over a period of many years. It will be a great internal tragedy in the midst of war.

We hear much said about disunity; it is asserted that the poll tax is calculated to bring about disunity, when it has been in effect for 150 years; yet no mention is made of the disunity that is caused by Democrats attempting to force down Democratic throats such legislation as this.

So, Mr. President, for my part, I shall fight to the last, to the bitter end, so long as I can stand and speak, against this legislation proposing to repeal by statute, not only the Federal Constitution but also the constitution of my State. The effort is all the more clearly unconstitutional since it was a custom, practice, and law in Georgia when my State approved the original Federal Constitution in 1778. If this bill be passed, it will wipe out the last right of the States. There would be no real excuse for their existence, and the State government would be a useless appendage.

I shall continue to denounce with all the vigor at my command those who assume and take the position that my people in Georgia

The Poll Tax

and those in other Southern States are in need of a Federal guardian sent down from Washington to tell them the type of legislation they shall enact within the State, and who undertake to prescribe rules and requirements covering the life of my people at the behest and insistence of those who either hate them or who would capitalize politically on legislation directed at them. My people in Georgia are the peers of any in this Nation. They are doing their part in this war, as they have ever done in the past. There is no condition which deserves the odium this legislation would heap upon them, and they deserve better and fairer treatment at the hands of their fellow Americans.

President Harry S. Truman's Civil Rights Commission
23 March 1948

In 1944 the Supreme Court ruled that denying African Americans participation in so-called "white" primaries was unconstitutional. Two years later, the Court determined that passengers could not be segregated by race when crossing state lines in public transportation. To placate most Georgia voters, Senator Russell opposed any efforts by Presidents Franklin D. Roosevelt and Harry S. Truman to pass civil rights legislation. In this speech, opposing "professional agitators," Russell led a quartet of southern senators in a series of radio broadcasts over WOL and the Mutual Network in opposition to legislation initiated by Truman's Civil Rights Commission.[3] The other senators participating were Burnet R. Maybank of South Carolina, Clyde R. Hoey of North Carolina, and Lister B. Hill of Alabama.

* * * * * * * * * *

The slogan—"civil rights"—is appealing. The report of President Truman's commission bears an attractive label. All Americans believe in the protection of individual rights and liberties. I would advise you, however, to look the President's gift horse in the mouth. It will be well for every citizen everywhere who is truly interested in individual rights and liberties to carefully examine the contents of this package labeled "civil rights." Otherwise you will find after delivery that you have been badly cheated. An examination will reveal that under the guise of protecting the rights of various minority groups the enforcement of the commission's recommendations will have the effect of wiping out

---

[3]Text of speech from Speech File, Speech and Media Series, Richard B. Russell Collection, RRLPRS.

the rights of the States and seriously impairing some of your individual rights which have long been considered sacred.

What about this commission and the reasons behind their unusual presentation? The commission was a carefully selected body. The views of the individual members, as well as those of the professional staff who prepared the report, were generally known before their selection. No outstanding authority on the Constitution and constitutional rights was a member. It is therefore no surprise that the report embraces and approves every suggestion and theory brought forward by professional agitators whose vocation it is to represent the various minority pressure groups here in the national capital.

The report frankly admits that its conclusions are in the main directed at the Southern States. It proposes by Federal fiat to revolutionize the political, economic, and social relations between the whites and the Negroes in the South to make them conform to the views of the President and his commission.

In the effort to intimidate the Congress into enacting their proposals into law they are bringing into full play the power of political pressure of well organized minority groups. Though the recommendations will do more to disturb racial relations than anything suggested by Thad Stevens or Charles Sumner in the tragic era of reconstruction, not a single person whose views are truly representative of Southern majority opinion was appointed to the commission. Not an open hearing was held in any State at which a Governor or other responsible official or citizen was permitted to testify. No record of any evidence justifying the extreme conclusions and the vicious sanctions demanded against innocent and helpless Southern people has been made public. We are told that unless we supinely submit to having our lives and social order completely refashioned to the whim and fancy of reformers and zealots representing the minority pressure groups—that our old people are to be denied pensions; our sick and afflicted are to be refused medical care; the education of our children is to be crippled; we are not to be permitted to share any beneficial activities of our Federal Government.

In spite of this condign punishment we are to be compelled to continue to pay Federal taxes and defend our country just as anyone else. This is the sweeping verdict of a hand-picked jury reached in what amounted to Star Chamber sessions. We appeal from that verdict to the sense of decency and fair play of the American people.

We submit that the white people of the South, though widely misunderstood and oft maligned, have some few rights as American citizens. We are grateful to the Mutual Broadcasting Company for affording us this time to present our views.

To those of you who are tempted to turn away from this issue with a shrug and a "Let those Southerners squirm," let me point out that many phases of this drastic program directly affect you and your rights. If it is enacted into law the everyday life of all citizens will be in some measure regulated and controlled by Federal bureaus and bureaucrats in Washington. If Federal power strikes down the individuality of any one State or group of States the rights of your State will be invaded. If Federal law creates an entirely new right for a member of a minority group at the expense of an inalienable right of any other citizen, your security in the enjoyment of your right is endangered. The passage of these laws will strip the once proud States of this Union of their last remaining rights and reduce them to a state of abject vassalage to Washington. Local self government will become a mere fiction. Hordes of new Federal employees—to be supported by already overburdened taxpayers—will swarm over the country as Federal policemen to enforce these drastic laws. The Federal Government cannot embark upon such a program without concentrating police powers. Any such centralization will inevitably lead to complete regimentation and to that disastrous loss of personal liberties which marks the centralized police state.

Our Federal Constitution reserves to the several States and to the people all powers not specifically given to the Federal Government. This dual system of Government has caused America to grow great and strong. The States of the Union have served as forty-eight laboratories. In these laboratories we have tested new ideas and made the adjustments necessary to meet the varying needs of the people of different sections of our country without that violence to State and individual rights which overall Federal action always entails.

The fundamental rights guaranteed to the individual citizen by our Federal Constitution are those of life, liberty, and property. This guarantee protects all citizens, whether members of minorities or so-called majorities. Efforts to twist or distort these constitutional rights so as to penalize one citizen for the benefit of another is a dangerous procedure. Let me remind those of the so-called minorities that even if they accomplish their purpose and pass these bills they are likely to create a Frankenstein which will eventually destroy them.

Let us consider how this program will affect your rights if you happen to belong to what the President's commission regards as a majority group. In substance they advance the remarkable proposition that in a democracy members of the majority must be deprived of rights long considered as inalienable to enable minority citizens to enjoy newly created rights. The average citizen will be startled to know that in the view of this commission he has no right to choose his associates in business or in pleasure, in the education of his children or in any or all of his common everyday relations. The President's commission holds that the rights of choosing one's own associates should be denied the ordinary garden variety American citizen who cannot claim to be a member of a minority group.

If their wishes are attained—the Federal police power is to be invoked to compel one American citizen either to employ or work with or associate with other American citizens not of his choosing. If the poor garden variety fellow refuses to accept in the most intimate associations of life some person selected for him by a petty Federal official he is to be sent to Federal prison. What has become of the right of the garden variety American if such laws are enacted? We contend that it is unfair, unjust, and violative of the individual rights guaranteed by our Constitution to create these new rights for minority groups. It amounts to special privileges for minorities at the cost of rights long possessed by other individual Americans.

An effort has been made to create the impression that the white people of the South claim civil rights greater than those conceded Negroes. This is untrue. The enlightened Southerner believes in equality in administration of the law for all citizens without regard to race or creed. We do, however, insist upon the right that we regard as sacred and inalienable of choosing our own associates. We believe that the rights of no person have been violated so long as the members of both races, white and Negro, may maintain restaurants, hotels, swimming pools, where they may enjoy the right to associate only with members of their own race. We believe that white parents have a right to have their children associate in the schools with white children and be taught by white teachers. We believe that the Negro is entitled to his schools and to Negro teachers.

The Southern whites have a pride of race. They resent the efforts to employ the power of the Federal Government to force Negro children into the white schools. We believe our Negro citizens have a pride of race which will cause them to resent the efforts to take away from them the individuality of their schools and the opportunities of their teachers.

Before you condemn our view, I ask you to consider the fact that the solution of a racial problem is one thing in a community where the population is five percent Negro and ninety-five percent white, and quite a different proposition in another community where fifty percent of the people are Negroes and fifty percent are white. The Southerner is often accused of bigotry and intolerance because of his views. Bear in mind that while we do insist upon the right to build our own social order, based on our own experiences, we do not constantly assail the people of other States for holding a different view.

For example, under the constitution and laws of the State of New Jersey no State funds are available to schools unless they compel the intermingling of the races in the classrooms. Failure to serve Negroes and whites together in the hotels, restaurants, and all other public places is a violation of the criminal statutes of that State. If a proprietor of a skating rink or a swimming pool undertakes to cater to any special group or race he is subject to both civil suit and criminal punishment.

A recent news article carried a story to the effect that the white girl students of a school were insisting that the Negro boy students of that institution attend their school dances. There is of course no law in New Jersey against the intermarriage of the races such as we have in all of the Southern States. In frankness, the New Jersey social pattern is offensive to the South. Any policy of solving the grave racial problem of this nation by absorbing the Negro race through the process of amalgamation is abhorrent to us. Wherever this solution has been applied, degeneration has followed. We consider it a crime against our civilization and a sin against nature's God. I am sure that we feel as strongly about the New Jersey system as the people of New Jersey could feel about ours. But have you ever heard of a Southern Congressman undertaking to pass Federal legislation to repeal these New Jersey laws?

I would be the last to claim that every detail of our racial relations has been perfectly handled. But our progress has been steady and great, and any effort to compel radical changes by Federal legislation will do irreparable injury. The solution of our problem has been an immense task, undertaken under tremendous difficulties.

Let those who would be critical of the paucity of our educational and health facilities and economic opportunities for our Negro citizens bear in mind the great disparity existing as well between the opportunities and the health and educational facilities of the Southern white people as compared with those of more favored areas. We have long taxed ourselves more heavily in proportion to our means to provide these facilities for white and black alike than have the people of any other section. We are going ahead in spite of our handicaps. The greatest of these has been our economic situation—not social or racial problems. Within the lifetime of people living today the South suffered complete defeat in the most destructive war ever fought on this continent. No other American States have suffered comparably from the devastation of invasion, or lost anything like as much manpower and wealth. We did not share in the prosperity which followed in the wake of the War Between the States. We lived under the bayonets of victorious armies for twelve years, and since that time have suffered as a people, both black and white, the most severe forms of economic exploitation. It was 1940—eighty years—before the tax values in my own State of Georgia reached the taxable values of the tragic year of 1860. We had no Marshall Plan or other form of relief. Instead we were weighted down with punitive legislation. It has been a long and tedious process to pull ourselves up by our own bootstraps.

We have shared with the Negro, only recently freed from enslavement—the meager blessings of our poverty. We have paid a fearful penalty for having held to the institution of slavery after it was no longer profitable in the North. We have paid a fearful price for undertaking over eighty years ago to leave the Union. We accepted the verdict of that war in good faith, and ever since have had to grapple with a problem of greater complexity and magnitude than was ever thrust upon any other people in human history. We feel that we are entitled to better treatment at the hands of our fellow Americans than to be kicked as a political football in every election year, and to have our good name constantly bartered by political auctioneers in bidding for votes.

We have assumed our responsibilities in both war and peace since 1860 without complaint, believing in and cleaving to the Constitution that our forebears had so large a part in fashioning. We appeal to all of those in every section who still believe that the Constitution is the Ark of the Covenant of our liberties. Do not be deceived by platitudes, propaganda, or appeals to prejudice into a course which will threaten the blessings of our system and the individual liberties of all of our people.

Message to Constituents
24 January ca. 1950

In this speech, broadcast over WSB Radio in Atlanta, Senator Russell addressed issues he considered vital to Georgians and Americans, including taxation of oleomargarine, deficit spending, and civil rights proposals.[4] He discussed legislation underway to remove "unjust taxes" on oleomargarine, a topic of interest to Georgia farmers. He cautioned about the nation spending more than it collected in taxes. Russell opposed "civil rights" legislation. As in the past, the Senator spoke out against the "intermingl[ing]" of blacks and whites, and complained because he felt the South was becoming a "whipping boy for political purposes."

* * * * * * * * *

Good evening, Ladies and Gentlemen, I wish to thank station WSB for affording the representatives from Georgia to the National Congress to talk to our constituents about the national issues which will be before the Congress in this session. Since [Adolf] Hitler [of Germany] moved into Poland in 1939 the Congress has been in almost continuous session. I have missed my opportunities to get about over Georgia and talk to the people about the many matters to be decided in Washington which so vitally affect our lives and the future of the country.

I am sure most of you know that last week the Senate passed the bill removing the unjust taxes which have been imposed upon oleomargarine for the past sixty-four years. This has been a matter of agitation and debate in the Senate since I first came to that body seventeen years ago. The representatives from the cotton states have protested these discriminatory penalties each year. Having only about

---

[4]Text of speech from Speech File, Speech and Media Series, Richard B. Russell Collection, RRLPRS. The above date oddly indicates the precise day, but only an approximate year. The original copy of Russell's manuscript is dated in this way. The editors have chosen to leave it intact.

one-fourth of the members of the Senate, we were unable to correct this injustice until the consuming public demanded action from their representatives. The bill enacted contains provisions requested by the dairy industry and to which they were entitled which require the manufacturers of oleomargarine to clearly designate it as such. Both butter and oleo are legitimate commodities and are entitled to fair competition. The tax has been removed from oleo and the law assured to the dairy interests that no consumer will be deceived into buying oleomargarine as butter.

The national budget is undoubtedly the most vital issue before the Country. Your Government, during the current fiscal year, is spending more than five billion dollars more than we are collecting in taxes. The President's budget submitted to the Congress for the next fiscal year likewise shows a deficit of five billion dollars and there are some experts in fiscal affairs who predict that it will be nearer seven billion. This means that the national debt which has already reached the staggering sum of 258 billion dollars, will be increased by the amount of the deficit. Many of us do not believe that the Government is justified in borrowing money from its citizens and increasing the national debt so as to burden generations yet unborn—in a period of relative prosperity such as exists today. In the last session of the Congress several attempts were made to reduce some of the expenditures, but without success. The members of Congress spent some time with their people after adjournment last fall, and there is a stronger sentiment in favor of bringing the budget into closer balance than existed in the last Congress. If we are not to continue to pile up the public debt through deficit financing, we must either reduce expenditures to match income or increase taxes. This is a campaign year and it is highly unlikely that taxes will be materially increased, so the alternative is either to cut national spending or continue deficit financing.

I hope that we may be able to bring about substantial reductions in national spending. To my mind it is nothing short of folly to continue deficit financing under existing conditions. It is difficult for people to realize the problem which confronts those who wish to reduce Federal spending. In the first place, the interest on the national debt, the maintenance of adequate national defense, and the appropriation for the Veterans Administration and for other items which are due entirely to past wars amounts to seventy-one cents of every dollar which the Government spends. To substantially reduce the national defenses in the face of Russia's present aggressive drive for world conquest is to invite national disaster. The United States is the only nation of the earth that suffered reductions as great as eighty percent in their cotton acreage. As applied by the Department of Agriculture there are any number of hardship cases, while on the other hand allotments have been made to farmers who have no intention of planting any acreage at all. I have been urging the Committee on Agriculture and Forestry to report out a bill which will relieve those who have taken these unreasonable reductions and will permit reallocation of the acreage which will not be planted. Unless some relief is found, it will disorganize the operations of thousands of farmers and throw many people out of work. Up until now the Committee has not been able to agree on the form that the bill should take and how far it should go, but I hope that we will be able to get action within the next few days. Time, of course, is of the essence in this matter, and if it is delayed much longer it will be too late to prevent the damage which has been done in the system employed in allotting this acreage. There is also a great controversy here as to who is responsible for the allotment system, but it seems to me that this is not nearly as important as securing a directive from the Congress to straighten it out.

Just ahead of us lies a long and hard fight over the bills which are erroneously and euphoniously called civil rights. This being a campaign year, those who seek to use the South as a whipping boy for political purposes in other areas will press hard for the enactment of the misnamed FEPC [Fair Employment Practices Commission] and other so-called civil rights bills. Even if we are able to prevent the passage of these measures when they are brought up for consideration next month, we will undoubtedly be bedeviled by having them offered as amendments to nearly every other bill throughout the remainder of this session. The Administration leadership has selected the FEPC bill for their principal test. It is the most vicious of all of these bills and has the active if not violent support of fifty or sixty organizations representing minority groups throughout the nation. A so-called mobilization of several thousand advocates of the measure met in Washington last week with delegations from thirty-six states. They filled halls of office buildings and buttonholed. The bill has support from the dreamers and idealists who think that the Congress by passage of a law can immediately equalize everybody.

A number of other national organizations support it with the objective of destroying all forms and customs of separation of the races and to compel them to intermingle by Federal fiat. The socialists and the communists are unanimous in their support because they know it will cause internal confusion and result in the nationalization of all business and industry.

Much of its support in the Congress comes from those who know better. Many of them hope it will not be passed, but support it for political reasons. There is also opposition to this measure throughout the nation from the unorganized, and I believe it would be defeated in the ballot box if it were submitted to a national referendum of informed [citizens]. The fact that it is seriously pressed for passage shows how far we have come in this country to yielding to pressure groups who are vocal and whose votes are the balance of power in the larger and more populous states. The odds against us on this bill have increased since the last time it was pressed for passage in the long fight which occurred in 1946. I am hopeful, however, that there are still enough sane and courageous men in the Congress to enable us to defeat these politically inspired measures which can only bring confusion and disaster.

Civil Rights Referendum
2 July 1957

In this speech from the Senate floor Russell opposed the Eisenhower Administration's civil rights bill, and called for a national referendum on the measure.[5] He argued that the proposed legislation provided the federal government unchecked powers. The Senator discussed the role of the media in influencing citizens' attitudes toward the bill, and what he saw as the intimidation of the military and discrimination against the South. Russell opposed integrating black and white children in the "public schools of the South." The Senator called "talk about voting rights" for African Americans "a smokescreen to obscure the unlimited grant of powers" to the federal government.

* * * * * * * * *

Mr. President, for the first time since I have been a Member of the Senate, I respectfully request that I be not interrupted in the course of my prepared discussion. I shall be happy to yield to any Senator who wishes to discuss any phase of my remarks when I have finished.

In the course of the discussion of the so-called civil-rights bill when it was sent directly to the calendar I touched upon the propaganda campaign to deceive the American people as to the true purposes and effect of that measure. I charged that an effort was being made to sail this bill through the Senate under the false colors of a moderate bill to assure and protect the voting rights of American citizens, while obscuring the larger purposes of the bill.

I said then, Mr. President, and I reassert now that the bill is cunningly designed to vest in the Attorney General unprecedented

---

[5]Text of speech from *Congressional Record: Proceedings and Debates of the 85th Congress*, July 2, 1957, First Session, Vol. 103, Part 8, 10771-10775; the debate continued through 10778.

power to bring to bear the whole might of the Federal Government, including the Armed Forces if necessary, to force the commingling of white and Negro children in the State-supported public schools of the South.

Indeed, Mr. President, the unusual powers of this bill could be utilized to force the white people of the South at the point of a Federal bayonet to conform to almost any conceivable edict directed at the destruction of any of the local customs, laws, or practices separating the races in order to enforce a commingling of the races throughout the social order of the South.

This campaign of misrepresentation took shape even before the Senate took the unusual action of placing the bill directly on the calendar without committee consideration.

Proponents of the bill prepared the way for that action by speeches in which they consistently referred to it as a measure to assure the right to vote. The press, the radio, and television consistently parroted this propaganda line.

On the day following Senate action, I took occasion to listen to a number of radio and television broadcasts purporting to describe the bill and discuss the Senate action of bypassing the committee. Everyone that I heard referred to it as only a "moderate bill to assure voting rights for all citizens."

The great organs of the national press chorused this flagrant misrepresentation of the true character of the bill. . . .

Newsweek, which styles itself as the magazine of news significance, limited its description of the bill to this statement:

> Under the administration's civil-rights bill, the Attorney General would be given the power to seek an injunction in a Federal court against anyone who interfered with anyone else's right to vote. Those who violated the injunction would face charges of contempt of court.

Mr. President, I have always considered the *Christian Science Monitor* to be the most objective of our great national newspapers. But even the *Monitor* cautiously participated in the campaign in its

Civil Rights Referendum

editorial dealing with the Senate action by describing the bill as a plan to permit the Attorney General to obtain injunctions to prevent such things as denial of voting rights to Negroes.

These are samples of the misrepresentation of the scope and extent of the sweeping powers of this bill that came to my attention in the course of my daily reading. They are fair samples of the movement designed to inflame public sentiment in the rest of the Nation against the white people of the South and their representatives in the Congress, in order to force passage of the bill before the people generally understand all of its terms.

In my opinion, Mr. President, this campaign of deception as to what this bill proposes to accomplish constitutes an abuse of the constitutional guaranty of freedom of the press. It is as great an abuse of that constitutional right as abuses being practiced to deny to any segment of our population the constitutional right to exercise the franchise.

It is a much more widespread abuse, for in this country today there are very few areas where persons who are qualified under State law to vote find that right improperly limited or circumscribed. I can speak of personal knowledge of the condition in my own State. Within recent months, at a primary in our capital city, a Negro citizen was re-elected over a single white opponent to serve in an important office, by a city-wide primary vote, in a southern city where the colored population constitutes only about thirty percent of the total.

There is a very simple reason, Mr. President, for this studied misrepresentation of the sweeping powers to punish the South, as proposed by this bill. Let me say in passing that in all of its implications it is as much of an actual force bill as the measures proposed by [Charles] Sumner and [Thaddeus] Stevens in reconstruction days in their avowed drive "to put black heels on white necks." The powers are there, even though more cunningly contrived than the forthright legislation aimed at the South in the tragic era of reconstruction.

The simple reason for confining the description to a voting bill is that the American people generally are opposed to any denial of the right of ballot to any qualified citizen. It is easy to array them in support of a bill represented as confined to this purpose.

The more sweeping powers which this bill gives to the Attorney General, to exercise his will, are obscured because in this country outside the South there are millions of people who would not approve of another reconstruction at bayonet point of a peaceful and patriotic South.

There are many people in every State of the Union, including thousands who do not favor the social order which exists in the Southern States, who would not approve the use of their tax money to throw the whole might of the Federal Government, including the military forces, behind a force law designed to compel the intermingling of the races in the public schools and in all public places of entertainment in the Southern States.

There are many Americans everywhere who would look askance at denying the white people of the South the ordinary rights guaranteed all Americans everywhere, as is proposed in this cunningly contrived bill.

There are many Americans who know that constitutional guaranties cannot be denied to the white South without endangering the loss of those guaranties by all the people of this Nation.

There are others who do not believe in indicting and convicting the whole people of a great section of this land on the charge, unsupported by evidence, that all of them would forswear themselves as jurors.

Now, Mr. President, I shall undertake to examine some aspects of this measure, so glibly advertised as a moderate bill to assure the right to vote. I shall undertake to do so in language which the layman can understand. I shall cite sections of the code, in order that my brethren of the bar may have the opportunity to study what I believe to be the most classic example of cunning draftsmanship ever presented to the American Congress.

Mr. President, let us go first to the one part of the bill which does deal with voting rights. It is appropriate that the part of this drastic bill which deals solely with voting rights should be part IV of a four-part bill. Weighed against the important and far-reaching effect of the other provisions of the bill, it is meet and proper that the voting provision should be the last part of the bill, even though it is the only one that has been emphasized in the presentation of this wickedly designed measure to the American people. . . .

Mr. President, part IV undoubtedly deals with voting rights. I shall not at this time discuss the full effect of this language. At an appropriate time I shall undertake to show that there are already on the statutes of the United States any number of laws to assure the right to vote, including criminal statutes which punish by fine and imprisonment any person who interferes with that right.

Leaving part IV, the voting part, I shall now proceed to that section of the bill which clearly stamps it as a force bill of unprecedented powers aimed at the white South. I shall demonstrate by explaining part III of the bill that the talk about voting rights is a smokescreen to obscure the unlimited grant of powers to the Attorney General of the United States to govern by injunction and Federal bayonet. This section of the bill strikes at our whole theory of a government of law and proposes to create a government of men. It grants to one man or to men sweeping powers to deny individual rights by wholesale and to jail and imprison peaceful American citizens according to the whim or caprice of the man or men exercising the power.

The heart of this bill is found in part III. Part III is the most cunningly devised and contrived piece of legislation I have ever seen. It is the ultimate in the technique of legislative draftsmanship to obscure purpose while creating and conferring power. By a process of amending one statute or existing law by reference and taking this statute or law and incorporating it, by reference to a number, into another law, without anywhere spelling out the total effect of the proposed law in express terms, it cunningly obscures its real scope and purpose.

When I was engaged in the active practice of law I thought I was a fair lawyer, but it has taken me a great deal of study to comprehend thoroughly the full magnitude of the objectives of the drafters of this part of the bill.

I understand it completely now. I unhesitatingly assert that part III of the bill was deliberately drawn to enable the use of the military forces to destroy the system of separation of the races in the Southern States at the point of a bayonet, if it should be found necessary to take this step.

I assert that this bill vests in one man, the Attorney General of the United States, greater powers over the American people than any other man, including any President elected by the people, has ever possessed.

This part of the bill is a potential instrument of tyranny and persecution. It can be used to jail and imprison American citizens and to deny them elemental rights inherent to all our people if it accords with the political inclinations of any Attorney General who possesses the confidence of the President. . . .

Mr. President, the Attorney General of the United States does not ordinarily participate in civil suits for damages between individual citizens of the United States. His primary duty is to enforce the penal or criminal laws passed by the Congress. In studying this matter, I was greatly puzzled by the fact that this proposed new law, which gave the Attorney General the power to sue, in the name of the United States, at the expense of the American taxpayer, in civil actions should have been included in and made a part of the old law defining a tort action or a suit for damages when there were so many criminal statutes available.

I of course apprehended that the bill would be far-reaching in its effects. This bill would authorize the Attorney General to bring suits whether the aggrieved party wished him to sue or not. It has always been the duty of the Attorney General to prosecute for criminal violations whether the aggrieved party desired a prosecution to be entered or not, but it is unusual for him to seek powers under a damage suit law when there were so many other clearer statutes, including criminal statutes, available for use in seeking civil injunctions if that should be a necessary or proper proceeding.

I knew that under the clever wording of this section injunction suits could result in the jailing of American citizens for an indeterminate period without the benefit of jury trial. I soon found that the proposed act struck down all Federal and State administrative or other remedies that must ordinarily be pursued by private citizens.

But it was difficult to dig out the purpose of the draftsman in using this particular law which defines not a crime, but a cause of action or case for damages as the base for this far-reaching bill. . . .

Mr. President, I now undertake to show that the real purpose of this bill is to enforce judicial law dealing with separation of the races in the Southern States. Let me explain that judicial law is law that is written by the courts rather than by the Congress.

We have had an unusual spate of judicial law recently. The present Supreme Court is writing more judicial law than the Congress is making through the ordinary process of legislation.

I shall resist the temptation to deal with some of the recent excursions of the Supreme Court into the legislative field which we had heretofore considered as reserved to the Congress.

For the purposes of this exposé, I must say that we can expect the present occupants of the marble building constructed to house a Supreme Court of the United States to go to any requested length to make the white people of the Southern States conform to their psychologically inspired and supported decisions as to what the social order of the South should be.

With this I return to the subtle cunning of the draftsman of this act in seeking to use a law authorizing a suit for damages between individual Americans as a vehicle to vest these vast powers in the Attorney General. I assert, Mr. President, that this bill was specifically drawn in this peculiar fashion so as to authorize the use of the military forces of the United States against the white people of the South to compel them, if necessary at bayonet point, to do away with any separation of the races in any phase of public life. . . .

Mark well, Mr. President, that section 1985, the old reconstruction law creating the right to sue for damages, is specifically mentioned in this authorization of the use of military forces, whereas it is not mentioned in any of the other statutes describing a crime or any civil action that might lie in a case of this kind. None of these other statutes on which the Attorney General would ordinarily rely are mentioned in this section of the code, providing for the use of military forces. The devious purpose in undertaking to have the Congress legislate by reference and cross reference, and by numbers of references to sections of the code, was to tie this whole proposition into a law authorizing the use of troops to integrate southern schools, and not for the purpose of assuring the right of any citizen of this country to vote.

I might point out that the voting section of the code is not tied in with the use of military forces, whereas that section which will be utilized to force the mixing of the races in the schools and in the public places of amusement is tied in with the statute authorizing the use of military forces. . . .

Under this bill, if the Attorney General should contend that separate eating places, places of amusement, and the like in the South, licensed by State or municipal law, constituted a denial of equal privileges and immunities, he could move in with all the vast powers of this bill, even if the person denied accommodation or admission did not request him to do so and was opposed to his taking that action. The white people who operated the places of amusement could be jailed without benefit of jury trial and kept in jail until they either rotted or until they conformed to the edict to integrate their places of business. There is no limit on the punishment for contempt. A person convicted of contempt of court stays in jail until he purges himself of the contempt.

If a group of white people were to gather in front of the restaurant or theater or other place of amusement after its operators had been jailed, and there protested and resisted the commingling of the races in such places, the Attorney General could invoke the use of the military and naval forces of the United States to subdue, suppress, arrest, and jail every person who so gathered to protest and resist the commingling of races on the ground that they were guilty of conspiracy. That could be done if this bill should ever be enacted into law in its present form.

I have already said that the widely advertised voting section of the bill is not even remotely tied in with the use of military forces. The school enforcement section is. That affords a measure of the true importance of the voting right clause, as compared to the power sought to integrate the schools and destroy the separate system for the races on which the social order of the Southern States is built.

Who can doubt for a moment that some Attorney General, yielding to the demands of such organizations as the NAACP [National Association for the Advancement of Colored People] and the ADA [Americans for Democratic Action], who have been most zealous in pushing this proposal, would move into the South to compel the communities to integrate white and Negro children in the schools?

If that were done, town meetings would be held, of the white citizens of those communities. They have already taxed or obligated themselves for bond issues to establish separate and equal schools for the children of the two races, as the law specifically provided for nearly 100 years.

At the outset of such a meeting the Attorney General and the courts might recognize the right of the participating citizens to peaceable assemblage, and to petition for the redress of grievances. However, it is certain that there would be many at the meeting who would advocate closing the schools rather than commingling their children.

What would happen then? If certain citizens should vote to close the schools, would they not all become subject to the conspiracy statute, and liable to being gathered up and jailed for violating the Attorney General's writ?

This purported moderate bill would give to the Attorney General the authority to apply these vast powers in the community, on his own volition and indiscriminately, even, as I have said, if all the people of both races residing in the community should oppose the use of Federal power and military might.

Part III is the heart, soul, and body of this so-called moderate measure. I assert that any fair-minded law[y]er who studies the cross references must conclude that it could result in placing many southern communities under martial law if they should fail to submit to what they regard as the destruction of their society at the time and in the manner demanded by whoever might be acting as Attorney General of the United States.

If this be a moderate bill, just what would be embraced within a drastic bill? I suppose some persons would regard it as a proper law to require all southern white people opposed to forcible race mixing to wear a tag, to declare all those tagged to be wild animals, and prescribe a year-round open season on such persons, with an annual bag limit of twenty-four white males and twelve white females.

I shall not elaborate at this time upon the policy which the bill proposes to establish, of saddling the American taxpayer with lawyers' fees and costs of litigation in innumerable cases between individual citizens.

Neither shall I deal today with the ingenious method employed in the proposed legislation to abolish the right of trial by jury.

I shall not dwell on the fact that the bill is a gratuitous insult to the integrity of every white southern citizen. Without exception, it indicts and convicts them all on the unsupported charge that southern jurors will not do their duty, but will forswear themselves in any case in which the rights of a Negro citizen are involved. Such indictment and conviction are without evidence to support them.

I should also like to note that this charge is most vigorously and frequently voiced by citizens who represent areas where there has admittedly been, within recent years, a complete breakdown of the processes of law and order. It has come from communities which have seen periods of domination by gangsters and racketeers, communities which have passed through the experience of having all their mediums of law enforcement and their public officials subservient to gang leaders.

What I say now is in no sense a threat. I speak in a spirit of great sadness. If Congress is driven to pass this bill in its present form, it will cause unspeakable confusion, bitterness, and bloodshed in a great section of our common country. If it is proposed to move into the South in this fashion, the concentration camps may as well be prepared now, because there will not be enough jails to hold the people of the South who will oppose the use of raw Federal power forcibly to commingle white and Negro children in the same schools and places of public entertainment.

I suppose that we may now expect to be told that President Eisenhower believes in moderation, and that he would not use the provisions of this bill to send the military forces into the Southern States to compel southern white people to conform to the views of the present Supreme Court and of other sections of the United States as to their social order, which, by custom and State law, has always required separate schools, eating places, swimming pools, hotels, and the like, for the two races.

I would be less than frank if I did not say that I doubt very much whether the full implications of the bill have ever been explained to President Eisenhower. I base that statement on my analysis of his answers to questions at press conferences relating to this measure. At first he apparently did not know that it would abolish the right of trial by jury. Someone must have referred him to a comment President Taft had made with respect to contempt of court. He used that comment in another press conference. Let me say in passing that I doubt whether any lawyer would insist on a jury trial for a contempt which was committed in the presence of the court.

Without regard to what may be contended as to the uses to which the bill, if enacted, might be put, this is supposed to be a government of law and not a government of men. Jefferson said: "In questions of power, let no more be said of confidence in man."

Any idea of legislating and passing permanent statutes on the basis of the statement of intentions of any man, however great, fair, and just, who may happen to occupy the White House is wholly contrary to our entire system of government. I repeat that if this bill is used to the utmost, neither Sumner nor Stevens, in the persecution of the South in the twelve tragic years of reconstruction, ever cooked up any such devil's broth as is proposed in this misnamed civil-rights bill.

I make this statement today because I know that if any statement is made after a motion is made to proceed to the consideration of the bill, it will be clouded by cries of "Southern filibuster," which will ring throughout the land from the moment the motion is made.

Several years ago I was asked, with respect to a prolonged discussion on a certain bill, whether or not it constituted a filibuster. I think I coined the expression that it was "a lengthy educational campaign."

So far as this bill is concerned, in view of the campaign of misrepresentation which has been waged, it seems highly probable that we shall be largely confined to the *Congressional Record* as our medium to attempt to disseminate the truth about the measure. The circulation of the *Congressional Record* is limited, and we shall require a long time to get the facts across to the country. I hope that our colleagues will not be intolerant of us as we seek to discharge our duty to the American people of our States who have honored us by sending us here, even as the people of other States have honored other Senators.

I say to all the other Members of this body: If there should ever be presented here a bill which proposed to deal so harshly with the people of their States as this bill would deal with the people of my States, if they did not fight it to the very death, they would be unworthy of the people who sent them here.

If it is ever proposed to use the military forces of this Nation to compel the people represented by other Senators to conform their lives and social order to the views of the rest of the country, those Senators need not be afraid of the word filibuster or of attempting to exercise all their rights under the rules. I hope that no one who lives outside the South will ever be faced with the experience that lies before us. However, if there should ever be presented a measure which would deal so harshly with the people of other parts of our country as this bill deals with the people of the South, and at the time I am a Member of the Senate, I hope Providence will give me the strength and the courage to stand by their side, even if the great majority of the people of my State should happen to favor a measure so unfair.

Mr. President, there are millions of God-fearing, law-abiding citizens in the Southern States who believe as strongly in their right to send their children to schools attended by children of their own race, as the victims of destroyed Lidice or the Hungarians who fell in the streets of Budapest believed in the rights for which they died.

The social order of the South, with the separation of the races in the South, was accepted and protected by the laws of the land for nearly a hundred years. It is the only system the present generation has ever known. It was overturned in the twinkling of an eye, not by an act of Congress, after debate and explanation, but by action of the Supreme Court in striking down long-established law.

Mr. President, it is a monstrous proposal to establish the power to bring the military forces of the United States to bear against the white South, to compel them to change at once a way of life long supported by law and the only one under which our people have ever lived.

It is a tragic fact that the misrepresentation of the South and the southern people should have assumed such proportions in this country. Nowhere in our history has any minority group in this country—with the possible exception of the persecution of the Mormons in the nineteenth century—been subject to a campaign which compared to that being waged against the white people of the South today.

We have become mere pawns in a game of power politics. Other minority groups have apparently convinced the leaders of both political parties that the presidential election of 1960 will go to the political party willing to go the furthest in the drive to humiliate and punish the white South.

I say, Mr. President, that the white people of the Southern States deserve better at the hands of their fellow Americans of all races than to be subjected to the treatment which will inevitably follow if the bill is enacted in its present form.

Since Appomattox, this country has engaged in four wars in which the sons of the South have sealed the compact of reunion with their blood. Nearly every conceivable charge has been brought against us except that we are a cowardly people. I thank God I have not heard that charge. I would not resort to invidious comparisons, but I refer the Senate to the list of those who have won the Congressional Medal of Honor, the Distinguished Service Cross, and all the other decorations which are given for bravery in action—yes; and to the casualty lists—for evidence that the South has done her part in the armed services of the United States when our common country has been threatened.

Mr. President, politicians may be stampeded into supporting proposed legislation of this type. Pressures may be brought to bear that can compel those who control radio and television to distort and misrepresent. But, Mr. President, I have an abiding faith in the sense of fairness of all the American people when they know the facts. Before the outrage possible in this bill is inflicted upon a helpless people, I shall demand an amendment which will submit this issue to the American people in a national referendum.

It may be said that there may not be any precedent for such action, but there is certainly no worthy precedent for the disasters that the enactment of this bill in its present form are certain to bring.

I concede that it will be difficult to get the facts about this bill to all the American people under present conditions, but we will undertake to do it by word of mouth, if we must, and if that is the only way available to us.

If they understand it, the American people will reject this proposition overwhelmingly at the polls in any fair plebiscite. Pressure groups cannot work both sides of the street where the whole people are involved, as they can when they deal in terms of the number of votes they can deliver in given wards, counties, and States to the holders of public office.

This is not a partisan question. It is not one to be decided in terms of who will be elected to Congress, or governor of a State, or even President of all these United States. It is a problem that goes to the peace and tranquility of our whole land.

The South was finally freed of the bayonet rules of reconstruction days through the efforts of northern men. There was less bitterness and hate between the soldiers than between the civilians in the War Between the States. Northerners who had been subjected to the waving of the bloody shirt came South in the forces of occupation. They found the truth about the South, and their hearts were touched with compassion at the treatment accorded their late enemies during the reconstruction era. It was really the veterans of the war and those who served in the forces who occupied the South for 12 years who finally broke the chains forged for the South by Sumner and Stevens.

I am not afraid to have this issue submitted to the people of the North and West in a clearcut and fairly presented plebiscite. I shall appeal to my colleagues at the proper time to let the whole people of this country pass upon this question before millions of white people in the South are subjected to the outrageous and un-American treatment contemplated by this bill.

Georgia General Assembly
8 February 1960

When the high school in Clinton, Tennessee was racially integrated in October 1958, "three explosions rocked" the school.[6] By February 1959, social disorder caused President Eisenhower to request that Congress "make it a federal crime to use force or mob violence to block integration of schools under court orders."[7] By 1960 African Americans were employing the "sit-in" as a means of segregating lunch counters.

In this speech, Russell noted the importance of military preparedness for the nation's security, and addressed civil rights measures.[8] He drew "ringing applause" from Georgia legislators when he promised "to protect the Sovereign State of Georgia and to preserve the way of life of our people."[9] He ridiculed the federal Attorney General's proposal to place "voting referees" at "southern ballot boxes." At the same time, Russell appeared to be preparing Georgians for social change that was increasingly inevitable. "We face great odds in Congress," he cautioned. In response to those who would close rather than racially integrate the public schools, women in the gallery listening to the speech held signs proclaiming: "We Want Public Schools."[10]

* * * * * * * * *

I am happy and honored to have the opportunity of returning to this historic chamber and for the privilege of visiting with my good friends of the General Assembly.

---

[6]*Atlanta Constitution*, October 6, 1958.
[7]*Atlanta Constitution*, February 6, 1959.
[8]Text of speech from Speech File, Speech and Media Series, Richard B. Russell Collection, RRLPRS.
[9]*Atlanta Journal*, February 9, 1960.
[10]*Atlanta Constitution*, February 8, 1960.

It is ever a proud yet humbling experience to speak in this hall—where great men and great events have met to shape and mold the destiny of Georgia.

It is also a sentimental occasion for me to return to this chamber. Ten of the most memorable and fruitful years of my life were spent as a member of the Georgia House of Representatives. During four of those years, it was my honor to serve as Speaker of the House.

Your people have placed a sacred trust and a grave responsibility in you who have been chosen as their representatives. You have been selected to perform a far larger service than the term representative implies. You represent your people, of course. But you also serve as the spokesman for their interests, the watchdog of their rights and the champion of their causes.

I know that the members of the present General Assembly are living up to the trust that has been placed in you and are discharging your duties fully, faithfully and well. The record bespeaks eloquently of your efforts. I commend and salute each and every member of the House and Senate for the dedicated service that you are rendering to your people and to your State.

Dark days and difficult decisions may lie ahead of you. You probably will be called upon to resolve stormy and far-reaching issues. There will be—as there always have been differences among you as to how those issues should be resolved.

There is, however, one common bond that holds all of you—indeed, all of us—firmly together in mind and spirit. That is the unflagging love and devotion that all of us have for this great State of our's—for our beloved Georgia.

On that, there is no division. On that, we are of one accord.

I am doubly pleased to be here with you today. Again this year, I am privileged to share your kind invitation with my good friend and able colleague, Senator [Herman] Talmadge.

No group in Georgia knows Herman Talmadge better than do the members of this General Assembly. It is a pleasure for me to tell you that his ability, intelligence, and courage are recognized and respected in the United States Senate. He is a tower of strength to our little band of southern patriots and continues to grow in national stature.

Our southern group is sadly lacking in numbers but we strive to overcome this deficiency by our determination. We are likewise sustained by the knowledge that our cause is just.

Whatever the odds, we will continue to fight to the limit of our ability against the increasing forces who are apparently willing to wreck the Constitution of the United States for political ends if this is necessary to bring success to their conspiracy against the South.

. . . This is destined to be a fateful year for Georgia and the South. Our enemies are marshalling their forces against us at every turn. In many respects, 1960 may be one of the most momentous and crucial years for the South since 1860.

The insidious campaign to harass the southern people and to destroy the southern way of life is being pressed against us from all sides.

Those of us in Congress who cling to such fundamental beliefs as constitutional government and states' rights have felt the full brunt of this vicious attack for years. But the battle extends far beyond the confines of the Federal Congress in Washington. It has fanned out into our own State, and into every county and community in this State.

The people of Georgia—and you, their elected representatives and spokesmen—have come face-to-face with the devious drive to uproot our traditions and to destroy our institutions.

I have always had an abiding faith in the strength, courage and determination of Georgia's General Assembly and Governor to defend our State against all its enemies—foreign and domestic.

Let me assure you of this: I stand shoulder-to-shoulder with the members of this General Assembly and with the Governor in this battle to protect the sovereign State of Georgia and to preserve the way of life of our people.

The battle that lies ahead will be hard—both for you here and for Senator Talmadge and myself in Washington. The situation confronting our people and our state will demand the best of each of us.

In frankness, I must say that we face great odds in Congress against the conglomeration of mis-called civil rights legislation that has been introduced to punish and harass the South.

Georgia General Assembly 351

Since this is a presidential election year, there will be greater pressure than ever to make the South the nation's political football. The NAACP [National Association for the Advancement of Colored People] and the ADA [Americans for Democratic Action] and similar rag-tag, left-wing groups are pulling the strings on their puppet politicians and demanding passage of the most extreme and vicious legislation.

A stable of presidential and vice-presidential hopefuls—wearing both party labels—are eagerly dancing to the tune of the pressure groups in hope of currying favor with the minority bloc vote.

Congress has been deluged with all manner of proposals under the catch-all banner of civil rights. More are being introduced every day. As soon as one of the moguls of the NAACP or the ADA thinks up a new scheme, there is a stampede among the radicals for the dubious honor of sponsoring it. It often happens that the same bill is introduced several times by different sponsors.

The current fad in civil rights circles is some form of legislation to place under federal control and operation the election machinery that belongs to state and local government.

This shows a startling lack of originality on the part of those who scheme up these civil rights proposals. Federal control of elections got a pretty good tryout—and became a national disgrace—during the first reconstruction. Under those earlier laws, local elections were taken over in the North as well as the South and a presidential election was stolen.

The sponsors of these iniquitous proposals can't decide on the best way to go about federalizing the elective process. One group, including Senator [Jacob] Javits, wants to do it through a system of federal "registrars." The Attorney General, on the other hand, proposes to put "voting referees" in charge of southern ballot boxes.

These proposals, though differing in approach, have the same end result. They would put the counting of the votes under the direction of federal bureaucrats.

Their passage, in effect, would be a declaration that all state and local government is bankrupt and should be placed in the hands of a federal receiver. Sooner or later, all the elections would be decided in

Washington. If that tragic day ever comes, we will have traded our birthright of constitutional government for a federal dictatorship.

The proposals to federalize the election process should be opposed by thinking people in all parts of the country. True, these bills are aimed at the people of the South today. Tomorrow, another section of the country might find itself the victim of the on-rushing federal juggernaut.

These vicious schemes must be fought—and will be fought—to the end.

I pledge to you that I will oppose them to the limit of my endurance and to the extent of my ability.

We will leave no stone unturned—no rule of the Senate unused—in this battle to protect states' rights and constitutional government.

I confess I do not know how much longer the South must serve as the doormat for the ambitious leaders of both national parties.

Certainly there is no comfort for us in the ranks of the Republican Party. The heir apparent to the GOP crown already has taken his stand with the NAACP. He is, in fact, one of their most prominent honorary members.

Our own party has virtually deserted us. The proud democracy of Jefferson and Jackson has become the captive of a left-wing element that is barely democratic even in name, but which is trying to recast the party in its image.

Many of this gang of phoney liberals and party-wreckers have publicly advocated driving the South from the house of our fathers.

The South is entitled to better treatment from the party that it has nurtured, supported, and revered for almost as long as it has the Constitution. We are entitled to the measure of respect and influence within the party that our years of loyalty have earned.

No section of the country can rival the South's long record of democratic loyalty. But party loyalty is a two-way street. Those who kick the South in the teeth at every opportunity must not expect us to keep turning the other cheek forever.

The South has no intention of abandoning its loyalty to the democratic principles that it has ever held. But it owes no loyalty to self-styled democrats who flout and despise the true democratic faith.

The patron saints of the democracy—giants like Jefferson, Madison, and Jackson—built the party upon the solid rock of the Constitution.

That is where the South stands today. Others may seek to subvert that fundamental premise of the Democratic Party, but the South will keep the faith.

We have taken our stand on the Constitution of the United States. And there we propose to remain.

Coosa Valley Area
Planning and Development Commission
15 July 1964

In this address, Senator Russell climaxed the business session for one thousand persons gathered at Berry College in Rome, Georgia, for the Sixth Annual Meeting of the Coosa Valley Area Planning and Development Commission, an organization credited with contributing to the "rapid growth and development of industry in Northwest Georgia."[11] After recognizing the economic progress made by the South, Russell assessed the requirements of the recently passed 1964 Civil Rights Bill, legislation that desegregated public accommodations, provided more equitable opportunities for employment for blacks, and denied federal funds to institutions found guilty of racial discrimination. Unlike some southern leaders who had opposed civil rights legislation, in a widely publicized statement, the Senator advised that the laws were "now on the books and it becomes our duty as good citizens to learn to live with them for as long as they are there . . . to avoid all violence." The *Rome* [Georgia] *News-Tribune* editorialized that the Senator's support for obedience to the law was of "major significance."[12] The *Macon Telegraph* concluded that, of the "thousands of speeches" Russell has made during "this decade," the one at Berry College "stands out as one of the best." The editor advised that, "If Senator Russell . . . argues obedience and condemns defiance, who in this country has standing to suggest otherwise?"[13]

****

Not so long ago as time is reckoned, a great President of the United States [Franklin D. Roosevelt] described the South as the

---

[11]Text of speech from Speech File, Speech and Media Series, Richard B. Russell Collection, RRLPRS.
[12]*Rome News-Tribune*, July 15 and 16, 1964.
[13]*Macon Telegraph*, July 17, 1964.

Nation's "economic problem number one." Today, a quarter century later, this dynamic region might well be called the nation's number one economic opportunity.

Everywhere the South is on the march. Tangible evidence of our progress may be seen on every hand—in the quickening pace of business and commerce, in the boom and bustle of cities and towns, in the green look of the land, and in the rise of a modern industrial complex.

We have broken the last of the chains that for almost a century bound the South in economic servitude. No longer is our industrial growth hampered by discriminatory freight rates. No longer are our young people denied opportunities of an adequate education. And no longer are our human and physical resources exploited for someone else's gain. We have become the masters of our own destiny.

The course of our progress has been long and tortuous. The ordeal of civil war and reconstruction left the South of yesterday a land of poverty and desolation almost beyond description. But with unswerving courage, determination and faith—characteristics exemplified by the great and noble lady who founded the college where we are today—the Southern people built a vibrant new South on the ruins of the old.

Today the prophesy of Henry Grady in large measure has been fulfilled. Our cities have become hives of industry. Our countrysides are yielding forth their treasure of resources, and our streams are alive with the whir of commerce and play.

A prophet of later times and lesser note has characterized the transformation taking place in the modern South as the movement of cotton West, cattle East, Negroes North, and industry South.

However it may be described, we are living in a new day. Never again will the South be content to play the red-haired stepchild of the economy. We intend to have our rightful place as a full and equal partner in the mainstream of the country's progress and growth.

As a Georgian, it is a matter of great pride to me that our state is helping lead the way in the economic renaissance of the Southland. Since the end of World War II, the value of manufacturing foods produced in Georgia has increased almost nine-fold. This is somewhat better than the rate of increase for the South as a region and double that for the nation as a whole.

I realize that this must be balanced against the fact that we started out considerably behind most of the rest of the country. But it shows nonetheless that industry is expanding faster in Georgia than in the country generally.

This great Coosa River Valley of Northwest Georgia is in the forefront of Georgia's industrial expansion and is making a major contribution to our overall growth.

The Coosa Valley, of course, has always been one of the principal industrial areas of the state, and almost half of its total employment is manufacturing. But this has not deterred you from actively seeking additional industrial jobs to offset the continuing decline in agricultural employment.

I was interested to note in your Association's Annual report for the previous year that twenty-eight new industrial plants had been established in the area during the twelve-month period. This is a remarkable achievement, one that speaks eloquently for the activities of this Association.

I salute the counties that make up the Association for their foresight and common sense in working together to advance the mutual interests of the entire Coosa Valley. Certainly this Association is setting an example that might profit others to follow. You are proving that solid achievements can come from cooperation, intelligent planning, and hard work.

Although our industrial and economic growth of recent years is gratifying, we must not be satisfied to rest on past accomplishments. We must keep our eye on the future and remain dedicated to the task of keeping Georgia forging ahead.

There is much to be done. Although Georgians today earn more money than ever before, our per capita income still lags substantially below the average for the nation. We have made steady progress in recent years in closing the gap; our average income per person is now slightly more than three-fourths of the average for the country. But we must not be satisfied until we close the gap completely and move ahead of the national norm. I am confident we can do it. Indeed, I believe the door is open to the brightest economic era in Georgia's history if we will accept the challenges and seize the opportunities that lie before us. One of these opportunities—and challenges—lies in expanding and strengthening our research efforts in all fields. . . .

I cannot close my remarks without making some reference to the longest and most intensive legislative conflict of our history that resulted in the passage by the Senate of the so-called civil rights statute. This statute is now on the books despite the last-ditch opposition of our small group of Senators. We put everything we had into the fight, but the odds against us mounted from day to day until we were finally gagged and overwhelmed.

The signature of President [Lyndon B.] Johnson has placed it on the statute books of our country. This enactment is the most far-reaching federal force bill that the central power of the federal government has ever sought to impose upon the people of this land.

It is the understatement of the year to say that I do not like these statutes. There are hundreds of thousands of people in this country who feel as I do about them. However, they are now on the books and it becomes our duty as good citizens to learn to live with them for as long as they are there. The constitutionality of some of the provisions will be tested immediately in the courts. While it is being adjudicated, all good citizens will learn to live with the statute and abide by its final adjudication, even though we reserve the right to advocate by legal means its repeal or modification.

Time after time during the three-and-a-half months of the agonizing legislative struggle, I was highly critical of the growing disrespect for law and order generated by the campaign of civil disobedience by extremist groups. Time and again, I was shocked to hear persons in high authority not only condone but urge the breaking of established laws because someone had decided that they were either immoral or personally repugnant.

Most shocking of all, our ambassador to the United Nations in a commencement address, claimed it to be a "proud achievement" to spend time in jail for violating local laws with which the violator did not agree.

This strange doctrine that a citizen may pick and choose the laws he will obey and ignore those he does not like is, to me, totally reprehensible. It is a form of anarchy to say that a person need not comply with a particular statute with which he disagrees. Ours is a government of laws, not of men, and our system cannot tolerate the philosophy that obedience to law rests upon the personal likes or dislikes of any individual citizen, whether he supports or opposes the statute in question. This is true even if the body which now passes as our Supreme Court gives tacit approval to mass violations of local laws in one section of the country while enforcing them ruthlessly in others, as their predilections and preconceptions may dictate.

It is therefore our duty as good and patriotic citizens, in a period that will undoubtedly be marked by tension and unrest as this statute is implemented, to avoid all violence.

Violence and law violation will only compound our difficulties and increase our troubles. I am sure that the vast majority of the people of Georgia were shocked and outraged by the brutal and senseless murder of a Negro Reserve officer upon our public highways a few days ago. I am convinced that this cowardly act was generated by a demented mind and I trust that the guilty party will soon be apprehended so that we may demonstrate to the world that assassins, even if demented, will not be tolerated in Georgia. If our highways are not safe for all, they are not safe for any of us.

I have no apologies to anyone for the fight that I made against the federal force bill. I only regret that we did not prevail. I opposed it because of a profound conviction that, in the long run, this measure could only prove harmful to the country and curtail and destroy the rights of all Americans of every race. I still have faith in the soundness of our free institutions and in the inherent good judgment of the American people. I can but believe that in time the people of this nation will turn back the trend toward statism and enforced conformity in every activity of life.

Violence and defiance are no substitute for the long campaign of reason and logic we must wage to overcome the prejudices and misconceptions which now influence the majority of the American people in this field.

Index

Act of Religious Freedom 106
Aderhold, O. C. 198
Africa 89, 140, 191, 213, 224, 227, 229, 234, 237, 241, 249, 279
African Americans 33, 307, 333, 348 *See also* Negro(es), blacks
agricultural commodities 23, 112, 118, 122, 146, 148-149
agricultural prices 148
agricultural production 22, 23, 121, 122-123, 135, 139, 140, 146, 147, 148, 149, 175, 177, 179-181, 183
agricultural research 23, 142, 150, 162, 171, 175, 180, 181, 183
Agricultural Adjustment Act 113, 146, 149
Agricultural Appropriations Bill 20, 122, 150
Agricultural Appropriations, Senate Committee on 162, 171
Agricultural Appropriations Subcommittee 119, 181
Agricultural Marketing Service 180-181

agriculture 2, 6, 11, 15, 20-23, 25, 32, 38, 109, 112-114, 116-119, 121, 130, 131, 137, 140, 142-147, 150, 152, 158, 161, 163, 167, 171, 173, 175-181, 183, 184, 196, 204, 271, 280, 331
Agriculture, Department of 113, 114, 140, 173, 180, 331
Agriculture and Forestry, Committee on 331
aircraft 25, 268, 279, 299, 302, 303
airmen 241, 290
airplanes 215, 227, 229-232
Alabama 13, 17, 18, 37, 85, 146, 188, 189, 192, 322
Alaska Purchase 239
Allen, Marion 212, 215
Allied cause 230, 231
Allied High Command 206
Allied Military leaders 225
Allied Military personnel 223
Allied nations 242, 248 *See also Allied Powers*
Allied Powers 225-226, 230-231, 242-243, 248
Allies 58, 64, 146, 153, 164, 206-208, 217, 223, 226, 233, 235-239, 242, 248,

246, 248, 251, 260, 264, 266, 283, 293
American dream 276
American Farm Bureau 142, 146
American ingenuity 134
American Legion 18, 26, 29, 203, 207-209, 256, 257, 259, 260
American way of life 70, 78, 80, 138, 214
Americanism 208, 209, 257
Anderson, Clinton 10
Anderson, Leeman 9
Anderson, William L. 218
Anglo-Saxon 42, 46, 77
Appomattox 43, 351
Appropriations 2, 10, 21, 23, 119, 122, 124, 142, 147, 150, 160, 162, 170, 171, 181, 190, 199, 268, 283, 302
Argonne 206
Armed Forces 19, 29, 92, 132, 133, 227, 228, 230, 237, 245, 257, 265, 266, 285, 334
Armed Services 3, 30, 163, 165, 199, 220, 266, 275, 345
Armistice Day 26, 27, 202, 203
Army 25, 27, 54, 70, 134, 139, 140, 186, 193, 205, 208, 225, 227, 230, 232, 233, 241, 242, 245, 246, 260, 262, 266, 298, 299, 308
Army Air Corps 299
Army Engineers 233
Ashburn, GA 167, 168
Asia 68, 127, 191, 256, 279, 289, 291-293
Atlanta 1, 2, 4, 7, 8, 12, 13, 16-18, 20, 22, 23, 26, 30, 31, 33, 34, 37, 40, 47, 64, 85, 111, 180, 192, 195, 197, 202, 218, 222, 288, 294, 298, 307, 329, 348
Atlanta Journal 4, 64, 294, 298, 348
Atlantic Charter 240
atomic accelerator 198
Atomic Age 60, 75, 247
atomic bomb 29, 70, 248, 259
atomic superiority 260
atomic war, warfare 28, 67, 244, 248, 253
atomic weapons 260, 275
atomic energy 2-3, 25, 252, 265
Atomic Energy Commission 197
Atomic Energy, Joint Committee on 275

Index 361

Atomic Energy, Senate Committee on 2-3
Atomic Energy, Special Committee on 247
Attorney General 57, 64, 74, 333-341, 351
Attorneys General 16, 29, 64, 67
Australia 69, 223, 227, 237, 240, 285
Axis Powers, nations 138, 141, 246, 264

ballot box 73, 332
Bankhead-Jones Act 123
Barkley, Alben W. 5, 7, 313
Bates, William M. 6, 13, 14
battlefields 297, 309
Belgium 285
Belleau Woods 206
belligerent group 156
Benson, Ezra Taft 22, 172, 173
Berlin 261, 262, 272
Bermuda 171, 182
Berry College 36, 37, 354
Bible 76, 103, 152, 191
blacks 34, 35, 36, 307, 311, 315, 318, 320, 327, 329, 333, 335, 354
blackmail 97
Bloch, Charles 71, 212
blockade 64, 69, 70

blocs 146
bloody shirt 42, 346
Board of Regents 1, 77, 244
Boll weevil 21, 50, 172
Bowen, Charles 270
bravery 42, 204, 218, 241, 345
Brett, James 218
Brewster, Ralph O. 223
British Crown 308
British Empire 234, 237, 242
British Food Commission 236
British government 235, 308
British people 67, 234-236, 249, 308
British soldiers 234
broadcasting 287-289, 324
Brougham, Lord 272
Browder, Earl 315
Brown v. Board of Education 36
Buford Dam 192
Bulgaria 177
Bunker Hill 261
Burdick, Fred 270
bureaucracy 281
business 3, 16-18, 27, 47, 51, 72, 73, 120, 127, 138, 145, 148, 151, 153, 154, 161, 167, 178-180, 187, 192, 199, 216, 236,

266, 267, 271, 308, 319, 325, 332, 340, 354, 355
Byrd, Harry Flood 5

Callaway Gardens, GA 287
Canada 54, 69, 285
Cannon, Clarence 187, 214
Capehart, Homer E. 23
capital 73, 93, 120, 130, 145, 177, 255, 280, 323, 335
Caribbean 291
carpetbaggers 310
Carroll, Charles 105
Carters Dam 25, 37, 185, 186, 189
Carters Dam Project 25, 185, 186
Castro, Fidel 270, 285, 291
Catholics 105
Chandler, Albert B. "Happy" 223
Chappel, Lucius 218
Chateau Thierry 206
Chennault, Claire 230, 232
Chief Executive 155, 160
children 21, 33, 49, 53, 62, 100, 116, 134, 152, 159, 162, 192, 193, 246, 288, 302, 308-310, 323, 325, 326, 333, 334, 341, 342, 344

China 69, 94, 106, 177, 178, 213, 224, 226, 227, 230-232, 242, 248, 262, 291, 292, 302
Chinese Communists 69
Christian institutions 91
Christian religion (Christianity) 96, 152
Christian Science Monitor 334
church 17, 41, 233
civil rights 2, 12, 15, 32, 35-38, 305, 322, 325, 329, 331, 333, 348, 350, 351, 354, 357
Civil War 18, 19, 43, 125, 309, 355
civilian 25, 32, 58, 163, 199, 214, 220, 221, 228, 234, 235, 241, 246, 267, 268, 273, 292, 296, 300, 301
Civilian Conservation Corps 19
Clark, Frank M. 11
Clark, Tom 57
Clark Hill Dam 10, 170
Cleere, George 188
Clinton, Tennessee 348
clothing 44, 48, 121, 130, 133, 137, 139, 140, 147, 148, 221, 234, 241, 279, 280
Coastal Plains Experiment Station 24, 182

Index 363

Cocke, Erle Jr. 8, 9, 13-15, 256
Cold War 29, 74, 264, 270, 272, 279
commerce 30, 37, 110-112, 167, 169, 197, 204, 205, 264, 355
Committee on Agriculture and Forestry 331
Commodity Credit Corporation 148, 149
Communism 2, 26, 29, 30, 44, 62, 65, 67-69, 88, 91, 96, 107, 152, 163, 178, 249, 250, 255, 260-262, 264, 265, 271, 276, 276-280, 283, 285, 291, 300, 302
Communist 29, 61, 65, 69, 87, 94, 99, 107, 161, 164, 177, 178, 249, 259, 261, 265, 272, 275, 282, 284-286, 290-293, 295, 296, 315
Confederacy 26, 27, 41, 43-45, 310
Confederate Fathers 45
Congo 89, 92
Congressional Medal of Honor 345
Congressional Record 5, 7, 11, 12, 17, 19, 22, 23, 25, 28, 31, 36, 37, 79, 85, 111, 212, 223, 307, 333, 344
constitution 2, 7, 8, 13, 16, 26, 33, 34, 36, 37, 47, 49, 51, 58-60, 63, 68, 75, 76, 80-83, 85, 91, 92, 95, 101, 106, 111, 134, 152, 166, 208, 250, 267, 270, 274, 307, 309-314, 317, 318, 320, 323-326, 328, 348, 350, 352, 353
constitutional principles 15, 38, 39
constitutional rights 166, 335, 337
Cook, Eugene 64, 220
Coosa Valley Commission 14
cotton 6, 19-21, 23, 33, 34, 111, 113-118, 120-123, 126, 145, 146, 148, 172, 180, 196, 329, 331, 355
cotton farmers 115, 123
courage 28, 43, 58, 61, 134, 141, 163, 204, 206, 207, 210, 214, 218, 228, 235, 296, 309, 344, 349, 350, 355
Cranston, Alan 9
crime 327, 339, 348
crimson clover 20, 27, 119
crops 21, 22, 116, 139, 145, 176, 182, 183, 289

Cuba 177, 270, 272, 285, 292
Czechoslovakia 27, 32, 212, 300, 302

Dalton High School 30, 270, 271
Darden, William H. 4-6, 12, 14, 15
Davis, Harold 4, 12
Davis, John W. 192
debt 2, 31, 99, 151, 154, 155, 173, 191, 294, 342, 331
Declaration of Independence 55, 58, 60, 105
Defense Appropriations Subcommittee 199
Defense, Department of 267
defiance 37, 354, 358
democracy 9, 17, 18, 48, 53, 55-57, 60-62, 104, 136, 137, 141, 156, 204, 208, 213-215, 230, 248, 249, 253-255, 325, 352
democratic 19, 26, 42, 44, 48-52, 54, 61, 71, 98, 103, 111, 125, 134, 136, 147, 152, 153, 158, 160, 162, 166, 195, 230, 304, 318, 320, 341, 351-353

Democrats 2, 9, 18, 23, 54, 55, 60, 147, 159, 160, 320
Democratic Party 71, 158, 162, 166, 318, 353
depression 1, 19, 21, 47, 51, 111, 119, 144, 146, 154, 160, 213, 279
desegregation 34, 35
detente 304
dictator(s) 58, 59, 98, 127, 156, 246
dictatorship(s) 59, 98, 248, 249, 352
Dirksen, Everett 12
disarming 44
disarmament 31, 207, 209, 251, 275
discrimination 24, 98, 117, 130, 199, 207, 208, 333, 354
Disraeli, Benjamin 102
Distinguished Service Cross 345
diversification 121, 146, 300
Divine Providence 107
Dixie 43, 46, 288
Dixon, Robert E. 218
Dominican Republic 287, 290, 291
draft 15, 17, 204, 209, 231, 301
du Pont, Renee 49, 53-55

Index 365

East Germany 177
economic progress 197, 354
economy 2, 3, 19, 24, 31, 47, 99, 119, 123, 144, 145, 149, 153-158, 160, 163, 164, 167, 168, 171, 178, 179, 183, 193, 197, 199, 250, 260, 281, 282, 284, 287, 355
education 1, 2, 16, 17, 30, 32, 36, 50, 132, 194, 264, 268, 271-273, 278, 280, 298, 303, 311, 323, 325, 355
Eighth Air Force 224, 228
Eisenhower, Dwight D. 2, 20, 22, 158, 160, 260, 333, 342, 343, 348
employment 35, 117, 154, 169, 297, 331, 354, 356
engineers 185, 186, 198, 223, 227, 233
England 65, 69, 105, 117, 199, 204, 207, 223, 224, 226, 228, 234, 236, 241, 242, 285
equality 35, 36, 53, 95, 123, 130, 131, 145, 146, 152, 238, 242, 253, 319, 325
Europe 27, 119, 127, 138, 140, 164, 178, 191, 209, 213, 219, 228, 244, 260, 278, 279
Executive Order 274

export 121, 122
Extension Service 151, 176, 183

factories 129, 149, 227, 241
Faires, Carl F. 218
farm(s) 2, 9, 20-23, 33, 51, 55, 73, 115, 119-125, 130, 131, 135-140, 142-144, 146, 148-152, 162, 167-169, 171-173, 175, 178-181, 183, 189, 206, 280
farmers 3, 8, 20-24, 34, 51, 112, 114-116, 119-126, 130, 133, 135, 139-145, 147-151, 167, 171-173, 175, 176, 180-182, 280, 329, 331
federal aid 146
Federal Building Speech 29
federal courts 50, 94, 95, 334
federal expenditures (spending) 25, 33, 147, 165, 265, 284, 298, 330
Federal Employment Practices Commission 35
federal funds 19, 23, 50, 125, 185, 342
federal government 17, 50, 64, 68, 71, 74, 75, 83, 98, 125, 173, 180, 198,

199, 250, 270, 274, 311, 314, 316, 317, 323, 326, 333, 336, 357
Federal Housing Administration 124
federal intervention 19
federal judiciary 74, 83, 84
Federal Land Bank 51
federal power 66-67, 324
federal programs 19, 47, 166, 180, 183
Federal School Lunch Program 21
federal work programs 25
federalism 81
fertilizer 21, 23, 139
filibuster 316, 343, 344
First Amendment 106
flag, American 58, 134, 141, 262, 292, 295, 301
flag, Confederate 42
flag-waving 16
food 11, 21, 58, 121, 129, 130, 133, 137-140, 146-148, 150, 160, 162, 171, 173, 177, 178, 180, 181, 221, 227, 234, 236, 279, 280
foreign aid 31, 99, 164, 265, 281-285
foreign markets 122
foreign nations 112
foreign trade 112
forestry 24, 182, 331

Forrestal, Admiral James 32, 298, 299, 302
Fort Benning, GA 24
Founding Fathers 66, 75, 81, 83, 95, 105, 130, 267
France 69, 127, 205-207, 209, 210, 241, 285
Franklin, Benjamin 18, 63
free enterprise 153, 279, 287, 289
free market 149
Freedom Train 57, 59, 60, 62
French North Africa 140
fruit 181, 182, 199, 251
Fulbright, J. William 9, 10, 31
"fundamentalists," political 79, 80

Gallup poll 104
gasoline 26, 139, 234, 238
George, Walter F. 6, 170
George III (King of England) 104, 307
Georgia 1-4, 6-13, 16-31, 33, 34, 36-38, 40, 41, 45-47, 49-57, 64, 71, 79, 95, 102, 105, 111, 119, 124, 128, 129, 135, 146, 153, 159, 167-172, 175, 176, 180-186, 188-194, 196-

200, 202, 203, 215, 217-219, 222, 228, 244, 245, 264, 271, 273, 277, 278, 287, 288, 298, 306-311, 313, 314, 317, 318, 320-322, 327, 329, 348-350, 354-356, 358
Georgia Crop Improvement Association 175
Georgia Department of Agriculture 180
Georgia editors 196
Georgia farmers 171, 172, 181, 329
Georgia General Assembly 1, 6, 23, 37, 348
Georgia Press Association 24, 194
German 27, 129, 132, 206, 212, 213, 219, 241, 278
Germans 61, 241
girls 50, 137, 152, 226, 232
God 29, 53, 67, 105-107, 117, 141, 152, 170, 208, 209, 253, 258, 327, 344, 345
Godlessness 29, 67
Goering, Hermann 229
GOP 352
Gordon, Hugh 277
Gordon, John B. 277-278
Gordon Cadet Corps 277
Gordon Institute 26
Gordon Military Academy (College) 203, 205, 211, 277-278, 286
Grady, Henry 195, 355
Great Britain 133, 250
Great Depression 1, 21, 47, 51, 111, 213
Greece 130, 261
Guam 240
Guantanamo Base 272

Haiti 282
Hale, Nathan 275
Hamilton, Alexander 275
Hamilton, Curtis 218
happiness 58, 276
Hawaii 27, 217, 223, 224, 257
health 16, 17, 50, 131, 132, 156, 221, 223, 225, 254, 273, 327
Henry, Patrick 133, 275
Herty, Charles 23
high school 30, 221, 268, 270-272, 348
Hill, Lister B. 13, 322
Hirohito 138
Hiroshima 60, 253, 248
Hitler, Adolph 27, 132, 133, 138, 265, 329
Ho Chi Minh 297
Hoey, Clyde R. 322
hog cholera 183

Holland 206
Holland, Spessard L. 12
Holmes, William F. 20, 21, 111
Holy Writ 80
home 3, 9, 17, 20, 24, 25, 41, 44, 51, 53, 55, 61, 124, 126, 130, 131, 135, 136, 138, 141, 142, 146, 152, 186, 188, 191, 195, 203, 205, 207, 209, 211, 219, 224, 226, 228, 231, 232, 235, 252-254, 258, 262, 271, 278, 286, 288, 294, 296, 297, 300, 303, 309, 310, 320
House of Representatives 1, 3, 8, 21, 123, 282, 349
Housing Authority 124
human rights 54, 65, 106, 213

Independence Hall 63
India 114, 117, 118, 224, 237
Indians 204, 308
individual 10, 17, 18, 35, 58, 59, 65, 66, 68, 75, 76, 80, 82, 88, 91, 98, 103, 106, 127, 152, 157, 164, 166, 208, 213, 228, 253, 258, 286, 289, 322-325, 328, 337-339, 342, 358

Indo-China 69, 262
industrial firms 169
industrial workers 120, 143, 148, 151
industries 117, 120, 133, 140, 145, 150, 157, 163, 168, 184, 192, 230, 300
industry 2, 15, 20, 23, 24, 32, 38, 109, 112, 116, 117, 120, 122, 139, 140, 145, 148, 149, 151, 153, 167, 169, 171, 176, 178, 179, 183, 184, 188, 189, 196-198, 204, 215, 221, 270, 271, 273, 280, 287, 289, 298, 299, 301, 330, 332, 354-356
insects 50, 144
Iron Curtain 60, 68, 76, 164
isolationism 28, 244, 248
Italy 27, 132, 207, 225, 229, 234, 237, 241, 248, 279

Jackson, Andrew 77, 275, 352
Jackson, Henry 4-7, 10, 13
Jacksonian philosophy 16
Jacobs, Randall 217
Japan 59, 132, 212, 230, 231, 239, 244, 248, 279
Japanese 27, 178, 217, 223, 228-231, 240, 242
Javits, Jacob 351

Index

Jaycees 102, 104
Jefferson, Thomas 14, 47, 52, 53, 76, 77, 82, 106, 195, 239, 275, 343, 352, 353
Jeffersonian 81
Jekyll Island, GA 20, 24, 25, 36, 194
Jews 105
Jim Crow 35
job-training 32, 298, 303
Johnson, Lyndon Baines 2, 10, 31, 292, 294, 357
Joint Chiefs of Staff 31
Judeo-Christian philosophy 103
jury trial 338, 340, 343
jute 111, 113-117

Kai-Shek, Chiang 230, 248
Katanga 87, 89-91, 93, 96, 97, 100
Kaye, Lambdin 288
Kennedy, John F. 2, 22, 85, 206, 292
Khan, Genghis 94
Khrushchev, Nikita 94, 174, 178, 265, 266, 270, 285
Knowland, William F. 79
Korea 29, 68, 69, 87, 164, 249, 256, 258-261, 265, 279, 281, 292
Korean people 69

Korean War 29, 64, 69, 162, 261, 292, 303
Kremlin 163, 165, 262, 263, 285, 286

labor 19, 21, 25, 57, 73, 112, 114, 116, 117, 120, 130, 139, 140, 145, 148, 149, 151, 155-157, 178, 181, 183, 215, 216, 233, 244, 247, 250, 252-255, 280
Landrum, Phil 187
Laos 278
law 16, 17, 36, 37, 57, 59, 60, 64-66, 68, 71, 72, 75, 77, 78, 80, 82, 84, 89, 91-93, 95, 99, 104, 122, 124, 148, 150, 153, 156, 157, 171, 194, 200, 204, 208, 253, 266, 274, 275, 300, 314, 319, 320, 323-326, 330, 332, 335-345, 354, 357, 358
Law Day 16, 17, 71
laws of the land 344
lawyers 16, 18, 64-66, 68, 72, 83
leadership 1, 2, 58, 67, 70, 75, 77, 78, 80, 107, 139, 162, 165, 166, 196, 271, 286, 304, 316, 319, 331
left-wing 351, 352

legal profession 70-72, 78
legislation 1, 5, 7, 21, 23, 35, 36, 52, 72, 73, 81-83, 85, 88, 90, 111, 120, 123, 125, 130, 137, 139, 142, 145-149, 153, 155, 157, 163, 164, 166, 187, 244, 254, 274, 280, 307, 315-322, 327, 329, 333, 335, 337, 339, 342, 345, 350, 351, 354
Lend-Lease 129, 236, 239, 241
Leonard, Earl T. 6, 8, 11, 12, 14, 15
liberal 194, 252, 253, 280
liberals 249, 352
liberties 54, 65, 68, 75-77, 80, 82, 88, 131-133, 213-215, 253, 258, 322, 324, 328
liberty 44, 45, 47, 49, 50, 52, 54, 57-60, 62, 66, 67, 70, 78, 103, 133, 152, 195, 261, 272, 289, 325
Liberty League 50
Library of Congress 9, 172
loans 51, 86, 119, 123, 124, 138, 142, 148, 149, 215, 248, 281
lobbyists 316, 318
London 244, 257
Long, Huey 190

Louisiana Purchase 239
love 42, 62, 130, 136, 140, 141, 143, 209, 245, 276, 349

machinery 48, 89, 117, 123, 139, 214, 246, 315, 316, 320, 351
Madison 249, 353
Magna Carta 60
Malaya 69, 217, 223
Manhattan 168
Manufactures 2
Marines 217, 226, 229, 259, 290, 291
Marshburn, Robert J. 283
Marx, Karl 278
Maybank, Burnet R. 322
McCormick, Margaret 5, 8, 9, 13-15
Melbourne, Australia 224, 257
Metropolitan Opera 288
Middle East 69, 233, 236
military 2, 10, 15, 17, 24-32, 38, 50, 62, 64, 87-94, 96, 100, 101, 119, 129, 161, 162, 199, 201, 203, 205, 209, 212, 217, 223, 225, 234, 236, 238, 241, 244, 246, 251, 252, 256, 259, 260, 264-268, 270, 275-277, 281, 285, 286,

Index   371

291, 292, 295, 297-301,
303, 309, 333, 336, 337,
339-342, 344, 345, 348
military preparedness 2, 15,
26, 38, 201, 260, 266,
299, 303
mills 48, 117
minority group 324, 325, 345
missiles 30, 193, 268, 270,
285, 298, 300
Missouri 59, 135, 247
mob 73, 348
Molotov, Vyacheslav 61
moral fiber 197
morality 103, 104
Mormons 345
Moscow 249, 262
Mudd, Roger 9, 12, 13

National Association for the
Advancement of Colored
People (N.A.A.C.P.) 316
national debt 99, 154, 155,
173, 330, 331
national defense 26, 133,
158, 164, 216, 276, 331
National Guard 52
National Security Industrial
Association 304
NATO 69
natural rights 16
Naval Affairs 2, 129, 229
Naval Affairs Committee 229

Naval aviation forces 299
naval blockade 64, 69
Naval Reserve 220, 221
navy 11, 28, 70, 129, 133,
139, 140, 159, 212, 214,
217-222, 227, 229, 230,
232-235, 242, 245, 246,
260, 262, 266, 298
Navy Seabees 233
Navy's Challenge for service
28, 217, 218
Nazis 132, 133, 279
Negro(es) 34, 307-309, 313,
316, 318, 319, 326- 328,
334, 335, 341, 342, 358
See also African Americans, blacks
Negro Reserve Officer 358
Negro-carpetbagger-scalawag
convention 309
New Caledonia 224, 240
New Deal 7, 8, 32, 33, 35,
47, 111, 307
New Delhi 224, 226
New Georgia 228
New South 18, 19, 21, 35,
41, 43, 46, 195, 196, 355
New Zealand 69
Newfoundland 223
newspaper 53, 88, 281
Nimitz, Chester William 218,
303
Nixon, Richard M. 2, 195
Norris, George W. 136

North (Northern states) 11, 322, 346, 351, 355
North Atlantic Treaty Organization 68, 69, 164
North Korea 256
North Vietnam 297, 294, 297, 302
North Vietnamese (people) 31, 302
Northwestern University 273
nut crops 182

Oglethorpe, James E. 50
Okinawa 261
Old South 41-44
Outerbridge, William 218
O'Neal, Ed 146

Pacific Ocean 133, 215, 217, 218, 224, 226-229, 231, 239, 240, 242, 298, 300
Pacific theater 226
Pannell, Charles A. 13
Paris 206, 257
parity for farmers 20, 115, 116, 119-122, 144, 148, 151, 152
Parker, William W. 219
patriotism 16, 41, 46, 62, 165, 207, 208, 211, 218, 257, 267, 299, 301

peace 28, 29, 53, 59, 60, 62, 70, 87, 90-92, 96, 137, 140, 153, 154, 163, 174, 203, 204, 206-208, 213, 230, 236, 238, 240, 242-244, 246-249, 251-253, 259, 261, 262, 264, 266, 275, 276, 278, 279, 283, 286, 290, 291, 300, 304, 328, 346
peaches 180, 181
peanuts 146, 180
Pearl Harbor 27, 139, 212, 217, 223, 230, 231, 246
people of color 97
people of Georgia 47, 52-56, 169, 191, 200, 311, 318, 358
per capita farm income 143, 172
per capita income 126, 143, 196, 312, 356
Persian Gulf 224, 227, 238
Pharris, Jackson C. 219
Phi Beta Kappa 2
Piedmont Soil and Water Conservation Experiment 24, 182
pilgrims 105
Plessy v. Ferguson 35
Poland 27, 93, 212, 329
political party 147, 345
poll tax 307-309, 311-314, 317, 318, 320

Index 373

Pope, James P. 114
"poor" whites 35
poultry 24, 180, 181
poverty 32, 237, 282, 303, 311, 328, 355
Pravda 249
Presidency 2, 23, 158
Presque Isle, Maine 223
press 2-7, 9, 19, 21, 24, 28, 35, 65, 89, 92, 94, 111, 112, 132, 136, 138, 148, 158, 166, 168, 186, 194, 195, 237, 242, 250, 331, 334, 335, 343
pressure groups 73, 81, 84, 146, 323, 332, 346, 351
price support 162, 173
processed foods 184
propaganda 44, 127, 165, 236, 249, 261, 284, 299, 328, 333, 334
property 2, 54, 65, 279, 325
Protestant 105
Prouty, Winston L. 3, 13
public debt 151, 155, 330
public officials 48, 77, 104, 195, 342
public schools 2, 36, 71, 169, 334, 336, 348
Public Works Committee 10
Puritans 105

Quakers 105

race 19, 34-36, 97, 132, 166, 274, 307, 315, 317-319, 322, 325-327, 342, 344, 358
races 35, 36, 162, 315, 318, 319, 326, 332, 334, 336, 337, 339-341, 343-345
racial problems 327
radio 7, 19, 28, 34, 47, 72, 137, 138, 158, 176, 217, 220, 227, 249, 250, 287-289, 322, 329, 334, 345
Raesly, Barboura G. 9, 10
Randolph, Walter 146
Rankin, John 137, 138
Rankin-Russell Bill 137
Raskob, John J. 49, 53-55
raw commodity 144
raw materials 106, 161, 163
rearmament 161, 163-165
Reconstruction 7, 18, 51, 309, 311, 318, 323, 335, 336, 339, 343, 346, 351, 355
Red Chinese 300
Red Cross 226, 232
Rededication Day 62
relief 12, 26, 32, 51, 116, 117, 123, 126, 192, 233, 234, 241, 327, 331
representative government 54, 75, 98

Republican 3, 20, 48, 49, 52, 54, 98, 147, 159-161, 165, 352
Republicans 23, 36, 51, 55, 60, 147, 160-162
research 1, 10, 21, 23, 24, 37, 41, 142, 150, 151, 162, 171, 172, 175, 176, 179-183, 198, 199, 273, 274, 357
Resor, Stanley 298
Reuter's (News Agency) 237
Revenue, Department of 155
Revolutionary War 308
Rheims 59
Romania 177
Rome, ancient 130
Rome, GA 36, 37, 188, 189, 222, 354
Roosevelt 2, 6, 8, 22, 28, 33, 34, 49, 53-55, 160, 212, 299, 322
Roosevelt, Theodore (T.R.) 160
Royal Air Force 235
Royal Navy 235
Runnymede 58
rural electrification 21, 22, 119, 141, 142, 149
Rural Electrification Act 21, 135,
Rural Electrification Administration (R.E.A.) 124, 135, 138, 139, 140, 162

Russia 28, 61, 89, 93, 96, 100, 132, 174, 178, 213, 236, 238, 242, 248-251, 253, 265, 272, 276, 278, 291, 292, 302, 314, 315
Russian 61, 174, 178, 179, 242, 248, 250, 253, 264, 272, 283-285, 300
Russians 60, 69, 224, 249, 284-286, 315

Sabbath 107
sacrifices 18, 41, 44, 47, 58, 62, 70, 78, 137, 163, 203, 210, 215, 229, 233, 234, 239, 242, 243, 246, 247, 259, 261, 265, 272, 285
sailors 58, 210, 217, 229, 290
Saltzbergers 105
Sanders, Carl 287
Sanford, S. V. 194, 245
Santiago, Chile 204
Saratoga 204
satellite 29, 61, 177, 264, 270, 291
scalawag 309-311, 318
Scerra, Joseph 294
school(s) 2, 5, 21, 25, 26, 30, 31, 35, 41, 53, 62, 71, 72, 77, 78, 81, 130, 131, 132, 142, 150, 152, 162,

Index 375

169, 198, 205, 211, 220-222, 245, 247, 253, 268, 270-272, 277, 278, 288, 311, 312, 326, 333, 334, 336, 340-344, 348
School Lunch Program 21, 150, 162
science 8, 15, 17, 30, 64, 66, 77, 137, 198, 268, 270, 271, 274, 290, 334
scientists 198, 247, 268
sectional hate 42
Security Council, United Nations 91, 95
security, general sense of 75, 78, 253, 260, 306, 336
security, international 69, 279
security, military 246, 254, 272
security, national 21, 27, 31, 59, 69, 87, 124, 161, 164, 205, 207, 215, 216, 259, 265, 268, 278, 279, 290, 294, 292-300, 303, 304, 336
self-government 17, 44, 77, 81, 98, 103, 106
Senate Armed Services Committee 30, 163, 266
Senate Judiciary Committee 313
separation of powers 81

separation of the races 332, 337, 339, 344
Shippey, Dorothy 14
Sibley, Celestine 12
slavery 29, 67, 76, 256, 259, 328
slaves 59, 75, 139, 219, 262, 308, 315, 319
Smith, Ashton B. 213
Smith, Margaret Chase 292
Smith, Marion 2, 238
Smoot-Hawley Tariff Act 111, 112
Social Security 125
soil 20, 22, 24, 45, 89, 122, 129-131, 133, 137, 142, 143, 146, 147, 162, 172, 182, 207, 241, 298, 309
soldiers 7, 21, 28, 29, 58, 85, 119, 141, 203, 206, 209, 210, 223, 230, 232, 234, 246, 259, 260, 272, 290- 292, 294, 310, 346
Solomon Islands 228
South Korea 262
South Koreans 69
South Pacific 226, 227, 229, 231
Southeast Asia 283, 285, 287
Southeastern Water Pollution Laboratory 182

Southern people 125, 195, 310, 318, 323, 345, 350, 355
Southern States 125, 185, 199, 307, 311, 314, 316-321, 323, 326, 336, 338-340, 343-345
Southern womanhood 42-44
Southerners 4, 18, 19, 36, 312, 324
Soviet Union 29, 30, 89, 95, 100, 177, 178, 264, 270
space 2, 3, 30, 268, 270, 273, 274, 288, 290
Spanish-American War 245, 312
Sparkman, John 85
specialization 72
spirit of democracy 254
spiritual values 152, 270, 276
Sputnik I 264, 270
Stabilization Act (1942) 148
State, Department of 69, 86, 169
Statesman 53, 102
states' rights 1, 12, 17, 350, 352
Statism 62, 249, 358
Stennis, John 298
Stevens, Thaddeus 323, 335, 343, 346
Stevenson, Adlai E. 20, 71, 158, 195
Stilwell, Joseph W. 230, 231
Suez Canal 69
Sumner, Charles 323, 335, 343, 346
Supreme Court 35, 36, 71, 74, 83, 94, 95, 159, 274, 322, 339, 343, 344, 358

Taft, Robert A. 22, 153, 160, 244, 319
Taft, Robert A. 22, 153, 160, 244, 319
Taft-Hartley Bill 153, 244
Talmadge, Eugene 6, 7, 26, 32-35, 47-49, 53, 55, 159, 307
Talmadge, Herman 95, 349, 350
tariffs 19, 116
tax collector 314
tax cut 165, 284
tax reduction 165
taxes 2, 50, 53, 113, 116, 133, 154, 155, 163, 165, 200, 215, 226, 281, 284, 323, 329, 330
television 72, 137, 174, 176, 274, 287-289, 334, 345
Tennessee Valley Authority 51
Tenth Amendment 16, 74
textbooks 2, 272
textile 116, 117, 153

Index 377

Thant, U 89
theaters of operations (World War II) 28, 35, 223, 225, 226, 232, 238
Tibet 94
Tifton, GA 218
Tifton (GA) Experiment Station 171, 172, 182
tobacco 146, 184
Toombs, Robert 53
Tories 308
Townsend, William B. 194
trade 72, 112, 115, 117, 121, 155, 156, 220
treaties 68
Truman, Harry S. 2, 28, 223, 256, 322
Turner County (GA) 110, 167, 168
tyranny 55, 68, 83, 133, 140, 163, 254, 256, 261, 278, 279, 338
United States Service Organization (U.S.O.) 226, 232, 233
United Daughters of the Confederacy 26, 27, 41, 43, 45
United Kingdom 26, 27, 41, 43, 45
United Nations 29, 57, 59-62, 68, 69, 85-101, 244, 248, 251-253, 255, 357

Universal Military Training 62, 260
University of Georgia 26, 28, 37, 71, 175, 181, 194, 197, 198, 244, 251
University of Georgia Law School 71
urbanization 303
utilities 184

values 18, 20, 276, 299, 327
veterans 26, 32, 73, 125, 232, 245,
Veteran's Administration 155, 331
Veteran's of Foreign Wars (V.F.W.) 294, 296, 331
Viet Cong 292, 302
Vietnam 31, 87, 107, 287, 290-297, 301, 303
Vietnam War 31, 32, 287, 294, 296, 301
Vinson, Carl 24, 199
violence 324, 348, 354, 358
vocational education 50
voters 3, 8, 20, 33, 83, 111, 173, 314, 322
voting 8, 11, 93, 96, 97, 308, 311, 314, 333-337, 340
voting rights 333-337

Wall Street 49, 289

Wallace, Henry A. 57
war 9, 18-20, 22, 27-29, 31, 32, 42-44, 52, 57-59, 62, 67-70, 74, 89, 91, 92, 98, 119, 125, 127-129, 132-135, 137-144, 146, 148, 151, 153, 154, 163, 168, 174, 196, 203-210, 212-215, 217-219, 221-228, 230-242, 244-248, 250-252, 254, 256, 257, 259-264, 270, 272, 275, 276, 278, 279, 283, 285, 287, 290, 292, 294-297, 299-303, 308-310, 312, 313, 320, 321, 327, 328, 346, 355
War Between the States 53, 245, 310, 312, 327, 346
War Department 232
war on poverty 303
Washington, George 17, 79, 80
Washington 4, 5, 7, 8, 14, 17, 23, 24, 28, 30, 32, 48-50, 52, 54, 68, 72, 75, 79, 80, 85, 88, 146, 158, 172, 217, 223, 224, 245, 274, 294, 298, 309, 311, 313, 316, 319, 321, 324, 329, 332, 350, 352
water 17, 24, 25, 45, 54, 129, 167, 169-172, 182, 185, 188, 189, 191-193

Watson, Thomas E. (Tom) 52, 53, 211
weaponry 17, 302, 303
weapons 30, 68, 70, 193, 216, 246, 247, 252, 259, 260, 264, 265, 268, 269, 275, 285, 294, 297, 300, 302, 303
Wedemeyer, Albert C. 64
Welling, A. C. 185, 186
Westmoreland, William 292
wheat 23, 114, 117, 120, 121, 126, 146
white 34, 35, 86, 89, 173, 191, 286, 290, 307, 309, 311, 315, 316, 318-320, 324-327, 333-337, 339-343, 345, 346
White, Edward 290
White, Walter 316, 318
White House 86, 173, 191, 286
"white primaries" 322
Whitfield County 271
Wilson, Woodrow 76
Winder, GA 7, 13, 159
Wingate, Lynnwood 146
woman 43, 53, 116, 133, 210, 214, 280
Woodruff, Jim Jr. 170, 171
workers 116, 120, 142, 143, 148, 151, 153, 180, 184, 244, 280, 307

world Communism 67, 260, 271, 291
World Court 54, 95
world peace 62, 70, 96, 238, 242, 249, 253, 264, 283
World War I 203, 245, 278, 300
World War II 9, 22, 27, 28, 57, 135, 142, 168, 196, 244-247, 256, 260, 264, 290, 300, 355
WSB Radio 34, 47, 329
Yorktown 204, 258